THE COLLEGE OF RIPON
AND YORK ST. JOHN
RIPON CAMPUS

AUTHOR *GODEFROY V.*

TITLE *THE DRAMATIC GENIUS*
OF VERDI

CLASS No. *782 VER*   ACCESS. No. *35167*

**Please return this book on or before
the date stamped below**

THE DRAMATIC GENIUS OF VERDI

THE DRAMATIC GENIUS
OF VERDI

Studies of Selected Operas

VOLUME I

by

VINCENT GODEFROY

With an Introduction by
Charles Osborne

LONDON
VICTOR GOLLANCZ LTD
1975

ISBN 0 575 01979 4

Printed in Great Britain by
The Camelot Press Ltd, Southampton

TO MY WIFE
ANN

Gott wird für die Seele, die ihn schauen darf, nicht ein geistiges Bild sein, sondern ein Schauspiel. Ein Schauspiel mit Musik! Vielleicht ist die Wonne der Oper etwas, was als schwache Vorform auf dieses herrliche Mysterium hindeutet.

Franz Werfel

(God will appear to the soul permitted to behold him not like a holy picture, but as a show. A musical show! Perhaps the rapture of the Opera is a pale advance preview of this glorious Mystery.)

ACKNOWLEDGMENTS

Queen Victoria's entry in her *Journal* after attending the first night of *I Masnadieri* is reproduced by gracious permission of Her Majesty the Queen.

My thanks are due to Mrs Ursula Vaughan Williams and to the Editor of *Opera* for allowing me to include the late Dr Ralph Vaughan Williams' delightful account of the last act of *Rigoletto*.

I also have to thank the Editor of *The Gramophone* for his permission to quote the 'Epigramophone' specially written by Hilaire Belloc for that magazine in 1929.

CONTENTS

All translations are my own, except where otherwise acknowledged. Reference notes on quoted material will be found at the end of each chapter.

V. G.

INTRODUCTION

WITH THE POSSIBLE exception of the two operas composed to French texts, *Les vêpres siciliennes* and *Don Carlos*, the operas of Verdi's maturity and old age have always been popular. It is only recently, however, that the pre-*Rigoletto* operas, those Verdi composed in what he called his years in the galleys, have come back into public favour. Now that many of them are being staged, and all of them being recorded, the opera-going public is really able to consider for the first time the shape and form of Verdi's complete *œuvre*, and to trace his musical and dramatic progress from *Oberto* to *Falstaff*. That his path was one of progress is obvious: no one thinks *Oberto* a greater opera than *La forza del destino*, or *Il giorno di regno* a more successful comedy than *Falstaff*. But there is a case to be made for *Oberto* as aesthetically more satisfactory in terms of form than *La forza del destino*, while *Il giorno di regno* works as well in its way as the later and greater comedy does on its, admittedly more exalted, level. The line of progress between the operas written by Verdi in his twenties and *Falstaff*, produced when he was eighty, is by no means a straight one.

In his pioneering volume of Verdi's life and works, published in 1931, Francis Toye not surprisingly skimmed over most of the earlier operas, to concentrate on the masterpieces from *Rigoletto* onwards. When I came to write about the operas, more than thirty years later, I quite deliberately sought to give as serious consideration to the early operas as to the later works. Now, for his examination of Verdi as a musical dramatist, Vincent Godefroy makes use only of the works of what might be thought of as the composer's first period, plus the three undisputed masterpieces which usher in his second period. At first thought, this might seem a perverse method of procedure, for the later operas are rich in musical characterization and constructed with more care than many of the earlier ones. Philip and Eboli in *Don Carlos*, Simon Boccanegra, Don

Carlo di Vargas in *La forza del destino*, a host of characters in *Aida*, *Otello* and *Falstaff*; a study of these would surely have rendered Mr Godefroy's task easier, would it not? He will turn to them in a further volume. But, on second thoughts, how valuable it is to have a number of Verdi's earlier musical characterizations examined in detail with such insight, freshness of mind and freedom from preconceptions.

Verdi said that his artistic career began with his third opera, *Nabucco*; Mr Godefroy takes him at his word and begins his study of the musical dramatist's art with that opera. Fair enough, though, *pace* the composer himself, in my view his artistic career began with his first opera to be staged. *Oberto*, though formally it could be by Bellini or Donizetti or any one of a dozen other composers of the period, is no mere student work, but original in the sense that its voice and its personality are original. Oberto and Leonora are the first, and worthily the first, in that magnificent series of fathers and daughters whose relationships Verdi was to explore with such compassionate genius throughout his entire career. *Un giorno di regno*, Verdi's second opera and his only comic opera until *Falstaff* a half-century later, is a work of great charm and melodic facility, and contains, in the character of the Marchesa del Poggio, a heroine as individual as many of Donizetti's. But *Nabucco* is, after all, an appropriate starting-point, for it is with the eponymous hero of that opera that the composer takes his first steps towards inventing the Verdian baritone, who is not only a type of voice, but a type of character in whose utterances we usually find somewhere a trace of the personality, the voice, of Verdi himself. Or so I like to fancy.

If I may indulge in the vice of self-quotation (a vice indulged in musically by Rossini and Donizetti much more than by the composer we are considering), 'Verdi's incredible achievement was that, over a period of nearly sixty years, he led Italian opera from relative Donizettian innocence to post-Wagernian wisdom. And he conducted this humanizing process entirely alone. A born man of the theatre, he created an operatic language in which the drama is carried by, yet gives form to, the melody. In this he shows himself to be as much a revolutionary as Wagner.' Mr Godefroy's achievement in this volume is that he enables us to examine with him Verdi's working methods in the first half of his life. I have derived both pleasure and instruction from reading *The Dramatic Genius of Verdi*, and it is with gratitude that I commend it to other potential readers.

CHARLES OSBORNE

FOREWORD

THIS BOOK IS an examination of the methods of Verdi the dramatist, the playwright with music as his language, the purveyor not so much of famous tunes and popular arias as emotional punch-lines, soaring phrases of triumph or despair, hatred or terror—all kinds of human passion. For although his operas adhere to the old system of division into 'set numbers', his sheer creative impulse has often inspired into these numbers an afflatus of such dramatic import that their original form is quite overwhelmed. One can find a parallel in the great poetic dramas of classical and romantic literature in which the basic metrical prosody is submerged under the rhythmic drive of the words, which nobody but a pedant would wish to halt in order to check on the scansion of the lines. It is because I feel that Verdi should be classed among the major figures in World Drama that I have set out to pursue this study.

Verdi, of course, did not actually write the verses of his own libretti, though he often dictated to his collaborators exactly what sort of words or lines he wanted. Thus he enjoyed some advantage over the do-it-yourself composers who insisted on compiling their own scenarios and poems. For they so often could not bring themselves to prune or jettison the verses they had so proudly fathered, and their operas for this reason could become weighed down by a double disadvantage—a verbose book set to musical prolixity. Verdi demanded a terse framework on the structure of which he could fasten his melodic emotions without danger of redundancy or cerebral padding. That is why, in the case of so many of his operas, we can read a long passage in the verse play, then listen to the aria or duet he has fashioned from it, and find that his librettist's few lines seem to have regained, in their musical clothing, all the dramatic weight of their literary original.

In order to examine this aspect of Verdi's genius I have selected some of his earlier operas, considering each one as a drama for music, relating it closely to its historical or literary sources, and discussing how he developed the protagonists from their documentary or theatrical beginnings into vital operatic characters. For Verdi, on his way to the top, had no compunction about offering us musical portraits of such eminent persons as Nebuchadnezzar the King, Attila the Hun, Macbeth and his Lady, Joan of Arc, and François Premier, not hesitating to transfer to the opera stage the prose and verse heroes and heroines of Shakespeare, Schiller and Hugo, Byron, Dumas and Gutiérrez. He never appears to have doubted his ability to present the lions of history or literature as *dramatis personae* adequately translated to a musical plane. He took them all seriously; and so must we.

I have tried, in these studies of ten of the earlier operas, to examine Verdi's methods of construction and portrayal; his insight into the dramas he had chosen; his homework with his librettists; and his use of music to distil the dramatic conflict which is the essence of his inspiration (not omitting his occasional lapses, oversights and miscalculations.) To anyone who searches diligently, countless nuances and subtleties of expression and reflection may be revealed. For genius offers profundity in the guise of clarity; and this is so true of Verdi that we can never be sure we have the measure of him.

SANDBANKS   VINCENT GODEFROY
1974

1

NEBUCHADNEZZAR

By the rivers of Babylon, there we sat down, yea, we wept,
when we remembered Zion. We hanged our harps upon the
willows in the midst thereof. For there they that carried us
away captive required of us a song; and they that wasted us
required of us mirth, saying, Sing us one of the songs of
Zion.
How shall we sing the Lord's song in a strange land?

PSALM CXXXVII. 1–4

THE CHORUS OF captive Jews that so stirred Verdi's early and reluctant
muse survived to be sung under Toscanini at his funeral sixty years later;
lived on to find itself listed under the heading *Patriotic Works* in the
catalogue of *La Voce del Padrone* at the time of Mussolini's rape of
Ethiopia; and after another thirteen years emerged to celebrate the
opening night of the new La Scala, rebuilt after the ravages of the Second
World War—an occasion of combined commemoration and hope. So it
has done the State some service—this little chorus of yearning exiles,
dreaming disconsolately of their lost land.

When *Nabucco* was first produced Verdi had to be content with
scenery and costumes out of stock; however, so keen was he to show the
Milanese that he could do better than *Oberto* and its unhappy *buffo*
successor, that he agreed to this disadvantage. But before he reached the
audience, Verdi had achieved his reward at the rehearsals. Years afterwards he told Stanford:[1]

The artistes were singing as badly as they knew how, and the
orchestra seemed bent only on drowning the noise of the workmen
who were busy making alterations to the building. Presently the
chorus began to sing, as carelessly as before, the *Va, pensiero*, but
before they had got through half a dozen bars the theatre was as still as
a church. The men had left off their work one by one, and they were
sitting about on ladders and scaffolding listening! When the number
was finished, they broke out into the noisiest applause I have ever
heard, crying *'Bravo, bravo, viva il maestro!'* and beating on the
woodwork with their tools. Then I knew what the future had in store
for me.

The scenery and costumes from stock may well have been those of Rossini's *Semiramide*. Its Halls in the Palace, Royal Apartments, Hanging Gardens and the like would have supplied the bulk of Verdi's requirements. Solera in his libretto referred loosely to Assyrians when he meant Babylonians and perhaps only archaeologists would worry about the difference. Both had Baal or Bel with exotic priests round whom to build stage rituals; the main difference being that the story of Semiramis is legendary, while Nebuchadnezzar is historical.*

One may wonder how Nebuchadnezzar became Nabucco. The title of the opera is in fact *Nabucodonosor*; but throughout the libretto the King of Babylon is called Nabucco, a convenient and accepted abbreviation, if a peculiar one. In the Septuagint and in the Vulgate he is Nabuchodonosor. In the Authorized Version he becomes Nebuchadnezzar; but our English Apocrypha retains the form of the Vulgate. Nabucco, if we were not now accustomed to it, might strike us as quaint and slightly irreverent. We may recall the late Sir Victor Gollancz's malicious chuckle at the expense of the Bournemuthian who called him Nabucker. Yet he was not so far out. Oriental scholars plump for Nabukudur. . . .[2]

There is one point of divergence between Rossini's work and Verdi's. Though both may be staged with full oriental splendour, *Semiramide* remains a fancy-dress Grand Opera while *Nabucco* has been widely credited with a sort of Biblical seriousness and authenticity. Indeed, its real model, as far as it had one, might have been that other oriental masterpiece of Rossini, *Mosé*, with which it shares its Biblical origin and its presumptuous creation of a fictitious story amid religious trappings. In this latter respect Rossini was more daring than Verdi; for he renamed Aaron *Elisero*, invented a sister for him and provided Moses with a daughter in love with Pharaoh's son. Verdi, too, accepted the inevitable love tangle between an Israelite and Nebuchadnezzar's daughter. Even as late as *Aida* he could take on this theatrical situation with all seriousness.

But in spite of its fairly preposterous plot, there clings to *Nabucco* an inescapable Biblicality. The High Priest Zaccaria, if not historically Jeremiah, is an eloquent epitome of that outspoken, unbudging, terrifying, ruthless yet wholly God-fearing figure: the Old Testament

* But see Julian Budden, *The Operas of Verdi*, vol. I, pp. 93–5. He points out that La Scala had mounted a ballet on the same subject only four years before *Nabucco*.

Prophet. In him speaks and gesticulates Samuel or Elijah, Ezekiel or Nahum, Isaiah or Baruch. The ferocious and amoral Abigaille is a veritable Jezebel, aggressively self-seeking and certain of a violent end. Ismaele and Fenena, whose romance gets little chance of developing, although its consummation is implicitly assured, are burdened with typically Biblical problems—the one 'cast out', the other 'passed over'.

In England, of course, regardless of any fictitious travesty, the 'Sacred Story' was forbidden by the Censorship. Henry Chorley wrote, 'We English are not so hard or so soft, as to be willing to see the personages of Holy Writ acted and sung in theatres.'[3] In fact, the only 'personage' thus qualified for censorship was Nabucco himself; for all the others, if true to type, are inventions. The King of Babylon alone figures in Holy Writ. All the same, we in London disguised him as *Nino, Re d'Assyria*, thus linking him once again with Semiramide, for Nino was her husband. The improbable plot thus unfolded had no meaning whatever. The impressive unaccompanied hymn at the end, 'Immenso Ieovha', now became 'Terribil Isido'. All that Solera's libretto really stood for—the sufferings of Israel justified by the unconquerable Truth for which they were undergone—vanished beneath the Victorian cloak of Puritan righteousness. Even as late as 1928 the Assyrian version was still being presented to gramophone devotees in the 'Opera at Home' volume of *His Master's Voice*.[4] But in 1846, in spite of Chorley's undeviating failure to find anything praiseworthy in Verdi's music, there was a growing appreciation that here was something eloquently sincere. Today in England we can, thanks to Non-conformist Wales, see *Nabucco* as Catholic Italy has always seen it—a moving tale of long ago with individual passions and mass-sufferings as modern as their setting is ancient.

Because of the sins which ye have committed before God, ye shall be led away captives into Babylon by Nabuchodonosor king of the Babylonians. So when ye be come to Babylon, ye shall remain there many years, and for a long season, namely, seven generations: and after that I will bring you away peaceably from thence. Now shall ye see in Babylon gods of silver, and of gold, and of wood, borne upon shoulders, which cause the nations to fear. Beware therefore that ye in no wise be like to strangers, neither be ye afraid of them, when ye see the multitude before them, worshipping them. But say ye in your hearts, O Lord, we must worship thee. For my angel is with you, and I myself caring for your souls. (BARUCH, VI.1–7)

Nebuchadnezzar—king, commander-in-chief, statesman, architect, philosopher, landscape-gardener, dreamer, lunatic—perhaps he is not the easiest of characters to present on the operatic stage. He stalks through the Old Testament, ranging among the chronicles and the prophets, a bogy to the Israelites before the conquest, an enlightened potentate after, larger than life in sickness and in health. In his power-clash with Egypt, Israel was the unhappy buffer-state. Yet the Bible as our main source of reference manages to present Jerusalem as the true focus of events. Egypt defeated and Babylon triumphant, for all their dramatic glamour, are on the periphery.

Solera's poem, though called *Nabucodonosor*, makes little attempt at portraying this fascinating monarch in the rich colours of his peculiar glory. The writer is understandably lured by the recurring Old Testament motif of Jewish suffering and steadfastness, of Jehovah challenged yet omnipotent. With the shameless facility of the romantic he had conjured up daughters in conflict and the inevitable amorous triangle with Hebrew apex and Babylonian hypotenuse. As in *Aida*, the woman scorned steals the show, her violent emotions submerging the limpid unity of the lovers. But Nabucco, whom nobody loves, looms inescapably. Though his appearances are somewhat disjointed and episodic, they make up for lack of development by their emotional variety. He comes through as the first of Verdi's illustrious line of baritones in whom dignity and pathos are so intermingled that their villainy (as far as they are villains) or their failings (as far as they are failures) cannot but suffuse a glow of tragic nobility. At the threshold of this gallery stands Nabucodonosor, Re di Babilonia.

It is well known that one line of Solera's had re-roused Verdi's creative interest—the opening of the chorus *Va, pensiero sull'ali dorate*. This sentimental passage appealed to him as he read it listlessly, undermining the defences he had erected against all musical temptation. There was little question of religious fervour, absolutely none of patriotic yearning—only the softening of a self-hardened heart. Verdi was indulging in a grand despondency brought on by the collapse of his young married career—all his pretty chickens and their dam at one fell swoop—and by the bitterness of an operatic failure, the unfair fiasco of *Un Giorno di Regno*. He himself had been King for a Day; lover, husband, father, composer—all these: and when the sun set, where were they? Wife and children buried; opera jeered at in La Scala. He was down, deranged, hopeless. It was not only the limpid line of Solera's pseudo-psalm that aroused his spirit; there was the story of Nabucodonosor himself, struck down at the height of his success and bullied out of his mind. Yet in the last the king revives and conquers. So Verdi, like Achilles between Troy and Scamander, stirred and strove and hoisted his fallen stature to its true poise.

The feelings of the composer can be sensed in this opera, for we can feel them in those characters and situations most akin to his own state. His obstinate loneliness is expressed in the dignified musings of the High Priest; his desolation in the disillusioned pathos of the dethroned monarch; his anger and rebellion against fate in Abigaille's fury and the spiteful imprecations of the Levites; his broken spirit in the Jewish lamentations; his defiant revival in the spirited retaliation of the abused Ismaele. The opera *Nabucco* is a young composer's breakthrough in more than one respect. Not only did its performances secure him international recognition; its music established his creative rebirth.

Nabucco is not a revolutionary work in the unfolding development of operatic history. While Verdi composed it, Wagner was engaged on *Rienzi*, Donizetti on *Linda di Chamounix*. Halévy and Auber were busy in France, while Meyerbeer was finishing *Le prophète* and dabbling at *L'Africaine*. The technical material of *Nabucco* was in no way ahead of its contemporaries—it was less ambitious than most. What was new was the man behind the work, an angry young man letting rip with chords and cadences against a fate that had nearly engulfed him, but from which his resilience had managed a miraculous escape. Not until *La Traviata* was Verdi again going to let his own feelings intrude into his music—and then a very different tale awaited the telling, and in very different music. Or was it to be so different? The accents of Verdi may have picked up new delicacies, nuances, refinements. But all along they were direct, unequivocal, sincere. He never wrote a cerebral bar. His metronome was his heart.

Nabucco is a manifesto, a demonstration, an opera of mass conflicts. The Hebrews, inflamed, defiant, suppliant, desperate, nostalgic, triumphant, explore all the choral emotions. The Levites are solemn and ruthless; the soldiers full of vigour and purpose; the Babylonian hierarchy proud and confident; the populace self-satisfied. All have their appropriate tunes, unerringly bestowed. Several of these are gathered for the fashioning of the overture, and their choice gives the piece a cohesion that places it above the level of a pot-pourri. We may not exactly read a programme into it, but it does, as is the function of a good overture, set the pace for the evening's drama. Trombones and tubas announce a demand for solemn attention, followed by two themes derived from the accompaniment to the High Priest of Jehovah's first solo. In these twenty-three bars is expressed:

The word that the Lord spake against Babylon and against the land of the Chaldeans by Jeremiah the prophet.

This is followed by the relentless theme of the Levites in their *maranatha* scorn for the assumed treachery of Ismaele and, by severe contrast, a woodwind interlude introducing rather dreamily the lamentation of the Hebrew exiles. This is soon swollen up by trumpets into a paean of triumphant release from sorrows, the flutes expectantly fluttering. The judicial Levites return briefly, to be swamped out by the swinging bravado of the Priests of Bel, which in turn gives way to a tune from the concerted finale which accompanies Zaccaria's spurning of the luckless Ismaele. Next comes a glimpse of the tune belonging to Abigaille's deceitful tricking of Nabucco in their big duet—the only passage in the overture not derived from sacerdotal or patriotic emotions. The concerted finale returns, and the angry Levites make the *stretto*. The overture ends noisily. Bonaventura pointed out that it contains 229 beats on the bass drum. Its relationship to the brass band of Busseto cannot be denied, but this is no anticipation of Sousa! Verdi was clearly trying to condition his audience for a drama compatible with the violence of the Book of Kings, the pathos of the Lamentations, and the prophetic nemesis of Jeremiah. For an Italian of the 1840s he did not do so badly.

The opera is divided into four parts. The first is entitled GERUSALEMME and shows us the interior of Solomon's Temple. It is packed with Hebrews taking shelter, for the legions of the Chaldees are already inside the city, and its fall is imminent. The libretto is here prefixed with a quotation from Jeremiah:

Thus saith the Lord . . . Behold I will give the city into the hand of the King of Babylon, and he shall burn it with fire.

The librettist gets his reference wrong, stating it to be from chapter xxxii when it is in fact from xxxiv. But his intention is manifest. He seeks authenticity for his Biblical paraphrase. Verdi's score is an exciting build-up to the inevitable entry of Nebuchadnezzar himself. Six scenes succeed each other rapidly, their contrast admirable. First there is the hymn of priests and populace, with the maidens' stanza faintly prophetic of the *Aida* victory parade. It is as rugged and sonorous an opening as any opera could wish for, its words echoing thoughts and phrases from the Pentateuch, from Samuel and Chronicles, the Psalms, Job, Jeremiah and the Minor Prophets. This is followed by the bass aria of Zaccaria with allusions to Exodus and Judges, the epitome of pontifical encouragement in days of darkness. It is broken into by Ismaele's tidings of the enemy's approach. A desperate *allegro* leads to the bass cabaletta, vigorous and implacable. A short interlude is given to Ismaele and Fenena. They pass as lovers in this turbulent and sexless plot. They are of course from opposite camps, snatching a stolen moment of reminiscence, pale prototypes of Fenton and Nannetta. Their meeting is blasted by the strident entry of Abigaille, storming in explosively like the Queen of the Night, only to soften surprisingly as she beholds Ismaele, the object of her secret passion. It is the situation that develops after *Celeste Aida*, but set to the strains of Bellini, the lyricism drawn out in contrast with the *agitatissimo* news that Nabucco himself is on his way. The orchestra reiterates a descending, cataclysmic theme as different sections of the chorus rush in, each bringing more desperate news, and all security seems to slide away under their feet. Here is the embryo of the crowd excitement during the *Otello* storm. Even Zaccaria's lone solo line bears the seeds of Iago's 'L'alvo frenetico del mar sia la sua tomba'.

The visual excitement continues as the Babylonian soldiers pour into the Temple, but musically the tension is unfortunately slackened by the intrusion of the Babylonian March, all sixty-four bars of it. Though it is no doubt intended to lead martially up to Nabucco's entry, it damps down the turbulence which was so well done before it starts. It will play its part as a motif in the opera, but its full-dress performance at this point jolts us back to the simplicities of *Norma* just as we were being carried away on the swell of panic. The March ends with Nabucco's appearance, judiciously delayed as a dramatic climax. He rides his war-horse to the very threshold of the Temple, an impious sacrilege. Francis Toye observed that Verdi's love of animals prevented him from ever introducing horses into his operas.[5] But it seems certain that the young composer set great store by this carefully prepared entry *a cavallo*. Zaccaria throws out his challenge 'O trema insano!' *Insano* . . . here is irony, for the insult is prophetic. When Zaccaria warns the king that this is the House of God, Nabucco enquires laconically, 'Who speaks of

God?' These are the first words he utters after all the long build-up, and they are unaccompanied. But they trigger off a sensational demonstration, for Zaccaria seizes his daughter Fenena and with a dagger at her throat challenges him to enter the Temple. Certainly some Old Testament prophets have records of bloodthirsty actions, but what priest of Jehovah would stab a girl inside the Temple? The outrageously theatrical threat has no effect on Nebuchadnezzar. He calmly dismounts and enters, murmuring that they will yet see him in his true colours. Then, *sotto voce*, he addresses the assembled people in a passage of studied yet foreboding calm. It is in fact the keystone of the concerted finale, but

in performance with its calculated rests it has all the effect of establishing that lordly detachment which is the king's political strength and personal weakness.

The ensuing ensemble is in the contemporary manner, but the florid and vitriolic Abigaille dominates intemperately, in contrast to the sombre self-control of her monarch and supposed father. When all have had their say, the conquering king declaims briefly in defiance of Jehovah, mocking him as Elijah mocked Baal on Mount Carmel. Zaccaria attempts to carry out his previous threat to Fenena, but is foiled by Ismaele. Nebuchadnezzar launches *con gioia feroce* into any angry stanza harking back to a passage in the overture. He orders his soldiers to carry out the operation described in the last chapters of Kings and Chronicles. The music resembles the chorus of Priests of Bel who in the next act will plot with Abigaille against the king. Whether Verdi intended this close relationship is not certain. What is more certain is that he did not realize he had lifted, almost note for note and in the same key, a part of Donizetti's finale to the second act of *Lucia di Lammermoor*.

So the curtain falls and Part One is over. The remainder of the drama will take place in and around Babylon. What we have seen is really a Prologue and as such it has been excellent. It has introduced all the characters, told us of their loves, hopes and hates, and has intimated that the ὕβρις of Abigaille and Nebuchadnezzar is riding for a tragic fall; also that Zaccaria will be an awkward captive. It is passably historical too. In

586 BC the Chaldeans did storm and destroy Jerusalem. The Bible, however, denies the presence of Nebuchadnezzar on this final occasion. It tells us that he entrusted the assault to his general Nebuzaradan.[6] Josephus adds the names of five more generals.[7] But the personal leadership of the king is essential to the drama, however inaccurate; and that, on the operatic stage, is how we would all wish it.

The Second Part, entitled L'EMPIO or 'The Ungodly One', has for its text Jeremiah, xxx.23:

> Behold the whirlwind of the Lord goeth forth with fury . . . and it shall fall on the head of the wicked.

Once again Nebuchadnezzar's entry will be delayed until the opening of the finale. This technically well-planned libretto holds the monarch back behind the scenes, to make his impact the more powerful. Abigaille, who has discovered that she is a slave by birth and not of royal blood, and that the feeble Fenena is heiress to the throne, is full of unrighteous indignation in her stormy recitative; full of self-pity in her aria. When the High Priest of Bel and his necromantic entourage bring her news that Fenena is actually liberating the Jewish captives, and acclaim her as Queen having put about a rumour that the king is dead, her anguish is switched cabaletta-wise to triumph.

From one violent enemy of Nebuchadnezzar we are now taken to listen to another; this time the dignified but equally vengeful prophet of Israel, Zaccaria. He is a splendidly fire-eating spokesman of all the apocalyptic dreams of the Books of the Captivity. As the Levite brings in the Tables of the Law we get a fleeting glimpse of Baruch:[8]

> This is the book of the commandments of God, and the law that endureth for ever: all they that keep it shall come to life; but such as leave it shall die.

But the severe accents of his prayer are more formidable than his Cassandra-like forecasts in which are reflected Jeremiah and Ezra. Here is the Rock of Ages set to music with not much more than a bass voice, a 'cello and some pizzicato. While Zaccaria retires to receive Fenena into the Jewish faith, the Levites snarl their hatred at the unfortunate Ismaele in a relentless, inexorable malediction that brutally wields a fragment of the Levitical Curse so fully expanded in Deuteronomy.[9] The desperate,

tortured cries of the tenor smarting under the bass lashes, brings
breathless realism to the scene. Operas, Verdi's included, are full of
curses. But though the victim may shudder, stagger, and mutter
'orrore!', he does not usually put up such vigorous resistance as Ismaele
in the face of his tormentors. The implacable Levites have a basic
relationship with some of the *Heldenleben* critics harping unpleasantly
and with narrow prejudice. In contrast the exasperated Ismaele, by no
means a hero, although repeating that he would willingly die to escape
their taunts, does so with such energy that his innocence seems to prevail.

When the stage begins to fill, and Fenena's briefly reported conversion
is followed by Abdallo's news of Abigaille's *coup d'état*, we have an
orchestral build-up bludgeoning its gracelessly un-Rossinian way to the
climax of Nebuchadnezzar's entry. As Abigaille demands the crown
from Fenena the king bursts in and forestalls an unseemly filial brawl by
taking the crown for himself. 'Terror generale'—for the propaganda
machine has broadcast his death. With excellent understanding of good
theatre Verdi refrains from a prolonged regal outburst. Instead, *sotto voce
a cupo* he begins the ensemble 'S'appresan gl'istanti'. He maintains his

quiet self-control until his final threat, which is flung out *tutta forza*. This
arresting melody, with the word 'terror' subtly emphasized by a
semitone drop where a whole tone would have been more likely, is
taken up almost in canon by Abigaille, then by Ismaele, then Fenena, and
finally by Zaccaria, Anna, Abdallo, the High Priest and the chorus.
There is no escaping the sensation, when the entire cast joins in the tune,
of the massive effect this music must have had that night in Milan when
the Rossini-Bellini-Donizetti-fed public found their auditorium ringing
with its sheer vitality and virility. Its cadence is resounding enough to
bring the curtain down. But immediately on its full close

Nebuchadnezzar, modulating into C major, challenges his own Bel, scorns the conquered Jehovah, and announces himself to be the One God. In a sternly repeated phrase he demands instant and complete

Il volto a ter—ra o—mai chi—na——te! me Nu—me

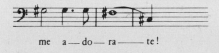

me a—do—ra——te!

obeisance. This triggers off a vigorous rebuff from Zaccaria and a defiant refusal from Fenena. Nebuchadnezzar snatches at her and orders her to her knees, for he is no longer king, but GOD.

And who is God but Nabuchodonosor? (JUDITH, VI.2)

Immediately there is a celestial demonstration in the shape of a thunderbolt which dislodges the Babylonian crown and dements its wearer. Verdi has an almighty orchestral crash of twelve bars swirling down four octaves. It is almost identical with the pandemonium sounded by Wagner when Hagen jumps into the Rhine in pursuit of the ring. Hagen never surfaced; but Nebuchadnezzar survives to conclude the act with a remarkable solo. He is out of his mind—not coloratura straws-in-the-hair mad, but schizophrenically deranged, carpet-chewing perhaps, self-pitying certainly. His aria contains within its framework a fine emotional display. It has in succession the markings: *allegro*; *adagio*; *allegro come prima*; *andante*; *adagio*. (The *andante* consists of 'Ah! Ah! perchè' and lasts for three bars.) The distracted victim of his own megalomania ranges from the bewildered

Chi pel cri-ne, ohimè, m'af-fer-ra?

to the hysterical

and then to the maudlin

with its accompaniment *dolce secondando il canto*. This is quickly followed by an *allegro* leap into terror as he sees grisly visions of archangelic flaming swords. Then once again the maudlin tune, and he trails off to faint mid-bar. Whereupon Abigaille seizes his crown; the orchestra whips up; and the curtain falls. This was surely, for Italian Opera, *new music*. Structurally it should have been a cabaletta, but Verdi has filled it with the stuff of dramatic monologue, breaking the mould. Certainly Chorley would have frowned as this was being performed, for in it he could hear the old school being slashed, if not yet torn to shreds.

The third part, entitled LA PROFEZIA, shows the ascendancy of Abigaille, who has usurped the throne and is keeping Nebuchadnezzar under open arrest, sufficiently confused in mind to have only the vaguest notion of what is afoot. Abigaille is enthroned and surrounded by her triumphant party under the leadership of the High Priest of Bel. Solera's text for this part is quoted as being from Jeremiah, li. It is in fact l.39 (abridged and adapted):

> The wild beasts of the desert shall have their dwelling place in Babylon together with the screech-owls, and the owls shall dwell there.

This forecast of ruined Babylon being reduced to a lair for wild creatures occurs, with minor variations, at least four times in Isaiah and Jeremiah, and once in Revelations.[10] The variations include dragons, lions, satyrs, doleful creatures, ostriches, devils, foul spirits, unclean and hateful birds. This depressing fate must be measured against the vast and glittering panache of Nebuchadnezzar's city. But the opera adds a new bird, *l'upupe*, which is naturally translated in the libretto of the Decca recording as *hoopoes*. This gorgeous bird, though immortalized by Aristophanes, does not actually occur in the Bible. One may wonder how the inventive Solera came by it. The answer is simple enough. In the Italian version of Jeremiah the word is not *upupe* but *ulule*—owls or 'doleful creatures'. In fact, 'the fatal bellman, which gives the stern'st good-night'.

For the new-crowned Abigaille the orchestra now plays the royal march of Nebuchadnezzar, as though to emphasize that she has successfully filched it from him. The scene, once the chorus has been dismissed, consists of a lengthy duet between the slave-usurper and the deposed king—the first of Verdi's famous collection of baritone-soprano duets. Abigaille remains throughout imperious, contemptuous and cruel. As though to underline the heady swagger of the upstart, the orchestra supports her with a brash, racing theme from the overture. Nebuchadnezzar's bewilderment is depicted by the orchestra with nervous comments, which alternate with strong chords as he pulls himself together. But when he rants, it is to no avail. The opportunist Abigaille holds all the aces. First she makes him sign the death-warrant of the Jews. He has misgivings, but she shames him into compliance. As soon as the guards have taken the proclamation to the High Priest, he remembers what was troubling his mind. His daughter Fenena has joined the Jews. He has sealed her doom. Abigaille reminds him that he has another daughter. The king, who carries about with him the documentary proof of her slave origin, now fumbles among his robes to confront her with it. But if we were attentive during her explosive recitative at the opening of the second act, we know Abigaille to be in possession of this damning parchment. With a run-up and a showy swoop-down she produces and destroys it.

Nebuchadnezzar in a subdued *andante* passage laments his impotence, pouring out those sad yet strong phrases in which Verdi excels when moved by the plight of his characters. With a key-switch Abigaille sweeps over his lament, ranging from B in alt down to middle C,

Ahi   mi-se-ran-do   ve ———— glio!

Leonora and Azucena all in one. With a keen sense of the pathetic Verdi
depicts the king's realization that he is a prisoner, the music held up at its
climax for him to reiterate the word 'prigionier', she to drive it cruelly
home. He then pleads in a sad stanza which is at once flooded over by her
forceful scorn (the overture theme again); and so the duet patterns on to
a conventional and noisy finish, the king importunate, the pseudo-queen
adamant. It has been a humiliating experience for one who has so
recently announced himself to be the One God. But Verdi has nowhere
allowed him to degenerate below a level of exasperated if suppliant
dignity. Here is just a touch of Lear—that evasive image about to haunt
the composer actively for twenty years and fitfully towards the very
close of his tireless career.

The next scene, by the banks of the Euphrates, is singularly treasured
by Verdians for its simple yet heart-rending chorus whose words coaxed
the desolated composer back from the shadows. Built purely on personal
emotion, it became the *Requiem* of his shattered past and the *Gloria* of his
abundant future. After seventeen bars of wistful *sotto voce* contemplation
comes a turning point as the chorus suddenly swells with the impulse of
resurrection. If it begins with reminiscences of Psalm cxxxvii, suddenly
now it is Psalm xxxii or lvii or cviii or any of those that sound paeans of
hope; and having expressed that hope, it moves into the serenity of self-
assurance, of strength arising out of suffering. Here was the tide of
Verdi's affairs which he took at the flood, and it led on to fortune. ('Then
I knew what the future had in store for me.')

The remainder of the scene cannot escape a charge of anti-climax.
Though Zaccaria's exhortation is broad and firm, reminding us
somewhat of an ensemble in *Favorita*, its development into the prophecy
of Babylon's overthrow does not really match up to a Biblical *maranatha*. We must remember in Verdi's favour that had he not put his foot
down, this scene as Solera wrote it would have petered out in an
undramatic love duet for Fenena and Ismaele. But Jeremiah's lurid 50th
and 51st chapters deserve a more terrifying musical setting than this. For
all Zaccaria's vehemence and prophetic vigour, it must be admitted that
the captive Jews could do better than comment 'Oh futuro!' and 'si, si,

si!' These accents are not portentous enough to shake Nebuchadnezzar's regime. It must be remembered that Psalm cxxxvii, for all its pathetic imagery of harps hanging on willows, ends thus:

> O daughter of Babylon, who art to be destroyed; happy shall he be, that rewardeth thee as thou hast served us. Happy shall he be, that taketh and dasheth thy little ones against the stones.

So we reach Part Four, L'IDOLO INFRANTO.

> Bel is confounded; his images are broken in pieces.
>   JEREMIAH, L.2. (not XLVIII as in the libretto)

The principal theme is now Nebuchadnezzar's recovery of his wits, prowess and authority. The curtain rises to reveal him sleeping, and though he is described as 'immerso in profondo sopore' the music at once tells us that it is a troubled sleep, with dream images flitting across his subconscious (as is recorded in the Book of Daniel).[11] First there comes a memory of that fearful moment when a supernatural power struck the crown from his head. This vanishes to be replaced by a fleeting echo of the love of Fenena and Ismaele, no solace to him but a cause for concern. It is quickly pushed out of his mind by the intrusion of his military march now usurped by Abigaille. Stirred by its sounds he leaps into the rushing fury that accompanied his call for the destruction of the Jewish Temple. The excitement of this awakens him. In a trice the dreams vanish and all he can remember is a nightmare sense of being pursued, a hunted animal, a glimpse of the grass-eating lycanthrope.

He hears a commotion outside. Instantly he feels the urge to take up arms as of old and ride at the head of his troops. The image of his horse brings a near-quotation from Job:[12]

> He paweth in the valley, and rejoiceth in his strength: he goeth on to meet the armed men. . . . He smelleth the battle afar off, the thunder of the captains, and the shouting.

He raves on about Jerusalem, his wits not yet fully recovered. The strains of a funeral march are heard, followed by his daughter's name. At this he rushes to the balcony and thus suffers the shock which restores him to sanity. He sees Fenena chained, being led to her execution. Desperately he tries to break out, but all the doors are bolted. Then with a cry he turns to the God of Israel. The 'cello and the trilling flute seem to echo the prelude to Zaccaria's prayer, recalling the solemnity of the religion he has mocked but now turns towards. His prayer is eloquent of his chastened mood, quite devoid of his customary rant. It may seem superficially to resemble his tune at the end of his duet with Abigaille. But before her he was the defeated fighter, exhausted yet still proud. Now before Jehovah he bares his soul and promises his own reformation. The accents take on a studied humility. The cabaletta which follows, when with sword in hand and loyal followers at his back he is poised to rescue his condemned daughter, is the raw material of 'Di quella pira'—one of those endearingly exhilarating pieces of near-vulgarity that make old operas swing when they are revived. That the orchestral postlude is the Babylonian March cannot be just chance. Nebuchadnezzar is back in warlike harness and the military initiative is once again his own.

We are transferred for our second visit to the Hanging Gardens. The funeral march already overheard by the imprisoned king is now played in full as a prelude, thirty-two bars in G minor, inescapably funereal and not without the effect of gathering doom. If it was originally something knocked up for a Busseto civic burial, it certainly conveys the solemnity of a public occasion. Fenena sings her modest prayer, unobtrusive like her humble role in the opera. It is moving, and contrives a dramatic lull before the anticipated entry of the king and his guards. When they burst in, Nebuchadnezzar's sword is brandished threateningly at the great statue of Bel. He orders it to be destroyed, but it collapses of its own accord. We have strayed again into the Book of Daniel, but somewhat haphazardly, for although the king of Babylon did erect a golden statue, he only *dreamed* of its collapse.

But this is enough for Nebuchadnezzar. He promises the Jews their freedom and return to their land (this is surely extra-Biblical). He announces that Abigaille has poisoned herself; then bids Fenena join him in worshipping Jehovah. An unaccompanied hymn in praise of the God of Israel seems to bring the opera to an impressive close. Its theme is based on Abraham's

> I have taken upon me to speak unto the Lord, which am but dust and ashes.[13]

All seems set for a fervent set-piece curtain, but Verdi has one card to play. Though Abigaille's suicide has been announced, a sudden oboe figure strikes the plaintive note that only an oboe can, and she is brought in for a dying aria. (Was this an addition?—an old libretto omits it.)*
We may perhaps feel satisfaction that this monstrously selfish and scheming impostor should in her final moments seek general forgiveness. Of course the Hebrews encourage her hopes of salvation. But Nebuchadnezzar has nothing to say. Zaccaria also is noticeably silent. Her last words are addressed to Jehovah: 'Do not send me to perdition.' The overall tenor of the Chronicles and Prophetic Books of the Old Testament makes us doubt whether her prayer will be acknowledged. Over her dead body Zaccaria greets Nebuchadnezzar, and we are left to assume that the end of the fourth chapter of Daniel has come to pass:

I Nebuchadnezzar lifted up mine eyes unto heaven, and mine understanding returned unto me, and I blessed the most High, and I praised and honoured him that liveth for ever. . . . At the same time my reason returned unto me; and for the glory of my kingdom, mine honour and brightness returned unto me. . . . Now I Nebuchadnezzar praise and extol and honour the King of heaven.

* See Budden, op. cit., pp. 92, 110 and 112.

NOTES

1 Stanford in the *Daily Graphic*, 14 January 1893.
2 Gollancz, *Journey Towards Music*, ch. 3, p. 59.
3 Chorley, *Thirty Years' Musical Recollections*, p. 268.
4 *Opera at Home* (4th edn, 1928), p. 309.
5 Toye, *Giuseppe Verdi, His Life and Works*, ch. XIX, p. 172.
6 2 Kings, xxv.
7 Josephus, *Antiquities of the Jews*, Book X, ch. viii.
8 Baruch, iv.1.
9 Deuteronomy, xxvii–xxviii.
10 Isaiah, xiii and xxxiv; Jeremiah, l and li; Revelations, xviii.
11 Daniel, ii and iv.
12 Job, xxxix.
13 Genesis, xviii.27.

2

FRANCESCO FOSCARI

It HAS BEEN customary for commentators to wonder why Verdi chose such a subject as Byron's *The Two Foscari*. He chose it no doubt partly because it appealed to him and partly because it was a slice of Venetian history and he was about to submit a subject to the Directors of La Fenice, where he must have supposed it would be acceptable. In fact Count Mocenigo turned it down. The nobles depicted in Byron's tragedy were the ancestors of families still surviving in Venice society. Mocenigo's own forebears had held the office of Doge; in fact the Doge immediately preceding Francesco Foscari had been a Mocenigo. The Count opted for a subject which would offend no local susceptibilities, and he got *Ernani*. But Verdi could not dismiss Byron's drama from his mind, and he used it for his very next opera, to be produced in Rome.

It has been suggested by some of those who are bewildered by Verdi's choice that Byron himself thought little of his own work. Yet in a letter to his publisher he wrote.[1]

I am much mortified that Gifford don't take to my new dramas. To be sure, they are as opposite to the English drama as one thing can be to another; but I have a notion that, if understood, they will, in time, find favour (though *not* on the stage) with the reader. The simplicity of plot is intentional, and the avoidance of rant also, as also the compression of speeches in the more severe situations. What I seek to show in 'The Foscaris' is the *suppressed* passions rather than the rant of the present day.

We can judge from this that Byron was trying to curb his style, reduce his histrionic excesses, and play down his theme. *The Two Foscari* is the careful exercise of a poet employing dramatic usage for what could well have been a narrative work. He called it 'An Historical Tragedy'. Only a profuse poet, his creative powers in full spate, could (like Milton) write a play not intended for performance. *The Two Foscari* is therefore very different from *Hernani*, in which Victor Hugo, his head also full of poetry, was exploiting theatrical possibilities and situations. But Byron was on safer ground, for if his play was not for the stage, its weaknesses could not be publicly exposed, only gauged in an armchair, and therefore a matter of opinion. If there have been those who found it a dull work, Verdi apparently was not among them. To him it was 'pieno di passione e musicabilissimo'. There can be little doubt that his visit to Venice for the production of *I Lombardi* and the première of *Ernani* had stimulated his interest in the subject and had given it priority in his mind. He could take a gondola along the Grand Canal and pass in turn the façades of the Palazzi Foscari, Contarini, Loredano and Barbarigo—the entire cast of his opera.

If Byron's drama is fundamentally different from Hugo's, the two works share one important constructional facet. The characters of both plays are trapped by the systems in which they live. Hugo's Spanish king and grandees are soaked in the code of ancient chivalry, honour and vengeance. Byron's Venetians are besotted by loyalty to their city-state, to their sacred soil and the immutable laws of its rulers. And in both cases the solitary female stands outside the bounds of protocol, wondering at the hide-bound ways of men—Doña Sol acquiescing; Marina rebelling. Notable in Byron's work is the part of Marina. She suffers, but she fights back exasperated by the appalling distortion of justice and loyalty she sees around her. All the men in her life behave as though mentally obsessed by their beliefs. She alone sees through them, says so in no uncertain terms, yet makes no converts. She alone has a sense of true values. Yet the drama is not called *Marina*; it is *The Two Foscari*. Marina is a Foscari by marriage only. The two Foscari are Francesco the Doge and his son Jacopo, her husband.

If Jacopo is a fairly conventional tenor-hero, a sort of Florestan but with an unhappy ending, his father the Doge, aged eighty and holder of the office for thirty-five years, is a dramatic gift for a composer toying with *King Lear*. Like Shakespeare's aged king, who was to occupy so much of Verdi's day-dreams, this Doge is beset by worries that he might have dismissed, problems that he might have solved, in his ducal maturity; but senile uncertainty has made him impotent in the face of those who torment him. Verdi must surely have seized on the character of Doge Foscari as a role eminently suitable for music. Music that would otherwise perhaps have gone into *Re Lear*.

Byron does not intrude his Doge until the second act. Verdi likewise postpones his appearance until the fourth scene of his first act. We are initially concerned with Jacopo the son, and his wife who is not now Marina but Lucrezia. The prelude contains themes associated with Jacopo and Lucrezia, but not with the Doge. It is their frustration that will provide the lyrical core of the work. The brooding pathos of old

Francesco, related yet separate, adds a sombre dignity to the plot. But he is not to dominate the drama until the very end, after his unhappy son is dead. They are the two Foscari; but when brought face to face they seem to be out of contact. There is no dramatic confrontation, for they are worlds apart. In Byron's scene at the end of his third act Marina has plenty to say, Jacopo laments a little, but the Doge does not utter one single complete pentameter line. Not even Piave could cook up a father-son duet of the kind that would have flowed so easily from Verdi's imagination.

Before the Doge's appearance on the stage we are introduced to the Venetian oligarchs, the dreaded Council of Ten with the Senators assembled for the further trial of Jacopo (trial by torture). Their theme, repeated when they return to the stage after their 'Question', is simple enough yet sufficiently coloured with grimness to suggest the crass, implacable nature of their thinking. This theme will blossom out with a sardonic dryness fifteen years later to depict the mutterings of the conspirators in *Un Ballo in Maschera*.

The Council's withdrawal into the Chamber is followed by a dialogue between Loredano and Barbarigo reduced from Byron who brings these two on from time to time as a sort of chorus, Loredano expanding his hatred, Barbarigo trying without real effort to water it down. Here Byron's Barbarigo asks

> Is it true
> That you have written in your books of commerce,
> (The wealthy practice of our highest nobles)
> 'Doge Foscari, my debtor for the deaths
> Of Marco and Pietro Loredano,
> My sire and uncle?'
> LOR: It is written thus.
> BAR: And will you leave it unerased?
> LOR: Till balanced.

Piave's précis alludes to this important account-book, but Verdi did not set the passage to music; so although it may be read in the libretto it does not appear in the score. Piave, however, prefaced his libretto with a two-page introduction, covering the drama's historical background. Operatic audiences must read this to find out what they have missed. Presumably Verdi did not fancy a recitative-dialogue so early in the opera, but he chose to omit what should be a key to Loredano's relentless pursuit of his Foscari-baiting. This must be accounted a curious oversight in one so particular that he faulted Piave for not having explained just why Jacopo is a prisoner, asking him to make this point more clear to the audience. Indeed the bloodthirsty book-keeping of Loredano is intended to enclose the portentous tragedy within the covers of his diary, a drama of infinite space bounded in a nutshell. Verdi seems to have missed this, though Piave did not. We shall see how at the final curtain this vengeful obsession of Loredano's was emphasized by Byron, but again played down by Verdi.

Loredano, glossed over at the start, stalks through the opera without a single solo number, not sufficient of a villain to have aroused Verdi's musical interest. But we very soon have arias, each with cabaletta, for Jacopo and Lucrezia, followed by the return of the Council, its deliberations duly completed. Lucrezia's aria is preceded by a chorus of her female attendants which contrasts briefly with the purposeful stanzas of the masculine Council. Jacopo's is an apostrophe of his beloved Venice, in the accompaniment of which Charles Osborne detects the lapping of the canal waters.[2] Both of these protagonists are introduced by their respective motifs: Jacopo's a clarinet lament, Lucrezia's an agitated flurry of strings. They will be repeated at intervals throughout the opera like musical identity cards, an idea which must have appealed momentarily to Verdi but which he did not pursue in subsequent operas with anything approaching this single-mindedness.

Now at last we are in the Doge's private apartment, and the powerless figure-head of state sits brooding in a great chair by candlelight, as Philip of Spain will be revealed in the fourth act of *Don Carlo*, weighed down with problems. Like his son and daughter-in-law he has his personal motif in the short orchestral prelude. It carries a superficial solemnity but is not memorable. From the opening accents of the recitative however, we are compelled to listen to the old man's haunted uneasiness. Sitting alone he feels the Ten have their eyes on him even in his own room. They seem to know all about him—thought, word and deed. In the final phrase of the recitative—'Prence e padre qui sono, prence e padre qui sono sventurato'—we catch a pre-echo of Philip. (My libretto, instead of this line, has 'Uno schiavo qui sono coronato!!!', which would seem to hark back to the Abigaille-ridden king of Babylon.)

The aria 'O vecchio cor, che batti' is like a miniature portrait of the worried old Doge, a crystallization of his pathetic, superannuated authority. With a precarious foothold in the repertoire of the baritone soloist it has long been just about our only aural contact with Verdi's score, recorded by Amato or Stracciari with fine, old-fashioned artistry about as moribund as the Doge himself. The aria, technically a *romanza* and in the manner of such pieces moving from minor to major and having no cabaletta, is musically contrasted with the preceding scenes for Jacopo and Lucrezia, lacking their lyricism and confining itself to a solemnity in which the sense of weary strain can be exactly caught. Though his entry into the opera is entirely static, as opposed to the aggressive mobility of Nabucco's first appearance, it creates a more profound if less exciting effect.

A servant announces Lucrezia. Before the obedient orchestra can thrum her *allegro* entrance theme Francesco has time to sigh 'another sufferer', and add solemnly 'Doge, forget not yourself'. Lucrezia opens with a disrespectful reference to the Council of Ten which receives his measured rebuke. In Byron's scene—a well-written one—Marina is far more outspoken, not mincing her words about the Ten or in addressing her father-in-law. Verdi's Lucrezia soon settles down into a routine pleading soprano, her repeated 'barbaro genitor' having no acid, though the Doge gently replies 'Non insultarmi'. The duet is appealing and constructed with a sure hand, but insufficiently firm. Lucrezia admittedly does call the Ten hoary tigers, but it is she who should be the tigress. When after the stanza 'Tu pur lo sai che giudice' he begins his 'Oltri ogni umano credere' the change of key brings a steadying contrast, but this could have been more so if she had indulged in anything like Byron's invective. The recitative bridge to the *prestissimo* finale breaks into one of those dialogue exchanges at which Verdi always excelled because he never prolonged them beyond their effective brevity. The Doge's last phrase has the decisive, declamatory ring of an argument between Philip and Posa. Though the excited *allegro prestissimo*

of Lucrezia may be a trifle too tunefully lilting for her desperation, his answer, *moderato*, maintains his contrasted dignity to the end, as she implores him to go with her and plead for his son, and so prove that the father may succeed where the Doge cannot. When he weeps, she seems jubilant, for she is single-minded in her fight for her doomed husband. In Byron he does not weep. He remains inflexible in the face of Marina's outspoken tirades. But what operatic composer can resist the tug of 'piangi' and 'lagrima'?

The second act takes place in the dungeons linked to the Palace by the Bridge of Sighs. Here were the infamous *Pozzi* of the state prison, deep down, one beneath another, admitting no light. In Byron Jacopo is just able to discern the scribbled graffiti of previous victims, and dutifully he adds his own name for posterity. Piave's Jacopo, more traditionally operatic, is deliriously troubled by spectres, until one detaches itself and advances, carrying its severed head in one hand and splashing its blood into his face with the other. In his imagination he sees it to be Carmagnola, the illustrious general imprisoned and executed by Francesco Foscari not many years before.

In his aria he addresses the ghost of the hero, telling him who he is and how fraudulently he is condemned, son of a feeble Doge who cannot act in his defence. Piave's introduction of this allusion to Carmagnola is a deft historical touch. This is not in Byron; and when one considers that librettists, Piave by no means excluded, habitually pared down or excised all political references, one may applaud this as a singular invention. Verdi of course, with a dark prison for scenario and an anguished tenor within it, gets straight into his stride. Once the Jacopo theme has been played through there is a progression of chilling shakes in the bass; and during the hysterical recitative the up-sliding *acciaccature* are menacing enough to remind us of Gluck's Cerberus. The aria is marked *andante agitato* and it literally pulses with the raised heart-beats of Jacopo's terror. At its conclusion he collapses. No wonder that when Lucrezia arrives he does not recognize her, even though the orchestra has dutifully played through her now familiar theme. But when he has recovered from his delirium, the comforting accents of his wife coax him to participate in a duet as lyrically lovely as Verdi knew how, and the rest of their scene is sheer melodious delight, with a brief off-stage snatch of passing gondoliers thrown in to make more wistful the dreams of liberty and reunion. Verdi seems always to be moved by the doomed happiness of his characters, as though floods of his own pity are drenching their plight. The melody starting at the words 'Speranza dolce ancora', especially when they repeat it *sottovoce* in unison over harp arpeggios, arrests passion for a moment in its sheer sense of serenity. I cannot recall another Verdian passage quite like this except perhaps in a duet for Arrigo and Elena in *I Vespri Siciliani*.

Yet in his rapturous tenor-soprano duet Verdi has strayed far from Byron. The poet's Jacopo is so obsessed by his love for Venice, and his wife so exasperated at his inability to think himself out of his bonds, that their scene ends thus:

> MAR.: . . . Thus far I am also the state's debtor,
>   And shall be more so when I see us both
>   Floating on the free waves—away—away—
>   Be it to the earth's end, from this abhorr'd,
>   Unjust, and—
> JAC.:   Curse it not. If I am silent,
>   Who dares accuse my country?
> MAR.:   Men and angels!
>   The blood of myriads reeking up to heaven,
>   The groans of slaves in chains, and men in dungeons,
>   Mothers, and wives, and sons, and sires, and subjects,
>   Held in the bondage of ten bald-heads . . .

In Byron's play no gondoliers glide by on the canal. Piave and Verdi have heavily sugared Byron's acrimonious pill. Commentators usually note that in this opera the expected cabaletta is often missing, and conclude that Verdi was deliberately aiming at a sense of solemnity in his slow-drawn plot. Perhaps he has been over-careful. In order to be true to the original Marina, Lucrezia should have nothing but cabalettas all through, full of 'odio' and 'furibondo'.

And now the Doge enters the prison. He comes black-robed and with a lighted torch, but instead of his solemn theme in the orchestra the music gears itself up into an *allegro agitato* almost flippant in its effect, no doubt intended by Verdi to denote the excitement of family reunion but a shade too rollicking for the occasion. When the three Foscari finally settle down to their trio Jacopo and Lucrezia continue to contribute attractive tunes, while the Doge plays his sombre part, his helplessness perhaps reflected in his lack of musical opportunity. The break-up of the trio gives him a chance to reiterate his inflexible, uncompromising attitude to their fate as in two final phrases he gives his son no comfort. Then Loredano enters to fetch the prisoner away to hear his sentence. But this is decidedly not one of Verdi's classic quartets. Jacopo and Lucrezia unite to sing a rising 'Ah!', steadying themselves to plunge into a 3/4 *presto*, into which the Doge is dragged, reluctantly perhaps since he starts by singing A nineteen times before joining their tune. Loredano then, *regarding them with contempt*—as well he might—contributes twenty C's in his opening. The quartet now swings along unashamedly. One wonders why Charles Mackerras did not include it in his *Lady and the Fool*. Charles Osborne quotes from Herbert Weinstock's *Donizetti* that it caused laughter in the Vienna Opera, so Straussian is its lilt.[3] Thus a scene that began with such dramatic effect ends very much on the wrong note.

The second scene of the act takes place in the Hall of the Council of Ten and we at once have their motif in the orchestra followed by their chorus condemning Jacopo Foscari.

> Parta l'iniquo Foscari
> Ucciso egli ha un Donato

they sing. In a letter to Piave Verdi had pointed out that the reason for Jacopo's imprisonment and sentence needed clarifying. Presumably this couplet was Piave's method of putting right the deficiency. We shall see again and again in the libretti how important items of information are tucked into simple little statements that are usually sung before their content can be grasped. Evidently it was considered sufficient for the libretto to contain the information, however brief. So long as it was written in, the course of the drama could be considered complete. Words or music—even Strauss' *Capriccio* could offer no final solution. But with Verdi it was certainly the music. How else could he have agreed to fit Piave's *Aroldo* to the score of *Stiffelio*? What counts here is the repetition of the Council of Ten's 'giustizia—giustizia incorrutibile' as a sort of ironical embellishment of the cruel state machine which insists on destroying the lives and happiness of the Foscari family. The short piece is effective, for Verdi has astutely avoided the traditional swinging tune of the men's chorus, constructing it instead from a menacing, self-satisfied phrase, repeated again and again, with a pugnacious, timpani-thudded chord to set it going.

As the postlude dies away the Doge enters with Loredano and all the

Court Officials. He proceeds solemnly to his throne. The effect of this grave assembly gathering in robed splendour while the music of the previous number dwindles away is one of impressive foreboding. Usually there would be a full close; then a fanfare and a key-change would usher in the pompous entrance. Somehow by the simple means of bringing them on stage during the run-down of the chorus' theme Verdi has contrived to make their convening surreptitious. The Doge opens by addressing the assembly in a recitative barely accompanied, the sparse orchestral comment isolating his voice as he himself is isolated from the proceedings over which he presides. 'I shall look like the Doge, but be the father under it,' he sighs. Then, as the door opens to admit his son, he prays in a brief, moving phrase, for self-control.

Four guards bring Jacopo before the Court, and his theme is duly played. Loredano hands him his written sentence of exile. He proclaims that exile will mean death to him and turns desperately to his father. The Council hastily observe that in their court-room law and justice reign. The Doge rises, and the Court with him. It is his terrible moment of decision.

At this climacteric the sacrosanct Hall of the Ten is invaded by Lucrezia, her two children, Pisana her maid, and a retinue of lady friends. This is a point of great interest to the student of operatic drama. In Byron's play, Marina, outside the Council Chamber, announces her intention of breaking in on their secrecy. Although cautioned against so desperate an action, she enters the Chamber. Shortly afterwards Barbarigo and Loredano come out, with the words:

BAR.: That were too much; believe me, 'twas not meet
The trial should go further at this moment.
LOR.: And so the Council must break up, and Justice
Pause in her full career, because a woman
Breaks in on our deliberations?

Barbarigo goes on to insist that Jacopo has been tortured beyond endurance, but we sense that Marina's intrusion has scandalized the Council more than her husband's pain. Yet the impact of the action is heightened by its occurrence off-stage. The sinister unity of the Ten is more relentless because we never actually see them. Such is good poetic drama from Aeschylus onwards.

Opera, however, is built on different foundations. It is music, and so must exploit sound. Voices can blend in harmony and volume, in complete contrast to the solo spoken word. There is pleasure in the build-up of an ensemble; satisfaction in a sonorous finale. So in Verdi's version we not only see and hear the Ten and their Court, we can actually be inside the sanctum when Lucrezia bursts through the forbidden door. And what is more, for good choral measure Lucrezia can bring with her Pisana and her friends, not to mention her children. In fact she has omitted no device except her orchestral theme which, at this visual crisis, Verdi has seen fit to do without. Byron's careful, classical stage-restraint, his aim at showing 'suppressed passions', has been turned inside-out by opera's permissive liberties. Had he lived to see it, would he (like Hugo) have expressed outrage at the injury done to his work? Well, he did write (in Don Juan):[4]

> Oh! the long evenings of duets and trios!
> The admirations and the speculations;
> The 'Mamma Mia's!' and the 'Amor Mio's!'
> The 'Tanto palpiti's' on such occasions;
> The 'Lasciami's' and quavering 'Addio's!'
> Amongst our own most musical of nations. . . .

What, in fact, is the result of Lucrezia's gesture? After the conventional concerted expression of surprise, Jacopo, overwhelmed by the sight of his tearful children, presents them to the Doge their grandfather in an attempt to soften his resolve. Lucrezia herself turns to the Council and pleads with rather more spirit. Barbarigo suddenly springs to life and entreats, 'Let these tears speak to your heart,

Loredano.' This is an important line because, apart from Barbarigo's sudden contribution to an opera in which he has so far played an almost non-rôle, his remark triggers off the finale. For Loredano (with the Council supporting him) replies with a haughty phrase which exactly

portrays the almost boorish truculence of his anti-Foscari obsession. Perhaps here we have a dim preview of how the Egyptian priests will inform Radames that his fate is decided. The same relentless swipe at the helpless victim. Above it Lucrezia and Jacopo of course, as tenor and soprano, are soon leading with a broad, swinging tune. The ensemble breaks off for Loredano to snatch the children from the arms of their father and hand them over to the officials. They are not to be allowed to go with him into exile. He pathetically asks the Doge to look after them; and the Doge, who throughout the ensemble has merely communed with himself, can now barely reply to his banished son. Verdi has deliberately refrained from making him the baritone-protagonist of this concerted finale. And rightly, for the initiative is not with him. His impotence has to be expressed in terms of the drama. Verdi does this simply by denying him musical prominence.

The third act opens on the Piazzetta di San Marco. The gondola-studded water is beyond, and in the distance the Isle of San Giorgio. It is, as Verdi stipulated to Piave, approaching sunset—a scenic stroke that appealed to him and would, he thought, be specially effective in the theatre. Perhaps too he took pleasure in its contemplation after Saragossa and Aix-la-Chapelle, Babylon and Antioch and Jerusalem. Were not Grande and Giudecca, canals of Venice, better than all the waters of Jordan or Euphrates?

Yet as is so often the case with a visually spectacular scene, the composer does not match his music with the spectacle. While the audience is lost in admiration for the *mise-en-scène* some exceptionally trivial choral work is afoot—the Venetians gathering for their carnival. The convention of gaiety ushering in a scene of pathos is common enough in opera. Usually the gay music is less skilfully handled than the pathetic; but this is quite to be expected. Communal jollification could well be a chore to a composer who is busy working up to his tragic dénouement.

Barbarigo comments to Loredano sarcastically, as well he might, on the rejoicing populace; to which Loredano replies that the people are quite indifferent as to whether Foscari or Malipiero is their Doge. This remark was considered by Piave and Verdi to be sufficient to notify the audience that an exchange of Doges is contemplated. For Loredano is a quick worker, and hot on Foscari's discomfiture he is persuading the Ten to force the old Doge out of office although his tenure is for life. This brief allusion to what should be an important development is suddenly swamped by the expected Barcarolle. A snatch of this has already been heard off-stage during the moving Jacopo-Lucrezia duet in the dungeon. Now that we have it in full it reveals itself to be devoid of that wistful sense of romance that goes (in theatres) with the gondolas of Venice. A lilt it certainly has, but inclined to be sober if not actually sombre. Rossini's solo gondolier, singing a snatch of Dante as he passes beneath Desdemona's window, is more memorable than this mass-evocation of Verdi's. And what is more—at least according to Byron who took note of such things—the Venetian canals used to reverberate with chunks of Tasso, the traditional text of the gondoliers' chanting.[5] So Rossini's wisp of Dante floating up from the lagoon was not so unlikely as it might seem. Verdi's choral Barcarolle is often supposed to be a deliberate attempt to cheer up the general gloominess of the plot. But it scarcely achieves this, and perhaps it was not meant to. It does not differ so very much in structure or style from the choruses of the Council of Ten. Sunset over the waters can be symbolically foreboding, even during a *festa* (for is not the sinister Loredano Master of Ceremonies?).

The embarkation of the exiled Jacopo follows. Trumpeters from the Palazzo Ducale give the signal, and the masked revellers retire to leave the Piazzetta clear. Likewise the gondolas are moved away from the waterfront. A galley flying the pennant of St Mark moves in. Guards accompany Jacopo to the gangway, his theme in the orchestra. Lucrezia follows him, forlorn, resigned, and without her motif. In the development of the scene she has a very subdued part. Jacopo as usual laments his fate. Loredano, who is masked for the carnival, reveals his hated identity, and the concerted finale begins. Jacopo leads with a moving melody which, as Lucrezia joins him in unison, seems to remind us of their duet in the prison. It is not a repetition of the music, but Verdi's feeling for these two has run very consistently throughout.

Amidst the general lamentations the relentless Loredano's contribution is:

> At last begins my vengeance
> For which long years I've waited;
> O Foscari so hated,
> Your suffering is my joy!

The stage directions at the fall of the curtain read:

> Jacopo, escorted by the Master of the Ship and the guards, embarks on the galley. Lucrezia swoons in Pisana's arms. Loredano enters the Doge's Palace. Barbarigo goes off in another direction. The people depart their several ways.

It is as though a scene which began in a whirl of pleasure has broken up and disintegrated. We have parted a long way from Byron. His drama, confined beneath palace roofs, breathes nothing of the open air. Jacopo, taking leave of his father, collapses and dies. Piave and Verdi, avoiding two consecutive death-scenes, have worked it so that news of Jacopo's death on the point of sailing is brought to the Doge in the final scene of the opera. So Francesco Foscari is not present to see his son embark; and this is sound construction, for it brings into greater contrast the final pages, with the old Doge alone in his private apartments, exactly as we saw him for the first time.

As though to emphasize this, there are the same ten bars of introduction. Since this theme has not accompanied the Doge in any of his subsequent appearances, it must be accounted not so much his personal motif as the expression of his tormented loneliness. He now has twenty-eight bars of recitative. It is a soliloquy of pure declamation which does not culminate in an aria. He has lost all his children. He admits Jacopo's innocence and his own inability to save him. Symbolically he removes from his head the Doge's traditional cap which has now become a ritual burden. This may reflect a similar, if more impulsive, action by Doge Marino Faliero in Donizetti's opera (also taken from Byron).

Barbarigo enters to tell him that Erizzo has confessed on his death-bed to the murder of Donato. This murder was the original charge against Jacopo. In Byron the confession is known all along to the Ten, who ignore it in pursuit of 'justice'. In Verdi the news is postponed until now, but makes little impact on an audience not vitally aware that there ever was a murdered Donato. However it induces another dramatic phrase from the Doge, deluded into thinking that now at last his son can be reprieved.

But right on top of his raised hopes comes Lucrezia with the shattering news of Jacopo's sudden death before the ship could sail. Once again she has entered without her theme. It is as though this was only necessary when she was fighting for her husband. Once her battle is lost, her motif ceases as if it portrayed her resolution only, not just her person. But what a way to make such a portentous announcement! This is how she tells him:

> Ah, no longer you have any sons . . .
> On departing the innocent died. . . .

It was a tendency of librettists to throw off important tidings in this telescopic manner. It was thus that Fenena's conversion was reported in *Nabucco*. The Doge, his brief joy dispelled in a flash, collapses into his chair, while Lucrezia sings her aria 'Più non vive!'

This tableau earned one of the opera's most appreciative comments from (of all people) Henry Chorley. When *I Due Foscari* was first performed at Her Majesty's Theatre in 1847 it drew from him the terse observation: 'an opera which England has declined to accept on any terms.' But he also qualified this by adding 'such small success as "I Due Foscari" gained at Her Majesty's Theatre, was referable to (Filippo Coletti's) appearance as the *Doge* in the last act of that dreary setting of what Moore happily called, in a letter to Byron, "one of those violent Venetian stories." In this, however, as I shall have to state in a future page, truly skilful and impressive as Signor Coletti proved himself to be, he was outdone by the only other representative of the character who has attempted it in England—Signor Ronconi.'[6]

It was in the same year, and in the Royal Italian Opera, Covent Garden's very first season, that Giorgio Ronconi sang the Doge. Ronconi had been Verdi's first Nabucco, and a very intelligent creator of the rôle. Some years later, when considering *Re Lear*, Verdi was to write 'in the name-part we would want a baritone who is also an artist in every sense of the word: an artist, for example, such as Giorgio Ronconi used to be'. It will be as well to quote at length what Chorley had to say about Ronconi's Doge.[7]

. . . it was Signor Ronconi's dignity and force, as the *Doge*, which saved 'I due Foscari' from utter commendation [*sic*—? condemnation] at the new theatre:—a feat all the more remarkable from his being grouped in that opera with Madame Grisi and Signor Mario; neither of whom found power in it to move the audience. The subtlety of his by-play in the last act was rare, original, and real. . . .

In this last act of 'I due Foscari,' the old, iron, noble *Doge*, tortured betwixt the heart of a father, and the duties of a Monarch, (half a slave to the jealous and corrupt and haughty folk who had invested him with supremacy,) has to sit mute, while the lady, distracted at the impending death of her lover (his son, doomed by the *Doge*), vents prayers, tears, and, these last being fruitless, maledictions, against the Sovereign who will not pardon—against the father, who is as deaf to the voice of Nature as the 'nether millstone;'—and the *Doge* is old, with a foretaste in him of Death, bred of the resolution which has decreed his son's death in obedience to his inexorable duty to Venice.—How the *Doge* of whom I am speaking sate in his chair of state, with a hand on each elbow of it as moveless and impassive as the thing of wood by Giovanni Bellini pictured in our National Gallery (a picture to haunt one); while the woman—not singing to him, but to the stalls—flung out her agony in a Verdi *cavatina*—I shall never forget.

But the modern ordinances [*sic*—? audiences] of Italian Opera, including Verdi's *cavatina*, will have everything done twice—will have the agony all over again—and, that the *prima donna* may take rest, (because her agony must be more agonized the second than the first time), the stupid form is that of making a loud noise during several bars,—a poor imitation of Signor Rossini's poor fillings-up.

During this pause, the hands of the *Doge* were unclenched from the elbows of his chair. He looked sad, weary, weak—leaned back, as if himself ready to give up the ghost; but when the woman, after the allotted bars of noise, began again her second-time agony, it was wondrous to see how the old Sovereign turned in his chair, with the regal endurance of one who says, '*I must endure to the end,*' and again gathered his own misery into his old father's heart, and shut it up close till the woman had ended.—Unable to grant her petition—unable to free his son—after such a scene, the aged man, when left alone, could only rave, till his heart broke.—Signor Ronconi's *Doge* is not to be forgotten by those who do not treat Art as a toy, or the singer's art as something entirely distinct from dramatic truth.

Allowing for the critic's traditional relish for the sub-acid, we can see that if Chorley could write thus fifteen years after the event, he must indeed have enjoyed that evening at Covent Garden, even though 'the music's only Verdi'. Yet one does wonder how neither Grisi nor Mario 'found power in it to move the audience'. What ought those two not to have done with the delicious melodies of Lucrezia and Jacopo?

From this speculation, however, we must return to the score. Lucrezia's aria over, she goes out, to be replaced by Loredano and the Council of Ten. Their sinister theme of *acciaccature* and semitones is now heard for the last time and has made its mark by repetition, as a theme is meant to do. The Council of Ten, notorious and infamous in Venetian political history, is in this opera a *dramatis persona*. Its findings are, as its decisions, unanimous. The extremist Loredano is its mouthpiece. He and they now confront the Doge. Loredano, tongue in cheek perhaps, offers sympathy. Verdi may have considered him incapable of this emotion, for he did not set the lines to music.

Foscari replaces the ducal cap on his head to listen to what Loredano has to say. Over a long tremolo Loredano announces that Council and Senate are united in insisting that the Doge has now earned a well-merited respite from the cares of office. They have come to receive back the ring of state—insignia of the Dogate. This is too much, and at last the docile and long-suffering Francesco, stung into defiance, recaptures a flash of the aggressive vitality that had qualified him for office thirty-five years ago. After a short recitative he embarks on the masterly 'Questa dunque è l'iniqua mercede' in which in a mere thirty bars he springs not to life but to operatic immortality. The alternate sextuplets and triplets of the accompaniment seem to throb with the emotional tension of a man thoroughly worked-up. It is an inspired climax. Into it the Doge packs all his waning authority, his octogenarian obstinacy, the final flicker of a decayed grandeur. For he cannot keep it up, and it ends in pathos. As Rigoletto's empty curses soon dissolve into tears, so Francesco Foscari, similarly opposed by a group of implacable enemies, is cornered into submission.

Yet he recovers his composure; sends a servant to fetch Lucrezia; and hands over his ring to one of the senators. Whereupon Loredano reaches out to snatch the ducal cap from his head. But Foscari turns on him, orders him to keep his hand off, and gives the cap deliberately to another senator, divesting himself at the same time of his cloak. Byron's Doge snubs Loredano more picturesquely. He asks for water. Barbarigo, Marino and Loredano offer it to him and he accepts it from Loredano because

> 'Tis said that our Venetian crystal has
> Such pure antipathy to poisons as
> To burst, if aught of venom touches it.
> You bore this goblet, and it is not broken.

There is calculated dignity in Byron's final pages, and Verdi matches up to this in the succession of declamatory phrases he gives to the Doge from this point on. Lucrezia's entry is for the last time accompanied by her urgent theme, as though having discarded it was too much for the composer, who felt bound to air it just once more. One is inclined to smile indulgently at this rather naïve device, but it usually has the merit of contrast, and particularly so at this point amid the sombre recitative of the deposed Doge, whose discomfiture is almost immediately completed by the sound of the great bell of St Mark's. In Byron it kills him, 'That bell!' he gasps, and dies. In an opera, of course, we must have music; and so the tolling, like Silva's horn, cannot make quite the impact. But it continues remorselessly at intervals to the end. Though it is being rung to announce the election of Malipiero, old Foscari realizes it is also his own death-knell. To be an ex-Doge and hear another man's elevation is more than he can stand. Even Lucrezia is so awed that she drops below the stave in a morose succession of flats, four C's and four B's.

The bell is also the signal for the finale. The Doge launches it in E flat minor, *nella massima commozione*. It is as lugubrious as Verdi meant it to be; yet when it slips into the major there is a last flicker of defiance with

the strings backing the ascending figure as though with a clenched fist. The ensemble seems to move with the swiftness of inevitability, its sense of doom perhaps enhanced by the absence of the *primo tenore* who would usually be a resounding asset. But Jacopo being dead, Barbarigo has been promoted to take the unison with Lucrezia; and a *comprimario* does not often emerge ringingly at the top of an ensemble. The vigorous finale breaks off with dramatic suddenness for the Doge's last solo phrase, and he falls dead. There is no sentimental exploitation (Verdi can never be accused of this). From his last words to the final curtain there are just seven bars. Lucrezia, Barbarigo and the chorus exclaim 'D'angoscia spirò!' Loredano, who has taken out a pocket-book, writes hastily in it, announcing at the same time 'Pagato ora sono!' Of course no one in the audience can single out this important declaration of Loredano's; yet the closing of the Foscari account in his balance sheet is the logical climax of his obsession. The whole sad drama may be considered as lying between the covers of his little book, as though he were standing outside the tragedy as producer-prompter.

Byron must have felt this, for he was anxious that the point should not be missed. His play ends:

BAR: (*turning to Lor. who is writing upon his tablets*)
> What art thou writing
> With such an earnest brow, upon thy tablets?
LOR: (*pointing to the Doge's body*)
> That *he* has paid me.

(*Curtain falls.*)

The half line is deliberate, and impressive. But Byron had doubts as to whether the dramatic point would be sufficiently clear; for in the margin he wrote:

If the last line should appear obscure to those who do not recollect the historical fact, mentioned in the first act, of Loredano's inscription in his book of 'Doge Foscari, debtor for the deaths of my father and uncle', you may add the following lines to the conclusion of the last act:—

CHIEF OF THE TEN: For what has he repaid thee?

LOR.:   For my father's

And father's brother's death—by his son's and own!

The printed version differs slightly, is in fact less explicit, though less involved than the poet's not very happy suggestion. Piave and Verdi have avoided the issue by hiding Loredano's exclamation inside the closing ensemble, leaving the curious listener to delve back into the Notice at the beginning of the libretto. This sketches in the historical background and records Loredano's obsession, including his final words. Verdi could very well have given Loredano a bar or two of solo recitative at the end, just to underline the point. (After all, Loredano, the *basso* of the piece, does not even get an aria.) Not many of the audience are likely to refer to a prose introduction in their libretti. And it must be remembered that Piave's dialogue in which Loredano explains his pocket-book's significance to Barbarigo was not set to music by Verdi.

This carelessness apart, *I Due Foscari* ends movingly. The deposed Doge, surrounded by grim and relentless enemies, perhaps recalls Richard II; yet the great age of Francesco Foscari makes his deposition far sadder, and it must be admitted that Richard did ask for it. We do not in the opera hear the cruel logic of Loredano, when he refuses to consider that the old man's advanced years deserve consideration. But we do witness the tragic superannuation and see dignity without dotage. The rôle of the elder Foscari is not considered among the plums of the baritone repertoire, but it must surely be a rewarding part in the theatre. It carries opportunities for subtle and careful acting. A performer can 'get inside' it and hold the stage in several scenes. Yet it is a rôle devoid of fireworks, largely declamatory, shorn of fiery passion, without cabalettas; but truly moulded in a musical frame. The great value of the part, in the theatre, is that it stands steadily amid the lyrical outpourings of the others. Disarming melodies decorate the periphery. The Doge is the centre. His old age is nearly drained of emotion. He declaims, soliloquizes, protests, but all the while is trapped in the political toils of his unenviable office. He has done the state some service, and they don't know it. So the bell of St Mark's booms across the *Piazza*, scattering the pigeons, reverberating his doom, while the Pasquale Malipiero whom we have not met waits in the wings for his ducal cap and ring. No other Doge suffered the humiliation of living to hear the bell announce his successor; and if in actual history he did survive rather longer than he is allowed to by Byron and Verdi, we are sure that his death comes as a blessing and a release, confounding those who would have gloated longer over his disgrace. Only Loredano enjoys complete satisfaction. He has his pound of flesh. One may wonder idly if he ever came across Shylock on the *Rialto*.

NOTES

1 *Byron's Works*, edn John Murray. *The Two Foscari: An Historical Tragedy*, p. 277, note: Letter from Lord Byron to Mr Murray.
2 Osborne, *The Complete Operas of Verdi*, p. 101.
3 Ibid., p. 103 (note).
4 *Don Juan*, Canto XVI, stanza xlv.
5 *Childe Harold's Pilgrimage*, Canto IV, stanza iii, and Appendix Note II (Murray's edn).
6 Chorley, op. cit., p. 298.
7 Chorley, op. cit., vol. 2, pp. 17–19.

3

JOAN OF ARC

On some days there has appeared a mobile organ of immense size, the largest ever made here at Milan. It has played practically the whole of *Giovanna d'Arco*. The overture sounded so well, it might have been performed by a real orchestra. At first the small organs used to play single extracts, but now we get the whole thing, including the finales and concerted numbers.

The police won't let it be played in the evening, because it collects such crowds that the traffic can't get through. But it is allowed in the day-time. However, the same trouble has already arisen, since what happened in the evenings is also going on by day. Everybody runs out into the street and gathers there when the organ appears.[1]

So wrote Emmanuele Muzio eighteen months after the première of *Giovanna d'Arco*. Where is that giant organ now? And where is the opera *Giovanna d'Arco*? It was all the rage in its early days when Erminia Frezzolini sang in it and received 'all kinds of bouquets from a score of white-robed girls, including what I would term a maxi-bouquet so colossal that two of the theatre staff had to carry it.' (Muzio again.)[2] The enormous organ recalls only too sadly the worn epithet 'Verdi-gurdy'. Typical is Chorley's remark when remembering the arrival in London of *I Lombardi* in 1846: 'The sickly cavatina for the tenor, which the barrel-organs made me hate ere "Il balen" was thought of. . . .'[3] These probably dreadful machines could have been no ambassadors for Verdi's art, but they were all the people had in the pre-Edison era. At least they were unable to murder the vocal score. One may feel with Hilaire Belloc[4]

> The owners of the Gramophone rejoice
> To hear it likened to the human voice.
> The owners of the human voice disown
> Its least resemblance to the Gramophone.

This extravagant prototype at Milan was only, to be sure, the groping fore-runner of the tape-recorder and the LP record, 1846 version. In the history of musical reproduction *Giovanna d'Arco* holds this pioneering place. Yet its success and popularity proved meteoric, soon to be lost in the dusk of oblivion. Nevertheless the rapidly learning Verdi had written into it a careful and true portrait of a girl carried out of her depth; a portrait well worth examining.

Giovanna d'Arco is the first of Verdi's operas to be named after its story's heroine. It is thus in line with *Semiramide*, *Norma* and *Lucia* as a self-declared prima donna's evening. It promises a great soprano rôle, stealing the show, taking endless curtains, sweeping the applause into armfuls of tribute. But the rôle has not achieved immortality. Neither Frezzolini nor Patti could affix the seal to their diploma which would enshrine it for posterity's approval and delight. The fault is usually ascribed to its curious plot; and Schiller was responsible for this.

Schiller's verse drama *Die Jungfrau von Orleans* is long and complex, consisting of a prologue and five acts. There are twenty-seven characters, plus many extras depicting officials of church and state, soldiers, people, etc. There is plenty of poetic licence and various conflicts are presented, contrasted and interwoven with a master's skill. But one invention overshadows all. The world knows Joan of Arc was burnt at the stake. Schiller had her killed in battle. The historic Joan died a near-martyr, gruesomely. The Schillerified Joan achieved battle-honours and a posthumous accolade. Inaccurate history on the stage can be enjoyed indulgently when it serves a good plot. Schiller himself, for instance, could outrage only pedants by bringing in Medina Sidonia to report the loss of the Armada to Philip nearly thirty years before it actually happened. Far wilder twists have been perpetrated in film-land, for the fleeting satisfaction of an uncritical public. But to rob Joan of her stake in the square at Rouen as illustrated in every history book seems audacious to the point of becoming artistically discreditable. As well mount a play, one might think, showing Charles I killed at Naseby.

It is understood to be the essence of romanticism that bare fact should be suffused with the colours of imagination; that an historical play must soar above the mere transcription of verbatim documents; that uninteresting motives may be reshaped to command greater attention. We need go no further than Shakespeare in pursuit of this theme. But if we explore Donizetti we will find a whole portrait gallery of Tudor England in which the people we learnt about at school come alive, accurately costumed and amid impeccable period architecture and furnishings, yet perform in a manner wholly alien to our home-grown conception of the facts. Yet England under Donizetti's Tudors is no more offensive than in *The Yeoman of the Guard*. Joan of Arc, however, with her spiritual overtones, her diabolical undertones, and her devastating impact on Anglo-French diplomacy, quite apart from her subsequent canonization, can be tampered with only at great risk. We may rhapsodize with the Romantics, be naughtily scurrilous with Voltaire, or bigotedly propagandist with Shakespeare. But we must respect the truth, as Shaw did so triumphantly, that she *was* tried, condemned, and burnt.

Yet a deeper study of Schiller's intention reveals a purpose not superficially apparent. The saga of the medieval Joan correctly ends, not at her death, but with her 'rehabilitation'. For such we term the formal reprieve and pardon bestowed on her memory twenty-five years later. This solemn declaration reversed the verdict of the trial, clearing the prisoner and condemning her accusers. It was not inspired by a humane desire to right wrongs or atone for past crimes; rather it was a political expedient, designed to prove to the French, now at last free from English occupation, that their victorious king had been crowned at Rheims not by a witch from hell, but by a deliverer endowed with heaven's blessing. This laying of the ghost was Joan's true end which, as Schiller saw, implied a resurrection and an ascension. So by a theatrical liberty he projected her *tod* into a *verklärung*. At the end of his play the Maid is carried in 'ohne Zeichen des Lebens'. Both the King and Burgundy speak lines that are couched in the language of epitaph. This is her death. Then Joan rises and declares

> Nein, ich bin keine Zauberin! Gewiss,
> Ich bin nicht.

To which the King replies

> Du bist heilig wie die Engel.

This is her resurrection. As a symbol of her rehabilitation she is given back her banner. A rosy glow suffuses the heavens. Joan's final words leave no doubt that she is being translated to the skies. 'Hinauf—hinauf,' she exclaims in ecstasy. It is her ascension. In a brief scene of total unhistoricality Schiller has traced in his own time-free element the *post mortem* triumph of the Maid of Orleans. What is more, Burgundy is present, establishing the final unity of the French, their enemies defeated, their heroine vindicated. But in the opera there is no Burgundy, nothing really symbolical, just plain bad history, with Joan singing after her funeral march has been played and so adding very combustible fuel to the bonfires that blaze so heretically in the breasts of those who find opera an 'irrational form of entertainment'.

Writing of Schiller's *Jungfrau* Carlyle averred it 'will remain one of the very finest of modern dramas'. In our own times Professor Allardyce Nicoll considered that 'we cannot esteem it a great play'.[5] Bernard Shaw, who enjoyed the qualification of professional rivalry, described Schiller's Maid to have been 'drowned in a witch's caldron of raging romance'. It would seem that those who have written about Joan, whether in prose or verse, have set themselves to swing the pendulum away from the prevailing view. Shakespeare even contradicted himself in the same play (if he wrote it at all). Schiller's 'caldron' was supposed to boil away Voltaire's indecent spite. Quicherat answered Schiller with documentary logic. Anatole France debunked Quicherat. Andrew Lang contradicted Anatole France. . . . All this is lucidly explained in Shaw's Preface.[6] He holds that you cannot understand Joan except by recognizing that she was a product of the Middle Ages; cannot write her into subsequent centuries and hierarchies. Then in his own play he proceeds to present her as the product of an age he did not even live to see.

And what of Verdi's contribution? We find Dyneley Hussey's verdict—'impossible to contemplate a modern revival of the piece'[7]—somewhat at variance with Charles Osborne's 'a perfectly viable and hugely enjoyable work of art in a style which modern audiences are learning to appreciate'.[8] It is such fluctuations of taste that make works like Verdi's *Giovanna d'Arco* worthy of consideration. *They are dead but they won't lie down* can be set against *Here today and gone tomorrow*. Like meteors in their courses they must be plotted and photographed while their orbit is in our ken, for assuredly they will swim away all too quickly into their uncharted limbo.*

Verdi gives *Giovanna d'Arco* a full-dress overture. His previous three operas do not have this distinction. One could indeed write much on the subject of why composers were so unreliable in their decisions about the necessity for overtures. Rossini seems to have regarded them as

* But since this was written, a complete recording has, rather surprisingly, been issued by EMI.

indispensable, but kept his stock in a working float whence they could be withdrawn and attached to new operas for which they had not been written. Donizetti pieced together some very serviceable overtures with orchestration much more subtle than that of the scores they were to precede—some with an almost Germanic flavour of efficiency—yet *Lucia* and *Lucrezia Borgia*, to name a couple of his most famous operas, have only short preludes. Verdi began with overtures, then discarded them, then took them up again, then abandoned them—a bewildering sequence until for *La Forza del Destino* he wrote the overture-to-end-all-overtures. And it did. For with some isolated and slender exceptions by Wolf-Ferrari and Mascagni we find no more in the Italian theatre.

Giovanna d'Arco, however, has an overture that is very nearly a splendid one. It sets at once the dramatic atmosphere of the story to be unfolded, starting with twenty-four bars of bass tremolo expanding from *pp* to *ff* under a menacing theme that might be either approaching storm or battle, the crisis of which then bursts and spends itself, to be replaced by a long woodwind *andante pastorale* which forms a restful interlude before a return to the turbulent music of the opening. In Schiller Joan has a long, poetic monode behind which, according to his stage directions, these very instruments—flutes and hautboys—are to be played. Schiller at one point in this passage demands a 'soft, moving melody'. Verdi in his overture dutifully obliges. The remainder of the piece consists of a resolute if jerky tune in D major. If we equate the *pastorale* with Joan's rustic beginnings, we may read into the finale her transformation into a female soldier. It would be too clever to suggest that the rousing tune is a little weak because Joan's military career ended in failure. Strauss might have handled that, but scarcely the young Verdi at the start of his so-called 'galley-years'. But one cannot deny this overture has a dramatic shapeliness that prepares the audience for the type of opera it is about to see and hear. Strongly influenced by Rossini's *Tell* it certainly is; but there is one thing Verdi *never* did better than Rossini—write an overture!

If in the theatre we have listened to this Sinfonia dutifully we will have absorbed some of the crude medieval blusterings of the Joan of Arc story. The curtain now rises on the Prologue. An overture *and* a prologue could be claimed as generous; but Schiller has a prologue and so must Solera. The librettist's lay-out here is the familiar one. The opening scene has a chorus of explanation with a generally male slant, the prima donna's entry being held back until after the first interval. Piave did this in his

Ernani and Cammarano in *Lucia*. It will be found again in *Macbeth*, *Rigoletto* and *Trovatore*. We have now a recitative, aria and cabaletta for the tenor, Charles, uncrowned king of France, despondent at the losing trend of the war with England. Verdi does his best, especially with the chorus, to strike an atmosphere of sub-Gothic gloom and supernatural mystery, but this is partly offset by the king's mellifluous lyricism; for the composer's new tenor, like Jacopo Foscari, is full of disarming tunes.

The second scene is a forest. The stage directions demand a shrine on a cliff, an oak-tree with a stone seat beneath it, a cave in the background, a dark and stormy sky, and a bell tolling for a Mass for the Dead. Into this Gothic setting comes Giacomo (Thibaut in Schiller) an important person in the drama though quite obscure in history, the father of Joan. The music of the short prelude is in accord with the stage scene and very much resembles, without quoting, the turbulent opening of the overture. Giacomo is spying on the curious behaviour of his problem daughter. He fears the oak with its reputation as a meeting-place for a witches' coven. Up on the cliff Joan, unseen by her father, appears and kneels before the shrine in a flash of lightning. Such is our sinister introduction to the Maid of Orleans. This is very different from Schiller's play. Thibaut has a scene with his three daughters in which he discusses their several fortunes in the manner of Lear. This, in fact, is better theatre; it does not often fall to the lot of an operatic heroine to wait on stage for more than fifty bars before starting to sing. During those fifty bars Giacomo has concluded his recitative, and without the expected aria has gone into the cave to watch for Joan, who now has the scene to herself and immediately takes advantage of it.

In her recitative she likens the stormy heavens to the turbulent state of France, lamenting that she has the heart of a man in the body of a woman and so is prevented from taking part in the war. As she sings the word *battaglia* the orchestra comments with a few bars marked *marziale*. But anyone in the theatre who has not got the score open on his knees may be forgiven for missing the point which Verdi is making. The military flavour is elusive, but it is an honest try at a leitmotif! Joan goes on to wonder if the accoutrements of battle would perhaps be too heavy for her. But in her aria 'Sempre all'alba ed alla sera' she starts to pray quietly, until in her prayer she requests a sword and a helmet. Now she sings *con energia* and the flourish with which she utters the word *spada* is so like a weapon being unsheathed that the very orchestra which has been jogging along placidly suddenly thrusts pugnaciously into the aria. Little did

Verdi know how close he was getting here to Wagner's *Ring,* wherein a wished-for sword is adumbrated in the music before it is even forged!

However, Solera has not provided a smithy. Joan is to obtain her arms in a far less spectacular fashion than Siegfried. At the end of her aria with its sword-motif and robust cadenza she has evidently outdone her feminine strength, for she sits down beneath the oak and goes to sleep. It is now our turn to be reminded of Brünnhilde. Sleep overcomes her as her martial theme, damped down into sixths and thirds on the woodwind, trips *leggierissimo e staccato* while Joan, *con voce quasi spenta,* drowses away. The effect, after the brief pugnacity of her aria, is greater than the means employed to sustain it (as so often with Verdi). It is now the turn of Charles to occupy the stage. He comes in, impelled by prophecy, to offer up his helmet and sword before the shrine on the cliff. Joan has prayed for arms and pat—like a story out of Grimm or Hans Andersen—they are to hand. But while Charles prays, she sleeps; a curious point of inactivity in a romantic drama.

Solera is not nodding, however. For to Joan in her sleep come the Voices—not St Catherine or St Margaret or St Michael, but choruses of demons and blessed spirits. Opera librettists will always fall for a chorus, given the occasion. The three witches and the three murderers in *Macbeth* become choruses. The three Gentlemen in *Othello* are multiplied by Boito into the populace of Cyprus. So this chorus of spirits instead of the lone promptings of St Catherine and St Margaret is not so bizarre. But we do not find them in Schiller, surprisingly enough. Not that he shied away from the supernatural. His *Jungfrau* is in one strange scene encountered by a Black Knight who warns her not to enter Rheims and then sinks into the ground accompanied by thunder and lightning. We still do not really know what Schiller had in mind.

Giovanna's spirits are *voces et praeterea nihil.* Quaintly accompanied as though emanating from an under-endowed religious institution, they make their respective points with the utmost simplicity. The demons are disarming, conjuring up seductive naughtiness like Peter Quint and Miss Jessel. The goodies are pure salvationists. Curiously Verdi has opted for them to be contraltos in unison. But no great matter as to their composition, for they are only in Joan's imagination and the simple country maid from Domrémy is not likely to have been visited in her artless mind by avant-garde themes. To my thinking Verdi's spirit-music has an authentic ring of naïve, earthy, medieval culture, its message primitive, its point inescapable. It could even be the source of Boito's

Mefistofele prologue. George Martin relates that 'in the theatre everyone's foot starts tapping and he smiles at his neighbour as the demon choruses come to terrify Joan'.[9] But of course! The Devil has not only the best tunes, but also the most lucid and palatable propaganda. Those who tap and smile are the real seduced—not Joan, who is suddenly roused and seems poised for a cabaletta when she spots the king's helmet and sword and scales the cliff to secure them. Charles, his orisons thus unexpectedly interrupted, reasonably enquires who she may be. Her cabaletta is his answer and it sweeps him off his feet. For she declaims 'I am the warrior maid inviting you to glory', and continues *in atto profetico*

> O loyal men of Orleans, be brave!
> With sword and helmet I am at your head!
> At last the banners of the French will wave
> Over the bodies of the English dead!

So an enthusiastic Dauphin joins whole-heartedly in her cabaletta, which brings old Giacomo out of the cave. (What has occupied him in there through twenty-four pages of the score?) To their enthusiastic unison he adds his own voice, putting an anxious parent's typical construction on what he sees. The Prologue thus ends in the conventional operatic manner—tenor and soprano rush off together, baritone falls to the ground *oppresso dal dolore*.

Devotees of Schiller will find little to admire in Solera's adaptation, for he has already wandered about as far from the original as a librettist could go. Having reduced the play's *dramatis personae* from twenty-seven to five, he must overwork these five to keep his pot boiling. Bernard Shaw, in merging two historical persons into one, claimed that he was 'thereby saving the theatre manager a salary and a suit of armour'.[10] Opera librettists are past masters at this. Solera's Delil is Dunois, Duchatel and La Hire rolled into one, and even then reduced to the merest handful of bars to sing.

So we have had the Dauphin meeting Joan in the Prologue, which quite spoils the true progress of the Maid on her way to the top. Now in Act One we are to find her father Giacomo in the English camp, offering his services (such as they may be) to Talbot, in an attempt to topple his wayward daughter from her unnatural pinnacle. Schiller, for all his distortions of history, never thought of this! Unless we are blind devotees of the baritone voice, we may by now be thinking we have had enough of Joan's father, but there is plenty more to come. This little scene is usually noticed for the curious resemblance of the English Soldiers' chorus to our song *Hearts of Oak*. In an age when Anne Boleyn can sing *Home Sweet Home* on the way to the execution block, this sort of thing is possible. But a far more interesting feature here is the strong link between the opening orchestral passage, later repeated by Talbot, and the 'Dies Irae' of the *Requiem*.

For this is in fact the requiem of England's lost initiative. Orleans has been liberated. The tide has turned.

> The poor condemned English,
> Like sacrifices, by their watchful fires
> Sit patiently, and inly ruminate
> The morning's danger; and their gesture sad
> Investing lank-lean cheeks, and war-torn coats,
> Presenteth them unto the gazing moon
> So many horrid ghosts.

But now there is no 'little touch of Harry in the night'. They have only the stolid, unfortunate Talbot to follow; and this brief, doom-laden pre-echo of the 'Dies Irae' is a rare flash of truth.

The sneaky Giacomo having said his pathetic piece, we are back with his daughter in the next scene. Joan is now at Rheims. She stands in the royal garden armed, helmeted and cuirassed, but below the waist all-feminine, a Gallic Valkyrie. One of the major charges at her trial was that of wearing men's clothes, then the very essence of corruption. But romantic drama prefers a sort of Britannia-figure, and this is certainly how Frezzolini and Patti fancied themselves. Yet Joan is in no warlike mood. A fit of nostalgia has overtaken her. She is out of her depth in the Court and longs for her father and her cottage life in the forest. It is a well-known emotion—this hankering by the worldly-successful for the lost simplicity of their origins. This scene is Solera-Verdi, not Schiller who, at this point in his long play (Act IV), has Joan in love with an English soldier she has spared on the battlefield. This love, not her yearning for Domrémy, is the weakness that undermines her moment of triumph. The opera version is of course more likely and its music is eloquent of how her emotion appealed to Verdi.

The prelude is all woodwind, the flute trilling and chattering, with snatches of the seduction tune of the demon spirits. For they conspire to lure Joan on to her destruction, from which her return home would have saved her. Through her plain recitative the delicate scoring continues, until at her words 'Why should I remain here? What is keeping me?' the full orchestra thunders out the demons' motif in a desperate attempt to restrain her. The pretty little *andantino* Romanza 'O fatidica foresta', in A flat, decorated with artless triplets, is a gem, 'like a water-colour sketch for the oil-painting of Aida's "O patria mia" ', writes Charles Osborne charmingly.[11] It is a pleasure to hear the real Joan who, once her brash snatching at the weapons of war has achieved its purpose, is now beneath her crested helm and plated bust giving voice to emotions of rural simplicity. The final cadence of her aria is that of Daphne *laureola* as imagined by Strauss. 'O fatidica foresta' indeed!

Now over a tripping *allegro vivo* Charles comes to plead with her not to abandon him. The duet which follows is wrought with both melodic and dramatic skill. First of all Charles sings her a stanza *con tutta la passione* at the end of which he declares his love. Moved, she echoes his outpouring but with caution, until over a return of the impulsive opening music he coaxes her to admit her love for him. Suddenly the F

major tune is cut into by the contralto angels singing four bars in C
minor. The warning is dolefully sinister. The effect it has on Joan is
instantaneous. She so registers her embarrassment that Charles is
bewildered by the sudden change in her. The orchestra punctuates his
astonished observations with a nagging figure played *ppp* eight times. It

is as though a blight has descended on his hopes. But he is nothing if not
persistent, for he proceeds to recover himself and woo her in a limpid
phrase calculated to melt any girl. Joan, however, still troubled as the
orchestra continues to show (p. 70), begs him to leave her for she is
accursed.

As she proceeds we hear the stirrings of that Verdian mastery such as
was soon to blossom in the murder duet at Inverness Castle. This is

Adagio

dramatic writing within the lyrical framework, and it is cast into dynamic relief by Charles' second attempt with his love-phrase. The duet slips into a conventional passage, Joan still insisting she is taboo, until the orchestra bustles to herald the entry of Delil and the chorus.

They come to conduct Charles to his coronation, for all is ready in the cathedral and the people are waiting. The good-natured simplicity of this sort of music will be heard again at the end of the Prologue in *Simon Boccanegra* where it is adjudged to be a serious flaw. Delil hands Joan the coronation standard which she takes automatically, showing no enthusiasm. When the deputation has departed, the Dauphin and his deliverer complete their interrupted duet. Charles, *mezza voce*, invites her to the cathedral and expresses his love. It is a disarming tune, coming after the bustling chorus. Although Joan's mind is still troubled, her repetition of the tune implies capitulation. Suddenly the gleeful demons are heard exulting. No longer do they have to tempt with a banal dance melody. This is their moment. Solera, straying into the realms of *Robert the Devil*, has given them a juicy purple patch. Verdi, anticipating the opening chorus of Richard Earl of Warwick's fatal ball, sets the demons jollificating exuberantly, a few sprinkled accidentals reminding us that it is not a *brindisi* but a *ridda*. Charles and Joan sing their lovely tune again (it must be remembered that Charles does not hear the demons). The infernal chorus, having gloated that

La femina è nostra!,

ends by enjoying a run of twelve *Vittorias*.

Act II opens with the scene of the Coronation Procession, the Meyerbeerian lure of which must have acted as a bait to Verdi who had not up till then attempted a scene of uninhibited state pomp. There is of course a stage band. Here Verdi really has caught up with Schiller, who demanded lavish musical effects at this point. His coronation march is to be heard behind the scenes, drawing nearer as the populace (including Joan's sisters and their swains) awaits in the square. Schiller describes his procession in detail. Flutes and hautboys introduce it, and inside the cathedral there are heard trumpets and drums. Solera too describes the procession, much in Schiller's elaborate terms. This was to be a pageant really worthy of La Scala's stage. The square outside the cathedral of St Denys is thronged with people who sing a chorus in praise of the miraculous Maid who has conquered the English. To accommodate this spectacle Verdi wrote a Grand March lasting for 124 bars* (the *Aida* one is only 43.) It greatly impressed Muzio. 'Quanto è bella,' he wrote.[12] But instead of being followed by another chorus or a ballet, it is no sooner over than Giacomo once again holds the stage. He has come all the way to Rheims, still in pursuit of his daughter. His solo, straight after the pomp and circumstance, cannot escape the charge of dramatic *ennui*, though its music may perhaps be welcome to those who are inclined to fidget through operatic marches. Giacomo's aria indeed develops into a broad Verdian tune marked *grandioso*, in which one senses his personal feelings of outrage. Trumpets and a hymn are heard within the cathedral. For a moment we may be excused for thinking we have strayed into the second act of *Lohengrin*, and are sitting outside the minster at Antwerp. But the illusion, though agreeable, does not last long. Soon Giacomo is at it again, expostulating in recitative.

But now, in contrast to the ceremonial build-up of the opening, the exodus from the cathedral, after what must be the shortest coronation on record, is sudden and unpredicted. For Joan has lost her nerve and is impulsively bent on escape from the exalted world into which she has so daringly intruded. Charles, duly crowned, is on her heels. With the support of the enthusiastic crowd he manages to halt her. He desperately tries to feed her ambition by bracketing her name with that of Saint Denys, patron saint of his kingdom. It is noteworthy that throughout this crisis Joan has kept silent, speechless with agitation. But her father, hearing the extravagant claim of the king, pushes himself into the centre

* Julian Budden makes it 137 bars. I returned to my score for a re-count, and now I raise my bid to 127. The advantage, so to speak, is still with me.

of the throng with a violent protest. Joan cries briefly 'Il padre mio!', the chorus repeating 'Ei suo padre!' just as Aida and the Egyptians at Thebes. But Giacomo, if he now holds the stage like Amonasro, is no such crafty dissembler. The old peasant (still *grandioso*) harangues his monarch and reviles his daughter, reducing the astonished onlookers to that hoary operatic comment 'Quale orror!' An ensemble develops, led off by Charles and Giacomo. It is not until the fifteenth bar that we hear the voice of Joan, breaking her embarrassed silence at last with a lovely passage of injured innocence carved into an appealing tune.

Andante

cantabile con semplicità

L'a—ma-ro   ca—li-ce   som—messa io be—vo

It is refreshing to hear her once more, her soprano shining like a good deed in a naughty world. That this phrase bears a very close resemblance to one of Charles' amorous expressions in the love duet must be a subconscious echo. It need not puzzle us as the opening bars of the *Rosenkavalier* trio are supposed to do. Charles in the love scene may have sounded designing; but now Joan melts us. It is perhaps at this moment that we really find ourselves her liege men, ready to follow her famous banner until all our ancestors are back across La Manche in what the libretto calls Anglia. But our allegiance is too late. Destiny is still on the side of that ignorant, persistent father of hers.

He takes her by the hand and thrice challenges her to admit her blasphemy. Each utterance is a monotone, A flat first, then B flat, finally B natural. The chorus comments: the king pleads. But Joan, like Radames similarly faced with a triple show of hostile ritual, keeps her silence. Her refusal to participate wins our further sympathy, which is greatly magnified when Giacomo, assuming the rôle of Elijah instead of Ramfis, succeeds in drawing down from the heavens a thunderclap of divine comment. The crowd now turns against her. All she can do is capitulate to her triumphant father amid the general curses. Her lone voice holds on to A for six bars after the others have stopped, then drooping exactly like Aida at the height of the Act II ensemble. Unfortunately this is repeated some pages further on, Verdi perhaps not grasping that a lone phrase may well be more effective in isolation. The act ends noisily, but the *allegro vivo* fails to assume those broad proportions of meaty ensemble we come to expect at a big Verdi curtain. Nor does it musically convey the mood of a chorus which is angrily calling the heroine 'donna maledetta, donna infame, donna impura'. For all the pageantry, procession, thunder and malediction, the most moving facet of this act is Joan's *silence*. This is not a normal observation to make when commenting on a prima donna rôle. Her refusal to join in the squabble is more impressive and telling than the furious cabaletta she might have launched in her self-defence.

The final act takes place inside an English fort. Joan, heavily chained beside the pyre erected for her burning, has been left by her captors who are now outside in action against the French. Solera has of course jumped over Schiller's head to reach this sudden conclusion. We are left to guess just how her fortunes have so deteriorated. After some opening chordal thumps a cannon is fired three times, which rouses Joan into consciousness. The orchestra then plays the martial music of which we heard a brief fragment during her first recitative in the Prologue. Usually in an operatic score such fragments are echoes of a previous statement; memories in fact, as when Nabucco dreams, or the mad Lucia recalls wisps of her love-duet. Here, however, the part precedes the whole. Joan in the Prologue has miraculously heard in advance the music of her final battle. Though in her special case this might not be impossible, it could hardly have been Verdi's conscious intention. Now over the pulsing orchestra she takes stock of her situation, then her desperate mind visualizes the battle raging beyond her confines. At this point her father enters. Possibly this is the least likely entry in all opera, even more unbelievable than that of another father, Germont, into the courtesans' party.

But the baritone-soprano duet that follows soon has us forgetting the weaknesses of libretto-construction—which is after all a principal function of operatic music. Joan first confesses in a prayer that her love for the king was only transitory and devoid of consummation. The Bellini-like tune with its simple wind accompaniment is taken up by Giacomo with a simple key-change. This transparent device emphasizes the old father's change of heart; for listening to his daughter's prayer he has at last been moved to pity. His stanza is in the nature of a private comment, for she is not yet aware of his presence. At the end of the *andante* section of the duet, during which she has brought us a delightful if somewhat inappropriate echo of a famous Johann Strauss waltz, Joan prays that her chains may be miraculously burst asunder, as used to happen to God's chosen in the Bible. (*Saul* is specified. Schiller's Jungfrau recalled Samson in her prayer at this point—a more likely allusion. How Solera came to prefer Saul to Samson we shall never know. If he really meant *Paul*, was this a subtle form of censorship, in the way in which *Salve* had to replace *Ave* in Giselda's prayer?)* At any rate the Jungfrau's invocation resulted in a miraculous severance of her bonds. In the opera, despite Joan's prayer, it is Giacomo who liberates her. We may smile at his sudden *volte face* after three acts of relentless vilification; but such is the stuff of romantic drama. Joan recognizes her father. In one of those exchanges that Verdi knew so well how to slip in between his tunes,

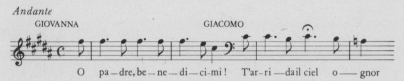

Andante

GIOVANNA   GIACOMO

O   pa—dre, be—ne—di—ci-mi!   T'ar-ri—dail ciel   o——gnor

daughter and father are reconciled. Then comes the cabaletta of the duet, resolute, determined, lacking in artificial ornament, yet fully expressive. Francis Toye considered that *Giovanna d'Arco* 'steadily deteriorates as it goes on'.[13] This father-daughter duet surely belies his assertion. And there is better to come.

Joan seizes her father's sword. As an old, pathetic peasant he is unlikely to have carried one, but she has been deprived of the one she obtained from Charles. Off she dashes into the battle, leaving Giacomo to climb the tower and give a running commentary. This is mirrored from Schiller, who has an anonymous soldier telling Queen Isabeau what is happening in the field. The battle music incorporates the martial motif we are now familiar with. It lasts for 73 bars while Giacomo describes how Joan mounts a white horse; is in a hundred places at once; rescues the king from the thick of the mêlée; routs the enemy in confusion—until a cloud of dust obscures his view and puts an end to his eye-witness account.

The French now storm the fort. Charles, in a bare recitative, declaims that once again he has been saved by the miraculous intervention of Joan. He tells Giacomo how his daughter bade him enter the stronghold and save her father. Delil arrives to announce the defeat of the enemy and the death of Joan. The king replies with a little aria 'Quale piu fido amico'

* But see Budden, op. cit., p. 220, where some interesting light is shed on the text.

accompanied by woodwind and 'cello, delicate and moving right to its last cadence, a gem among Verdi's tenor songs.

A funeral cortège now brings in the fallen Joan. The woodwind continues, with semi-quavers in octaves of fluttering lamentation. She regains consciousness and asks for her personal standard, which is at once given to her. Ecstatically she reaches for it, her beloved banner, symbol of her triumph. 'Oh mia bandiera!' she sings; and if it is coincidence that she sings these words to the opening phrase of Schubert's *Ave Maria* then it is one of the happiest coincidences in all music.

As Schiller's Jungfrau receives her banner the stage directions call for a roseate glow in the sky. This is not specifically asked for by Solera at this point. But the dying Joan is already halfway to heaven, with trills and arpeggios accompanying her broken phrases. It is these phrases, well sprinkled with rests, that cause the superficial listener to feel cheated; for a death scene should have a fine, round tune to make it memorable, during which our suspension of belief allows us all to admire a robust cantilena delivered at the moment of demise. Verdi's heroic Joan might thus have died amid melodic splendour. But she does not. Her vision of the Virgin might have incited her to a joyous outburst of triumphant self-vindication. But no. It is her king and her father who, with the chorus, carry along the closing ensemble. Joan's part is brief. Her few phrases do not develop into a tune. They are not even repeated. Discernible, but decorously subdued, are the good and evil spirits. The latter, robbed of their victim, can now make no impact. Their utterances are quite formal. Joan may just be hearing them as her consciousness floats away. Then at last comes the light from heaven, welcoming her soul.

In Schiller all the banners are dipped and then laid across her body, so that it is draped in military honours. This moving stage direction is not incorporated into the libretto, though it may be implied. The soldiers, we are told, lower their standards and kneel before the 'glorioso cadavere'.

It may be assumed that the failure of this opera, written in the age of the prima donna *assoluta*, can be ascribed partly to the lack of musical flamboyance in the heroine's rôle. Her arias are modest and finely chiselled; but it is this very quality which could have robbed them of their appeal to the old-time soprano diva who expected helmet and breastplate to go with a series of rampaging coloratura solos. Although this is in the truest sense a one-woman opera (Joan is one of the very few Verdi heroines who has neither duenna nor maid, nor female rival of any sort), the name-part does not carry the work on its shoulders. Verdi may have started with that in mind, but he seems to have grown into the understanding that the Maid of Orleans was more a girl with insuperable problems than a glittering Amazon. Hence his realization that the magnitude of her chosen career must indeed prove too much for her. The peripety of her tragedy comes early, at the beginning of the second act; far earlier than in Schiller's long and resounding chronicle. From that point her mind loses its repose and she never again occupies the musical centre of the work. Verdi has not been given sufficient (if any) credit for this intuitive handling of the story of Joan. Perhaps this is why Francis Toye found only deterioration in the opera. It is to be assumed that he never saw it performed; for given the period crudities of Verdi's formula on paper, it is easy enough to dismiss pedantically what may well strike home in the theatre. Muzio, privileged to hear *Giovanna d'Arco* being composed, no professional critic certainly, but a capable musician in the making, told Barezzi in a letter 'There are so many beautiful things that I would take all day to write about them.'[14] This hyperbole may recall the messenger in the *Persae* of Aeschylus. But Verdi, however careless in composition, could in those days be assured of one fervent fan. Muzio was one of those dream-pupils to whom the teacher is infallible. As the notes sprang from Verdi's pen they intoxicated the simple Muzio's senses. But about *Giovanna d'Arco* he was, despite his undiscriminating enthusiasm, not wrong. It *is* full of beautiful things.

A Rossini, finding his score languishing in the files of time, would have served it up tailored to a new libretto. Not so Verdi who, with the strange exception of *Stiffelio*, never fell into that temptation.* Without a qualm he left us a portrayal of Joan that, although inaccurate, must stand as an honest and intelligent, plausible and moving essay. Couched purely in the idiom of its time it certainly is. But if there is a Bellini-like gentleness in the music of Joan, it is rather the gentility of hidden strength. It was not the Maid alone who wore the helmet. According to Rossini, Verdi did too.[15]

* I have not forgotten *Jérusalem*; but this, for all the changes it contains, is still about the same Crusade.

NOTES

1 Muzio to Barezzi, 24 August 1846 (Luigi Garibaldi, *Giuseppe Verdi nelle Lettere di Emanuele Muzio ad Antonio Barezzi*, pp. 260–1).

2 Ibid., op. cit., p. 191, Muzio to Barezzi, 17 March 1845.
3 Chorley, op. cit., p. 270.
4 Hilaire Belloc, *Epigramophones* (*The Gramophone*, December 1929).
5 Allardyce Nicoll, *World Drama*, p. 427.
6 Shaw, *Saint Joan*, Preface—'The Maid in Literature'.
7 Hussey, *Verdi*, ch. IV, p. 42.
8 Osborne, op. cit., p. 117.
9 Martin, G., *Verdi, His Music, Life and Times*, ch. 12, p. 126.
10 Shaw, op. cit., Preface—'The Stage Limits of Historical Representation'.
11 Osborne, op. cit., p. 115.
12 Garibaldi, op. cit., p. 178, Muzio to Barezzi, 22 December 1844.
13 Toye, op. cit., p. 256.
14 Garibaldi, op. cit., p. 180, Muzio to Barezzi, 6 January 1845.
15 Pougin, A., *Giuseppe Verdi: Histoire Anecdotique de sa vie et de ses œuvres* (tr. J. E. Matthew), p. 288 (note).

4

ATTILA THE HUN

ALFRED LOEWENBERG, NOT over-given to the pleasures of quotation, prefaces his *Àttila* entry with two extracts:

> Cet opéra, un des plus faibles du maître, n'a pas eu de succès.
> (Clément-Larousse)

> None, perhaps, of Verdi's works has kindled more enthusiasm in Italy or crowned the fortunate composer with more abundant laurels than his *Attila*. (B. Lumley, 1864)

To these I must add a third:

> The other night *Attila*, a work full of boring and sometimes laughable crudities (literally laughable: the audience laughed), was revived at Sadler's Wells: and people were rushing about in the intervals asking wasn't it all really marvellous? (V. Gollancz, 1964)[1]

Attila the Hun has achieved immortality through being referred to as the 'Scourge of God'. His reputation looms very large for a military leader whose grand enterprise failed and who, having failed, made one vicious retaliatory gesture before retiring to suffer sudden and mysterious elimination. But he arose as the embodiment of a crisis in the affairs of men, the grim personification of that northern twilight that shadowed the sunlit world of Rome, from the Solway to the Danube's mouth. On the one hand there was the decaying grandeur of the effeminate Emperors in the autumn of their splendours. On the other, the seeping of the barbaric mists that rolled out of the uncharted hinterland beyond. It is always a powerful theme for the imagination to contemplate. To the Italians at *Risorgimento*-time it amounted to an obsession. To them the age-old saga of pitiless Nordic invaders gorging themselves on the plenty of fertile Italia was a political nightmare. It was more than just a fine theme for a drama. What Verdi was to plug deliberately in his blatant *Battaglia di Legnano* would in the loaded days before the '48 be at least subconsciously vital to his dramatic thinking. Yet he was too imbued with artistic integrity to write, at this point, a purely propaganda opera. Much has been said about the patriotic impact of certain choruses in *Nabucco*, *I Lombardi* and *Ernani*. Patriotism is a theme common to *I Due Foscari* and *Giovanna d'Arco*, and *Alzira* too. The confrontation of the Roman world with the invading hordes of Attila the Hun would surely strike sparks of patriotism. But the opera was far from conceived as a pot-boiler cry for liberty.

Verdi was clearly impressed by the theatrical possibilities offered by the story. In April 1844, with *I Due Foscari* still ahead in time, he was discussing the project in a letter to Piave:[2]

> Here's the sketch of Werner's tragedy for you. It is full of fine and effective things. You must read de Stael's *De l'Allemagne*. I'm planning to have a prologue and three acts. The curtain will rise to show Aquileja on fire with a chorus divided between citizens and Huns. One part is praying; the other provoking, etc. Then Ildegonda comes in. Then Attila, etc., and that concludes the prologue.
>
> The first act opens in Rome and, instead of the party, the scene will consist of Azzio soliloquizing in serious vein about his problems, etc., etc. The first act will conclude with Ildegonda disclosing to Attila that the goblet contains poison, which leads him to believe she has revealed it through love for him; when in fact she is motivated not by a desire to save him, but to avenge the deaths of her father and brothers, etc., etc.
>
> In the third act the whole scene of Leo on the Aventine while the fight goes on below will be magnificent. It is possible they won't allow it, but you must be careful to disguise it so that they do pass it. But the scene must be as it is.
>
> The finale to Act 4 I don't like, but here you must consider whether we can find some good in it. You look into it, while I get on with something else.
>
> Meanwhile there are three terrific characters. Attila whom it will not be necessary to alter at all; Ildegonda is a very good character, but plans to avenge her father, brothers and lover. Azzio is good and I particularly like his duet with Attila in which he suggests a division of the world, etc. Here we will have to think up a fourth character, and I am for keeping that Gualtiero who thinks Ildegonda dead. Perhaps you could put him either among the Huns or the Romans and give him the opportunity of a good scene with Ildegonda. Perhaps show him elated in the poison scene, but above all in the fourth act, at his

knowledge of Ildegonda's plot to kill Attila. I don't like Azzio dying first. He should take part in the quartet with Ildegonda, etc.

I believe we can make a good work of this. If you get down to it seriously it will become your best libretto. But you'll have to do a lot of research. I'll see you get the original Werner text in a few days. You ought to be able to adapt it, as it has some passages of very strong poetry. . . .

I suggest you study this subject well and get right inside it, the period, characters, etc., etc. Then make a draft, fully, scene by scene, with all the characters. . . .

Such were the detailed instructions to Piave about a libretto he was in fact never to write. Verdi knew what he wanted for his opera, whether Werner's play provided it or not; and he sensed besides that a portrayal of so famous a character as Attila must be preceded by careful spadework and a striving after truth. That he was well and truly bitten by the subject may be read in his letters towards the end of 1845, when he had resumed its preparation. To Escudier: 'Attila will start at Venice. It's a terrific subject! . . . Wouldn't it be a hit at the Paris Grand Opéra!'[3] To Ferretti: 'I'm deep in Attila. O what a fine theme! Let the critics say what they like, it's a marvellous libretto, I repeat!'[4] To Solera: 'I have great hopes of Attila. It is all ready except the recitatives and the scoring.'[5]

Only a few weeks before the première he wrote as follows to Luccardi:[6]

May I ask a big favour of you—I know there are in the Vatican either tapestries or frescoes by Raphael showing the meeting of Attila and Saint Leo. I want to know about Attila's appearance. Do me a couple of pen drawings and give me a verbal description of his costume and its colours; above all his head-dress. If you can do this for me you will have my sincerest thanks. . . .

This is our first glimpse of Verdi doing real research in pursuit of authenticity. He would of course have obtained a better idea of what he was enquiring about if he had gone to Rome himself. If we read his letters, and those of Muzio, we shall find him very much an invalid at this time. But he may not in any case have cared to visit the Vatican in person. Unfortunately we do not possess Luccardi's reply. The Raphael fresco is in the 'Room of Heliodorus' in the *Stanze di Raffaello*. In deference to the obligations of patronage Leo I has the body of Julius II

and the head of Leo X. There are Huns and horses, and Attila is cowed
by the figures of SS Peter and Paul, miraculously present to deter him.
Luccardi had plenty to absorb and copy for the composer. He might also
have gone into St Peter's, where the same theme is depicted in marble
relief on the ceiling above the altar of St Leo by Alessandro Algardi the
famous Bolognese sculptor. That Verdi wanted his production to be
influenced by works of this category is eloquent of his ambition to
impress.

We can get a genuine picture of Attila from the pen of Priscus, who
was a member of a Roman diplomatic embassy which visited him in his
remote headquarters beyond the Danube:[7]

> Forma brevis, lato pectore, capite grandiori minutis oculis, rarus
> barba, canis aspersus, simo naso, teter colore.

> (Short and squat, broad-chested, a huge beady-eyed head, a wisp of
> beard, flat-nosed, swarthy-complexioned.)

Curiously this shares some aspects of Verdi's ideal Iago as described by
him many years later. 'Small eyes set close together like a monkey's, a
high, receding forehead, and head well-developed at the back.'[8] And
moreover, if we remember that the *Nibelunglied* has some of its origins in
the Attila legend, we may be interested in Wagner's description of
Mime: 'His head is abnormally large, his face a dark, ashen colour and
wrinkled, his eyes small and piercing . . . his grey beard long and
scrubby. . . .'[9] So the (?prejudiced) Latin description of Attila conforms
to both Wagner's and Verdi's picture of an out-and-out villain. Yet, in
the cast of *Attila*, the King of the Huns and Scourge of God turns out
very favourably when compared with the other protagonists. To this is
often ascribed the comparative failure of the opera. The Huns and the
Romans are shown in diplomatic conflict—the *barbari* and the *cives* of our
old Latin Exercises. But the diplomacy of the *cives* is crooked all the way
through. The *barbari*, uncouth and bloodthirsty though they may be, are
innocent by comparison when it is a case of pacts, words of honour, or
marriage vows.

Naturally the plot is no more historical than Schiller's *Jungfrau von
Orleans*. Zacharias Werner was a disciple of Schiller. He copied his
model's extravagant romanticism, exceeding it even, but nowhere
improving on it. His *Attila* is a long play with an extensive canvas. He
roams over the political world in which his plot is set, using a large cast

and a chorus. Verdi had originally told Piave to take particular note of Werner's choruses. Like *Die Jungfrau*, it is too diffuse and complex for easy transfer to the opera house, and there was the usual problem of cast reduction. Verdi's *Attila* emerges with one soprano, one tenor, one baritone, one bass, one small-part servant, and Leo the Pope whose contribution is about on a par with a *Macbeth* apparition. The Roman Empire in its decadent sunset is not shown to us. The whole drama is worked out on its fringe. Verdi in fact never wrote an opera on a Roman theme. (What could he not have done with *Coriolanus*?)

The plot is hardly a tragedy. Attila the aggressor is foiled and slain, but his demise is not the classic result of his own shortcomings. He is the simple victim of a personal vendetta. Like Tamburlaine he is overbearing in his pride and arrogance but it does not lead to his fall. His inherent weakness is his superstitious nature. He is essentially primitive, impressed by signs and portents. It is this that breaks his enterprise, as Leo must have anticipated. The appearance of SS Peter and Paul, legendary if you like, was the trump card that really cowed and deflated the Hun. He may well have recalled too that the mighty Alaric, King of the Goths, did not long survive his march on Rome. He put absolute trust in his magic sword of divine origin, miraculously recovered from its burial-place—his Excalibur or Nothung. He stormed the impregnable Aquileia after he had already given the order to raise the long siege, when he suddenly saw the storks leaving the watch-tower. If the storks were abandoning the city, it was surely doomed. Attila knew this at once. In a few hours Aquileia, which had so long resisted, was his. No wonder the overwhelming spiritual demonstration of Pope and Apostles was too much for his credulous mind. He had to turn back. And soon he was no more.

In fact Attila was found dead in bed after his wedding feast. Since he was polygamous, his latest bride was no more than a new pawn in his composite matrimonial game. The poor girl suffered the cruel experience of taking part in a real *liebestod*. He broke a blood-vessel. Romance has naturally enough turned her into his murderess, a Bride of Lammermoor or a Judith. This distortion appealed to Verdi's melodramatic instinct. But as with Giovanna he missed an opportunity by copying the plot of a romantically over-ripe play. The true demise of the great Attila would have made a splendid operatic finale, complete with wedding music, brindisi, duet and death scene. But this was not Verdi's choice, as we shall see.

His portrayal of Attila is very much a study of a superstitious man plagued by warnings. But in deciding that the Hun should be a bass he chose a type of voice not naturally used in emotional parts. Basses are cardboard kings and priests, old men or tough pursuers of vengeance. They tend to be single-purpose characters, not subject to influence or deflection from their set course. Attila is the only Verdian bass who ranks as absolute *primo uomo*. It would seem to be a right choice for a man who earned the title 'Scourge of God'; but one feels that the solid grandeur of a bass voice is not compatible with such emotions as fear or indecision. Sorrow and disillusion a bass can well portray, but not weakness. Verdi's Attila *is* weak. He is a man out of his depth. In a way he resembles black Othello at sea in a white world. Both are muscular conquerors, but among the crafty schemers they are simpletons. Attila's strength is extrovert. His weakness, introspective groping. His own doubts bring him down. His vicious wife destroys him. These are not the natural instincts and destinies of a grand operatic bass.

The short Prelude, marked *largo*, opens solemnly as most of Verdi's openings do. This at once strikes the funereal atmosphere that is to pervade the opera. A tune develops in the strings, curving above the chordal thumps, in which we hear (via *Macbeth*) the pathos of *Traviata* with its semitone falling figure. Without actually using themes from his score, Verdi suggests the shape of things to come, a shape that threatens and brings no hope. It is a brief tale of doom, the decline of Rome and the fall of Attila.

We meet him first after the storming and destruction of Aquileia. He has previously punched his way around the Imperial perimeter, with a victory in the East and a strategic set-back in the West. Now, to blot out the fiasco at Châlons he has invaded Italy; and the walled stronghold of Aquileia, athwart his progress in the northern plains, has been reduced. In an opening chorus amid the ruins the Huns express their enjoyment of destruction and cruelty. Solera reminds us in his libretto that Aquileia has now been burning for four days; potentially a striking start to an opera.

We are, however, somewhat denied the full experience of this. The chorus which is meant to pave the way for Attila's Tamburlaine-like entry is more barbarous in text than music. The 'Unni, Eruli, Ostrogoti ecc.' here introduced by Solera (the ecc. presumably including the 'Gepidi, Turingi e Quadi-Druidi' mentioned in the libretto) could have made a mighty noise as they relish the pleasures of Attila, listed as 'howls,

pillage, groans, blood, rape, destruction, carnage and fire'. Soon we are
hearing such exotic names as Wodan and Valhalla. (Is this the sort of
thing Verdi had in mind when he originally urged Piave to soak himself
in de Stael's book on Germany?) It may be doubted whether Attila's league
of nations had any knowledge of the Nordic Saga. But the general effect
is an attempt at being barbaric and un-Latin. Verdi's music, however,
stays well within the conventions. The climax of Attila's entry comes too
soon. Here was a chance for a savage build-up to his appearance.

He finds his hordes prone in homage, and bids them rise. Biting the
dust is for the victims of war, not its heroes:

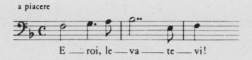

This first utterance of Attila presents his superior humility—an accurate
touch. The King of the Huns considered himself above his fellows, and
therefore free of their weaknesses. He eschewed finery and self-
indulgence. He affected a simplicity bordering on asceticism. His high
principles were those of ancient Rome, from whose archaic stoicism the
modern Empire was fast slithering down. So he does not rush on crying
'Esultate!' One might have expected, after so enthusiastic an opening
chorus, a swaggering order:

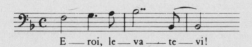

But instead, we find him gently chiding.

He bids them gather round for the hymn of victory, his latent fire
smouldering as he remarks that 'The sons of Attila come and conquer at
one blow. They are swifter than the path of lightning or the eagle's
flight.' There is an expansive bravura in his phrase, as he sits high on his
throne of shields and weapons while the Ostrogoths, Gepidi, etc., gather
round for the *Inno del vincitor*. This turns out to be a very tame anthem
indeed. It may be significant that Attila himself does not join in. If a sort
of dull servility is intended, then Verdi has managed to convey this. But
it is to be feared that he had no such intention and was essaying a barbaric
plaudit. Like his Crusaders, Bandits and Murderers, these trans-

Danubian tribesmen tend to fall into sloughs of banality. When they have finished, their terrible king does not utter a word of thanks, and small wonder.

Instead he descends from his throne to investigate the presence of a band of 'foreign maidens'. He had given orders that there should be no survivors, so who are these? Thus Attila is confronted by Odabella, the heroine of the plot, whose rôle it is to outplay the conqueror, check him, and check-mate him in a few outrageous moves. It is the tragedy of the ingenuous Attila to be faced with a trio of subtle enemies. Odabella is the first. She captivates him at once by a florid slide down two octaves, and then in a resolute stanza hurls defiance at him, taunting the barbarian women for their tearful passivity while the females of Italy roam the battlefield iron-breasted. This is just the stuff to appeal to Attila, with its markings of *con energia, declamato, grandioso e fiero*—not to mention a cadenza to match—and she knows it. His impulsive little *allegro* answer suggests his emotional submission. She soon wheedles a sword from him as a token of his admiration. Her excitement at receiving it leaves us in no doubt as to her intention. This music, one might think, is ripe for Joan of Arc. But its belligerence is extrovert. Verdi may have sensed Joan's ambitions to be spiritually inspired, for he cast her arias in a mould of artless purity. Odabella is obsessed with hate. Her cabaletta draws out a brief ensemble conventional in character, in which the chorus praises the king as Wodan-sent, while he in turn expresses admiration for Odabella. When this is over he turns to her and offers her an honoured place in his entourage. Odabella in an aside bids herself dissemble, welcomes her heaven-sent chance, and explains her motive in the concise operaticism:

O patria! Oh padre! Oh sposo mio perduto!

But unfortunately this vital key to the plot was not set to music. We are therefore left in some doubt as to Odabella's subsequent status and motivation. Verdi often assumed he would be understood, even though he had withheld an explanation. This might pass if the story was well-known; but he could not have expected his Italians to know Werner's remote play; and if any happened to be students of the later Western Empire, they still would not be familiar with Odabella, since she is purely fictitious.

Matters of state now take over. The Roman envoy awaits an audience and is summoned. Attila bids his warriors have patience. 'We must listen to him,' he explains, 'but he'll receive our reply on the Capitol.'

So Ezio makes his first appearance, the second of Attila's foes. Ezio is Aetius, the last great Roman general. But this is no confrontation of opposites, for Aetius and Attila had been on familiar terms in those declining days when the northern limits of Empire were no longer fortified frontiers. Aetius had been a hostage among the barbarians, could speak their language, and therefore could easily enough identify himself with them. Yet he had defeated Attila at Châlons—a defeat which had robbed the Hun of his dreams of conquering the Visigoths and the Gauls, and was, according to Sir Edward Creasy, one of the Fifteen Decisive Battles of the World. What a trick of fate, one might comment, that the mighty Aetius, victor of Châlons and conqueror of Attila the Hun, should emerge on the Italian operatic stage as Ezio, a two-faced and semi-anonymous baritone!

On his approach Attila bids the warriors withdraw. King of the Huns and Roman general face each other alone. Once again in Attila's approach there is impulsive open-handedness. Ezio, with no beating about the bush, refers to Theodosius, Emperor of the East, as old and feeble; and calls his own lord, the Emperor Valentinian, a cowardly boy. (This latter did indeed assassinate him later, but that is another story.) Ezio simply offers to divide the world between himself and Attila. 'Leave Italy to me,' he suggests, 'and you take all the rest.' It was at this point that the *risorgimento* audiences went mad with delight. This was an open challenge to Austria. Did Verdi intend it thus? If so, how did the Austrian censorship pass it? If we read the libretto, there are the lines

> Avrai tu l'universo,
> Resti l'Italia a me!

They come at the end of an eight-line stanza and do not stand out conspicuously. But if we look at the score, we find

which carries a flamboyant fling if no great musical climax. But at the end of Attila's answering stanza (rebuking Ezio for such treachery) the Roman sings it again; upon which the duet is patterned out with exchanges thus:

ATTILA: Là col flagello mio
EZIO: Avrai tu l'universo
ATTILA: rechi Wodan la fè, la fè,
EZIO: Resti l'Italia a me,
ATTILA: Wodan
EZIO: L'Italia a me
ATTILA: Wodan
    col flagello mio
{ EZIO: Avrai tu l'universo, avrai tu l'universo
{ ATTILA: rechi Wodan, Wodan la fè, si
{ EZIO: resti l'Italia a me, a me
{ ATTILA: là col flagello mio
{ EZIO: resti l'Italia a me, l'Italia a me, l'Italia a me
{ ATTILA: rechi Wodan, Wodan, rechi la fè, Wodan la fè
{ EZIO: resti l'Italia a me, l'Italia a me, l'Italia a me.
{ ATTILA: rechi Wodan la fè, rechi Wodan, Wodan la fè!

So what was not apparent to the libretto-reading censor came out pretty strongly in performance. Yet on the face of it the dramatic conflict is unexceptional. The two men voice their standpoints in an age-old operatic convention. The Roman repeats *Italia*; the Hun counters with *Wodan*. Presumably the Austrians, not identifying themselves with the Norse mythology, missed also the propaganda-value of Ezio's line. But Verdi's compatriots, also caring little for Wodan, heard their country's name (politically taboo) sung out loud *fourteen* times.

Ezio's attempted division of the world reaps the scorn of the Scourge of God. Both of Attila's replies are spirited; first his *mosso quasi allegro*, then his *allegro giusto*, a sort of cabaletta in which Ezio conventionally joins in unison. If not of a high musical order, this bass-baritone duet, with perhaps a suggestion of *Guillaume Tell* in it, makes a fine 'curtain' for the scene and gives us a foretaste of the great male duets yet unborn (Boccanegra-Fiesco; Posa-Philip). So the two part company; the invader to his tents, the would-be traitor to his further scheming. Four scenes are to pass before we meet him again. There will be two scenes before Attila re-appears. In them we meet his third enemy, Foresto.

The stage directions for the new scene indicate Verdi's desire to please his Venetian audience. He and Solera, quite independent of Werner, chose to show how the fugitives from Aquileia arrived amid the Adriatic lagoons to found their city.

Here and there above wooden piles rise some huts, linked by long planks fastened to boats. In front stand in the same manner a stone altar dedicated to St James. Farther on a bell hangs in a wooden turret, the forerunner of St James' campanile. Between the storm-clouds the darkness gradually gives way to a rosy light until (at the back of the scene) the sun suddenly floods everything, bringing a new loveliness to the clear sky and the blue water. The slow tolling of the bell greets the morning.

This, with a brief, sharp operatic storm in the orchestra, makes up a *son et lumière* cameo that Verdi must have enjoyed and no doubt the Venetians did. Some derision has been poured on the composition of the chorus. They are hermits, and they issue forth from the huts remarking 'Qual notte!' A *chorus* of hermits? These were early days, and if one reads Gibbon's thirty-seventh chapter one may consider it possible. However, the story of the opera is more concerned with the arrival of the refugees, led by Foresto, the tenor lover of Odabella. The remainder of the scene is given up to his aria and cabaletta. He begins by lamenting that he has lost her, and then prophesies that out of the destruction of Aquileia there will arise from the lagoons a greater and more beautiful city, a 'fenice novella'—no doubt the allusion was not lost on the opening night.

We have now met one by one Attila's three chief enemies. At the beginning of the first act, two of them unite to plan his doom. Odabella's B flat *Romanza*, with its flute ripples, vocal turns, and a chromatic run down from C to G flat near the end, gives us some momentary sympathy; but this is soon dispelled during her duet with Foresto. For when he naturally upbraids her for having apparently sold herself to the Huns, she reminds him of Judith the saviour of Israel. She has sworn to God to re-enact the story of Judith. 'Odabella, I throw myself before your feet!' cries Foresto, full of admiration. Woe unto Attila. . . .

Woe indeed. When we next meet with him he is asleep in his tent. His dreams waken him in terror. We now see the superstitious side of him which is to prove his undoing. To his Breton slave Uldino he confides his fearful nightmare. 'An old man seized me by the hair and spoke to me in a voice like wind blowing through a cave. . . .

> To be the scourge of mortals
> Is your sole mission planned.
> Go back! Beyond these portals
> The gods defend their land!'

As Attila repeats the warning to Uldino it sounds pious rather than terrifying, with more than a hint of the Frate's controversial utterance in *Don Carlos*. But its straightforward challenge is enough to trouble his barbaric mind at the defenceless moment of awakening. A broad Verdian tune seems to belie the fear he expresses. It conveys his latent toughness as, in a similar phrase, Macbeth at bay defies his gathering nemesis.

In a short recitative he pulls himself together and calls for his warriors. The voice like wind in his dream is quickly forgotten as he boasts to Uldino, 'Swifter than the winds I shall descend upon you, O evil Rome.' And away he leaps into a cabaletta. This is certainly the moment for a cabaletta, and when it is for Attila to sing, it should shake the world. It starts like the Scourge of God on the rampage, but after six rousing bars the tune weakens. Nabucco and Silva spring to mind; but their similar cabalettas forced their pugnacity through. Attila's seems to waver—doubly noticeable if both verses are sung.

Uldino now brings in the Captains and the Kings. Attila orders the war trumpets to sound for his march on Rome. The warriors excitedly shout to Wodan. For a brief, sonorous moment we can transport our minds to Hagen and his Vassals. But suddenly the mighty male paean breaks off to reveal the floating voices of a female chorus, chanting like the *Trovatore* nuns. Attila is dumbfounded. 'This,' he observes, 'is not the echo of my trumpets. Open up the tent!'

The canvas is rolled back dramatically to reveal the Hun camp. Amidst it a procession comes from a hill at the back. It is led by Leo and six *Anziani*, and consists of a band of Maidens and Girls robed in white and carrying palms. Attila's army is gathered round. Odabella is there; and Foresto her lover with his visor closed. Leo's procession advances. Attila's nightmare has suddenly materialized about him. The orchestra thumps as it did when Jacopo Foscari saw the ghost of Carmagnola in his prison cell. Then Leo pronounces the very words Attila heard in his sleep—to the self-same tune. Only this time the real Leo declaims in 3/4 instead of in 6/8, the added minims bringing greater gravity. The effect on Attila is instantaneous. He gazes into the heavens and sees towering above him two enormous figures with burning eyes and flaming swords. They are SS Peter and Paul. Before them Attila kneels and prays in a fine, broadly-opening phrase which, like the one in his previous aria, carries on its curve a heroic grandeur of its own. Attila halted is not

Attila defeated. The superiority is spiritual. His mind does reverence to divine authority; his heart is still indomitable.

A splendid ensemble arises from this situation. In it are mingled amazement that the mighty Attila is so baulked, with joy at the vindication of divine judgment. Thus the shepherd boy defeated Goliath. Attila meanwhile leading the movement, his bass voice breaking through mightily, continues his now self-assured acceptance of forces beyond his experience. The theatrical effect is most satisfying. At this point we feel that Verdi's unusual excursions into art and history have achieved their ends; even though he could not follow Raphael in arranging the confrontation on horseback. In the fresco Attila's white charger shies before the triple-tiara'd Leo and his scarlet Cardinals, the Apostles floating Da Vinci-like above, airborne without wings. The Pope, with such cover, is placidly invincible. For Attila worse things are in store. Of his fellow-singers in the ensemble Leo will play no further

part; Odabella and Foresto are committed to his destruction; Uldino
will turn against him. Only Ezio is missing, and his enmity is already
known.

In the turning back of the Hunnish king from the approaches to
Rome, Verdi has employed a disarming simplicity of method and
material. Attila and Leo might and could have opposed each other in a
ding-dong exchange, as Philip and the Inquisitor were later to do. Louis
De Wohl in his novel about Attila gives six pages of dialogue to the King
of the Huns and the Bishop of Rome at this crucial meeting.[10] It is
historically far more likely that some sort of summit conference took
place, than that an immediate show of Apocalyptic force won the day for
the Christian world. But as far as Verdi was concerned his time was not
yet come for insisting on and finding a second bass singer of front rank.
So Leo must remain a *comprimario* with only a few bars to sing; but those
bars concise enough to hold all the argument and defeat Attila's purpose.
If we think the Hun, after all his great plans, has given up too quickly,
we must remember not only the aerial threat but also the nightmare at
the beginning of the scene, in the silence of his tent before the scenic
panorama was revealed. He is already well shaken in advance. Physical
courage is insufficient to bolster up his superstitious nature.

The first scene of the second act is practically all Ezio's. It is high time
the baritone came back into the story. His aria is a real beauty and has a
cabaletta to match. Between the *andante* and the cabaletta a group of
slaves is brought in to invite him to a feast Attila is giving in honour of
the recent truce. Foresto, still disguised, joins him and divulges a plot to
assassinate Attila at the feast. Ezio throws in his lot with the conspiracy,
and dreams of a last fling in quest of glory. His final phrase

> Sopra l'ultimo romano
> Tutta Italia piangerà.

may have been good *Risorgimento* stuff, for he repeats it over 22 bars (34 if
the cabaletta is performed in full.) Once again a scene in which Attila
does not appear has been given over solely to the discussion of plans for
his overthrow by foul means.

We now attend the gala feast of Attila, who has marked the occasion
by setting up a hundred flambeaux amid the oak trees. The king seats
himself in the centre of his entourage of tribal royalty and nobility.
There are Druids and Priestesses; and Odabella is present in Amazonian
costume. Ezio arrives with Uldino and Foresto. Attila impulsively (as

usual) greets his Roman enemy, but his Druids gather round him and
warn him solemnly that the omens are full of dangerous portents. Attila
throws off a quick disclaimer.

Via, pro-fe–ti del mal !

If it seems to be a pre-echo, it can be fathered on the Gräfin's 'Morgen
mittag um elf' near the end of *Capriccio*: an irreverent and perhaps
irrelevant observation, but I cannot resist it. Yet the six ascending notes
do spring from a common emotion. They imply a sudden upsurge of
spontaneous feeling—the Gräfin's delight, the Hun's ridicule.

The priestesses then sing a short hymn. Attila surely had neither
Druids nor priestesses. Solera would have done better opera-wise had he
studied Priscus, who gives his own personal account of a diplomatic
dinner party *chez* Attila. After an appetizer they sat down according to
strict protocol. Then there were elaborate toasts, and afterwards the
dinner was served on silver plates with wine in gold and silver goblets
(but a wooden platter and tankard for the ascetic Attila). The there
were loyal toasts, and another course, and so on. When the torches were
lit as darkness fell, two singers entered and gave a recital of their own
compositions—*lieder* on the theme of Attila's prowess. The young were
excited; the elders moved to tears. After the singing a scythian come-
dian entertained; followed by Zercon the Moor—a fifth-century
Rigoletto.[11]

Out of this authentic material Verdi could have built up something
every bit as vivid as any librettist could have gleaned from Mme de Stael.
Here if ever was a situation for brindisi and ballet. But Verdi liked to get
on with things. *Prince Igor* is another world quite distinct from *Attila*.
Massenet perhaps would have made something of this banquet, with his
flair for presenting the exotic in Ancient History. Verdi quietly writes an
undistinguished little chant for the priestesses, which the enthusiastic
Muzio likened to Greek music. (He also called Attila's feast 'a sublime
and original poem, the like of which no one has ever before achieved'.)[12]
A sudden squall blows out most of the torches to the accompaniment of a
mighty orchestral *tutti* with Verdi's usual *morendo* quickly following.

This portent cows the barbarians, Druids, etc., but Attila himself is by now purged of fear. In the course of the ensemble which follows he receives another proposition from the persistent Ezio, which he indignantly rejects. Foresto explains to the gloating Odabella how it is planned for Uldino to bring a poisoned goblet to Attila. Uldino meanwhile informs us (*fra se*) that his Breton nationality cries out for the avenging of his people's sufferings. (How did Attila conquer Brittany? His furthest point west was Orleans.) Needless to say, all these observations, with their various shades of narrative importance, are lost in the sonority of the ensemble, which is chiefly interesting for its lambent accompaniment.

The passing of the freak wind is then noticed in a curious little unaccompanied phrase sung by Odabella, Foresto, Ezio and Attila, which leads to another general ensemble movement on the theme of the change in the weather. It is an intriguing passage, particularly as it dies away with the orchestra still fluttering. In its *diminuendo* and *morendo* bars it looks forward to 'Fuoco di gioia'. At Venice an encore was demanded, the whole house shouting, 'Maestro, Maestro, Verdi, Verdi.'[13]

During these concerted meteorological observations Attila has sung unobtrusively with the basses of the chorus. Now, with a change of key and tempo, he calls for the rekindling of the torches and a renewal of the festivities. A tripping tune suggests conviviality as Uldino brings in the bowl of wine. Attila raises it to Wodan. Odabella interposes with her warning about the poison. Foresto admits his plot, if not his guilt. The resourceful Odabella pleads for his life. Attila grants it and at the same time gives notice that he will marry her on the morrow. This spate of crucial developments flicks past quicker than we can keep up. There is in Attila's nuptial announcement a hint of that imperious solicitude which the King of Spain puts on for Elvira when he is wooing or abducting her. But it is fleeting; for now the King of the Huns slips from C major to E flat to announce to his warriors that the party is over and war is to be resumed. Ezio is ordered back to Rome to warn the Emperor. Leo and his Apostles are quite forgotten. Verdi's music here, though it moves along quickly and tunefully, is not that of a military ultimatum. In fact Charles Mackerras found it adaptable for his *Lady and the Fool*, where it is introduced briefly in the *Pas de cinq*. Soon Ezio, Odabella, Foresto and Uldino are addressing each other or soliloquizing, while the Huns, Ostrogoths, Gepidi, Herculi, etc., jubilantly anticipate further carnage and destruction. So this curious scene ends loud, if not clear; a scene of lost opportunities. Attila, however, emerges redoubtable and optimistic, though in the company of four people whose only interest is his downfall.

In the final act they are gathered for the kill. First Uldino tells Foresto that Attila's wedding festivities are in progress. Foresto's ensuing *Romanza* contains one of those plum Verdi phrases that in this opera each principal fairly gets in turn. Then Ezio arrives with the news that his soldiers are awaiting the signal. An off-stage chorus is heard. 'È il canto pronubo,' says Foresto dismally; 'Funereo diverrà,' comments Ezio; and he is nearer the mark as a music critic, for it carries with it not a vestige of nuptial jubilation. Odabella joins them, playing truant during the reception. Their misunderstandings are cleared up during the trio 'Te sol quest'anima', long the only piece known in this country through the HMV recording by Gigli, Rethberg and Pinza. It is not clear how Pinza came to take Ezio's baritone part, but it is a 'golden age' record if ever one may accurately use that expression. The music, though, is by no means that of three conspirators or would-be assassins. It is a tender moment before the catastrophe, but it comes too late to win our support.

No sooner is it concluded than Attila, outraged bridegroom, is after Odabella. But finding her in the company of Ezio and Foresto instead of at her wedding reception, he takes a blow more injurious than any defeat in the field. The orchestra depicts this blow as it staggers downwards:

As he turns to each one of them, aghast at their duplicity, his broken phrases reflect his amazement. Suddenly he pulls himself together and shouts

It is his last throw, the final crack of the scourge. For now the inevitable quartet begins and he, the bass, does not command it musically. While they have the tunes, he snarls his detestation, 'Rea donna . . . fellone . . . traditori!'—a Samson among the Philistines. In a symbolic gesture he hurls his crown away. Roman soldiers enter. Odabella, invoking her dead father, stabs Attila with the sword he gave her. 'And you, Odabella?' he sighs as he falls. Poor Scourge of God, he should have seen it coming. Her very first defiant phrases in the distant Prologue should have warned him. His tragedy is his simple barbarian faith in the code of the civilized. And down he goes before the joyous shouts of his massed enemies.

So ends Verdi's *Attila*, the only one of his operas whose scenes (with the exception of a tent) all take place out of doors, an opera of fields and forests, of lagoons and streams, of winds and clouds and storms and sunrise, of torches and smouldering ruins, of dreams and visions. Yet somehow the theatrical conception is more compelling than the musical score which supports it. And the sudden collapse of Attila is too quick. Here, if ever, there should have been a long and moving peroration, as in *Norma*. The King of the Huns deserves a more epic passing, as indeed history records.

He married a young wife named Ildico (Werner's Hildegunde), and after the wedding festivities at which he drank titanically he burst a blood-vessel in the marriage-bed. He was found next morning, choked by his own blood, his bride-widow sitting dazed and speechless at his side. Romance soon dubbed her his murderess. His end, melodramtic enough, was attended by the very stuff of operatic immolation. He lay in state in a silken tent, the Huns ceaselessly riding round him and singing a mighty paean celebrating his conquests, his defiance of the Roman world, and the colossal tribute the coward Emperors had paid him. So they rode and danced and sang, burying him at last and slaughtering the grave-diggers to conceal the treasure-laden site.

But this was not for Verdi. The forlorn Ildico was through the dark ages translated into Kriemhilde, and Attila became Etzel and then Siegfried. Another story; another world; another composer.

Wodan non falla,
Ecco il Valhalla.

NOTES

1 Gollancz, op. cit., ch. V. p. 75.
2 Cesare & Luzio, *I Copialettere di Giuseppe Verdi*, pp. 437–8. Verdi to Piave, 12 April 1844.
3 *Ibid.*, p. 439. 12 September 1845.
4 *Ibid.*, p. 432. 5 November 1845.
5 *Ibid.*, p. 440. 25 December 1845.
6 *Ibid.*, p. 441. 11 February 1846.
7 Jornandes, *De Rebus Geticis*, ch. XXXV.
8 *Copialettere*, pp. 317–18. Verdi to Morelli, 24 September 1881.
9 Newman, *Wagner Nights*, 'Siegfried', p. 573 (note).
10 De Wohl, *Attila*, Book III, ch. 4.
11 *Ex Historia Gothica Prisci Rhetoris et Sophistae*, ch. 3.
12 Garibaldi, op. cit. Muzio to Barezzi, 30 March 1846.
13 Garibaldi, op. cit., p. 83. Galeazzo Fontana-Pino to Verdi, 25 March 1846.

5

THE MACBETHS

The strangest alterations that Shakespeare was obliged to submit to, on his journey to the operatic stage, took place in the version composed by Verdi, in 1847, before he decided to follow Wagner into the domain of earnest librettos. *Macbeth*, with a ballet introduced, with Lady Macbeth singing a drinking-song, with a chorus of murderers, with Macduff singing a liberty song, must have been comical enough for any Shakespearean, but the Italians accepted it cordially, and the 'liberty-song' was received with frenzy, as a protest against Austrian tyranny.

THIS EXTRACT FROM *Shakespeare and Music* by L. C. Elson is quoted from the Furness Variorum Edition of *Macbeth*. It is the typical view of a Shakespearean scholar, the bit about Wagner being a bonus of ignorance. But this was written in 1901, when the Anglo-Saxon world had almost no experience of Verdi's *Macbeth*. It was the year of Verdi's death, and there were still thirty-seven more years to go before his opera would come home to an English theatre—and that was the young Glyndebourne where it broke sensationally into the Mozart ring.

But Shakespeare's *Macbeth* has been far more cavalierly treated by his own countrymen than by Italian Verdi. Already before the First Folio, passages by Middleton had been grafted on to its stock. Hecate had been brought to Scotland from mythological Greece to compère aspects of the story that needed no such assistance. These additions have in the course of 350 years assumed a patina of authenticity. But worse was to follow. The Restoration brought new theatrical techniques which made possible much that Shakespeare had been unable to do. *Macbeth* lent itself most readily of all to the lure of expansion. Stage apparatus had brought flying within reach of every theatrical witch, and flying ballets were very tempting. D'Avenant was the first to be seduced. His *Macbeth* was full of music and dancing. But D'Avenant did not stop at this. He added whole scenes of his own, giving dramatic prominence to the Macduffs, particularly Lady Macduff who even held a long dialogue with Lady Macbeth. And he removed the Porter.

Later Garrick would cut out D'Avenant's extraneous scenes for Lady Macduff, but he as actor-manager was tempted to add a new death scene for Macbeth. Kemble pared down the inflated witch scenes. Kean restored them, music and all. To this temptation Irving also succumbed, making even more of the music. While the purist will always take exception, it must be conceded that the theatre is naturally amenable to spectacle, and will go as far as mechanics permit. In Shakespeare's own day the elaborate Court Masques flourished in surroundings that the Globe could not compete with. The chorus in *Henry V* gives away the poet's own consciousness of his theatre's limitations. Had he been D'Avenant or Garrick or Kemble or Kean or Irving or Reinhardt or W. D. Griffiths or De Mille, he too would have fallen for spectacle where spectacle was possible. In *Macbeth*, though it is a tale of kings, there is no pageantry for painter and wardrobe. The challenge to the producer is mainly from the supernatural—what will he make of the witches, the ghosts, the apparitions, the various aspects that do not belong to our world *and yet are on't*? In this age of the camera lens trick photography has the last word. In the friendly daylight of the Globe there were very few horrific possibilities. Verdi's opera lies comfortably between, with gas-light and the magic lantern, a flying ballet and subterranean effects, but no modern scientific gimmicks to tempt eye and ear away from the basic drama.

Verdi's Macbeth opera was not the first nor the last, but it is the only one to survive. Hippolyte Chélard put on his *Macbeth* at Paris in 1827, and himself conducted a German version of it in London five years later with the famous Schröder-Devrient. It survived for a while in Germany, where another *Macbeth* by Wilhelm Taubert was produced in 1857. Twenty years later Lauro Rossi attempted to set the story in Scandinavia under the unrecognizable title of *Biorn*. In 1910 came Bloch's admired lyric drama.[1] In 1934 Lawrance Collingwood, conductor at the Old Vic, made a version faithful to Shakespeare as befitted an Old Vic production. Shostakovich's *Lady Macbeth of Mtsensk*, now masquerading under a less provocative title, was of course no relation. It is significant that none of the operas mentioned in this paragraph are included in Kobbé's *Complete Opera Book*, not even in the Earl of Harewood's revision; nor are any of the composers.

So when the opera world talks of *Macbeth*, it is Verdi. The guardians of our literature are entitled to wonder whether this is as it should be; whether Shakespeare's profound and terrible play has been treated adequately by him, or whether we wait for another. Verdi himself seems to have had few doubts. When he revised it eighteen years after he had written it, he left the bulk of the score as it was, making a few alterations, replacements and additions. So his *Macbeth*, like Shakespeare's, was tampered with early in its career. But in Verdi's case it was the creator who did the tampering, and for quite different reasons. He was not bringing the production up to date like D'Avenant or Garrick. He was improving its musical values, which he alone had the right to do.

Macbeth soon crossed the Atlantic, where it was performed in various countries of the New World. It was given all over Europe from Malta to St Petersburg, from Dublin to Constantinople; but not in England until 1938, more than sixty years after its first *Australian* production. It had been announced in London as a forthcoming attraction more than once; but it never forthcame. Those who saw it at Glyndebourne will recall the impact it made. Our knowledge of Verdi's *Macbeth*, unless we had picked it up in a foreign broadcast (usually German), was confined to what Bonavia and Toye had to tell us, together with one Battistini record, one Caruso, and perhaps if we were lucky the Chorus of Scottish Exiles and a truncated Sleepwalking Scene on German Telefunken and Polydor. It was scarcely possible for an Englishman to play the Caruso record of Macduff's aria and find in it the slightest relationship with the *Macbeth* of the Shakespeare text-books. But when Glyndebourne put it on, it suddenly came alive and marched with Shakespeare instead of debasing him. Even those parts of the score that seemed trivial on paper were now discovered to possess merits which even their composer is unlikely to have thought of. Since this may well be true of Shakespeare, who could not have been aware of all the plums his commentators have pulled out of his pie, it gives Verdi the benefit of that same posthumous acclaim, which is the prize of all the world's greatest artists.

In one sense *Macbeth* is a suitable play for turning into an opera. It is straightforward, with no sub-plot. Two towering protagonists carry the story. No other character comes anywhere near their stature. Those that do, or may, are promptly killed. The only survivors are those who have run away out of Scotland. Some of these never return; the rest do so only with outside help. So for operatic purposes all the lesser characters can go, or be merged with the chorus. No essential action need be lost; but scenes that do not belong to the main dramatic stream can be jettisoned without harm. The chief problem for the composer is to write music which compensates in the hearing for the lost poetry of the original. This is true of any opera based on poetic drama; but more true of

Shakespeare and particularly so to English-speaking audiences. Thus we get Collingwood who knew the text too well; and Verdi who did not know it at all (though he vehemently disputed this); and Collingwood's familiarity with the poetry was a handicap while Verdi's ignorance was an asset. For Verdi knew all the dramatic force of Shakespeare, without having experienced the sound of the word-music. This he had to match with his own, and this only genius can successfully accomplish.

Bernard Shaw, writing to Mrs Patrick Campbell, advised her:[2]

When you play Shakespear, don't worry about the character, but go for the music. It was by word-music that he expressed what he wanted to express; and if you get the music right, the whole thing will come right. And neither he nor any other musician ever wrote music without *fortissimi* and thundering ones too. It is only your second-rate people who write whole movements for muted strings and never let the trombones and the big drum go. It is not by tootling to him *con sordino* that Lady Macbeth makes Macbeth say 'Bring forth men children only'. She lashes him into murder.

And then you must modulate. Unless you can produce in speaking exactly the same effect that Mozart produces when he stops in C and then begins again in A flat, you cant play Shakespear.

One might almost suppose that Verdi had had a mystical preview of this. His score is so faithful to the harmonics of Shakespeare that he re-creates the passions and terrors of the characters in bar after bar and phrase after phrase with a libretto so innocent of poetic depth that it can in some places hardly be read without a smile; though as soon as it is sung, it assumes the mantle of tragic nobility. Verdi certainly 'knew' his Shakespeare by that same rare instinct through which Shakespeare 'knew' Cleopatra's Egypt. And instinct it certainly was; for although he told Cammarano in a letter that he had seen Shakespeare's *Macbeth* in London, this was after he had written the opera. The memory of that performance could only have influenced his later revision for Paris. The first inspiration of the *Macbeth* score was guided by that inborn awareness which is the rare gift of genius. Verdi and Shakespeare were partners in greatness.

But it will not do to expect Verdi's opera to match the play exactly. Opera as an art form has certain limitations which deny access to all that a play may do. It also enjoys opportunities that lie outside the scope of a

spoken drama. It should be within the capabilities of any competent
musician to invent a score with Shakespeare's dialogue as his libretto.
The speeches would of course have to be sheer declamation, sounding
either like synthetic Wagner or the tedious *verismo* monologues over a
long orchestral tremolo that shore up the rickety structure of many post-
Verdi Italian operas. To be the composer of *Ernani*, *I Due Foscari*,
Giovanna d'Arco, etc., and throw *Macbeth* effectively into your mould is
indeed tempting providence. Anyone knowing *Macbeth* as English
Literature might well have objected at the time that it could not decently
be done. Verdi himself had no doubts. He had already been matching his
creative mind against the challenge of *King Lear*. The project
confounded him finally; but in 1846 he was not to know this. He had
already used the works of Schiller, Voltaire, Byron and Hugo. He prized
Shakespeare far above these; reverenced him; and enjoyed the urge to
make a Verdi opera out of him. If Rossini could still fill the theatres with
his quite outrageous travesty of *Othello*, what could *he* not do with
Macbeth? His would be no travesty. He could not exploit the ignorance
of his public by presenting counterfeit. His *Macbeth* must *be Macbeth*. It
would be served up with *coro d'introduzione*, *cavatina-cabaletta*, *gran duetto*,
finale—the old routine. But within that accepted framework would
swell a Shakespearean Tragedy, testing the tensions for bursting-point.

This is an opera that could have started without a prelude. The
opening of Shakespeare's play is unique in its sudden, jolting effect.
Verdi too might have plunged us straight into the thunder and lightning
and the witches. His little prelude need not have been played first. Yet it
is a compact piece which introduces us briefly to the main elements of the
plot: the witches and the Macbeths. The wind instruments open with the
theme of 'Thrice the brinded Cat hath mew'd', with the trills and
repeated triplets that abound in the witch music. Then a deep brass
fanfare announces Macbeth the warrior hero, above whose earthy
virility the aerial witches seem to gyrate. Then the violins take over,
staccato, introducing the sinister tensions of Lady Macbeth. For four bars
we seem to hear a dialogue between them; Macbeth growling up from
the bass, his wife descending persuasively, until they meet in a full chord
and their resolutions join forces. Immediately Verdi pulls out his 'big'
tune—that of the prelude to the Sleepwalking Scene. The two return to
their dialogue, more intensely this time; and then *pppp* the sleepwalking
tune steals by again, to a conclusion as inevitable and hushed as the
Traviata death-scene prelude which certainly echoes it.

Then the curtain rises. For forty-three bars we have Shakespeare's thunder and lightning and the unmistakable presence of levitation. With each peal and flash a coven of witches materializes, until there are three: Verdi insisted on the triple formation of the witches, suggesting six to each group. We may call them covens, though a true coven had thirteen members. At any rate Verdi stipulates eighteen, all soprano; but although they address each other in sixes, they speak as one, their pronouns and verbs in the singular. Perhaps Verdi was not prepared to lose altogether the dramatic force of 'When fhall we three meet againe?' while at the same time availing himself of the fuller resources of the opera house. 'They must not forget they are witches speaking,' he wrote hopefully in the score.

They are interrupted, as in Shakespeare, by a *drum within*; and they promptly wheel into the mystical *ridda* of the witch-revels,

> Thrice to thine, and thrice to mine
> And thrice againe, to make vp nine.

(Fortunately Verdi knew better than to allow his *streghe* to indulge in mental arithmetic: their answer would have come to far more than nine.) In spite of the specific directions, they conclude in the old tonic-dominant gambit that ends so many legions of operatic choruses. Charitably, one may pretend that the routine signifies

> Peace, the Charme's wound vp.

Macbeth and Banquo enter, the former faithfully on his famous

> So foule and faire a day I haue not feene.

They challenge the assembled witches with equanimity, although severely outnumbered (which in the play they certainly are not). The covens greet them *in tuono profetico*. There was no difficulty in following Shakespeare here, which the libretto does down to and including

> So all haile *Macbeth*, and *Banquo*.
> *Banquo*, and *Macbeth*, all haile.

These lines are sung to a sudden *allegro* as they vanish, a deft musical splashing of Banquo's comment,

The Earth hath bubbles, as the Water ha's,
And thefe are of them: whither are they vanifh'd?

It may be suprising to hear 'Macbetto e Banco' since the opera is called *Macbeth* and was always so referred to by Verdi. Banquo is perfectly pronounceable by an Italian. But we also have Macduffo and Duncano. Most names remain as in Shakespeare for stage directions. Malcolm is not mentioned in the text except as 'figlio di Duncano', thus avoiding a small problem. Fleance, however, is Fleanzio in the stage directions. As for Lady Macbeth, she is consistently 'Lady', even in Verdi's letters, which has been indulgently accepted as a quaint curiosity. But in the First Folio she is Lady most of the time, and occasionally 'Macbeth's wife', but *never* Lady Macbeth.

A reassuring orchestral *allegro risoluto* at once dispels the sinister aftermath of the witches, as messengers (in place of Ross and Angus) come from the king to announce Macbeth's elevation to the title of Cawdor. Banquo in a horrified aside comments,

What, can the Deuill fpeake true?

It is the moment for a duet on the lines of Shakespeare's development, with Macbeth speaking his thoughts partly to Banquo, partly aside. Macbeth's opening stanza is uncommonly dramatic. Within the space of nine bars he has the instructions *sotto voce*, *quasi con ispavento*, *con esclamazione*, *cupo*, *esclamando*, *cupo* and *a voce aperta*. He is singing the equivalent of

Two Truths are told
As happy Prologues to the fwelling Act
Of the Imperial Theame. . . .
. . . why doe I yeeld to that fuggeftion,
Whofe horrid Image doth vnfixe my Heire. . . .
If Chance will haue me King,
Why Chance may Crowne me,
Without my ftirre.

In contrast to his melodic ruminations Banquo's *staccato*, worried comments complete the musical picture:

> Looke, how our Partner's rapt. . . .
>   . . . But 'tis ftrange:
> And oftentimes, to winne vs to our harme,
> The Inftruments of Darkneffe tell vs Truths,
> Winne vs with honeft Trifles, to betray's
> In deepeft confequence.

The messengers (although Ross and Angus say nothing at this point) add their weight to the duet as it closes, more or less developing Banquo's 'Looke how our Partner's rapt' with comments of their own.

It is sheer operatic licence that as soon as this all-male ensemble is over and the stage empty the witches should return for a curtain. Their re-assembly serves chiefly to give them the opportunity to sing 'fuggiam' thirty-four times; thus recalling the Shakespearean commentator's observation, 'The witches seem to be introduced for no other purpose than to tell us they are to meet again.'

What have we learnt so far? Verdi has not attempted to tell his audience anything about Macbeth. The roll of the *tamburo* is the sole suggestion that he is a soldier. The Arden Editor comments, 'It is curious that though Banquo and Macbeth are alone, their arrival is announced by a drum.' Here is a clear win for the operatic element! The epic scene in which Duncan is told of the military triumphs of 'braue *Macbeth* (well hee deferues that Name)' is omitted. Verdi has ducked the responsibility of presenting his hero as a superman in the field, where, according to the play's muddled and possibly spurious account, he has won three distinct battles in three different campaigns on the same day, outdoing the gods of Homer.

Except for this—and it could only have been included by enlarging the cast uneconomically—Verdi's Macbeth has been introduced to us with these essential pieces of information: the Cawdor prophecy has been fulfilled so quickly that the one about the throne must be seriously considered; the temptation to bring this about by getting rid of the existing king has risen in his mind—to be swiftly suppressed; Banquo is an interested party, but remains suspicious both of the witches and of Macbeth. A reasonably concise introduction to the tragedy.

It is now immediately the turn of Lady Macbeth. Her husband, on his first appearance, was denied the usual cavatina-cabaletta which is the chief singer's right. She now gets the full range of Verdi's growing power to present a strong-minded female. Abigaille and Odabella have

both opened their accounts with tough, florid, declamatory arias of
crucial impact. So now does Lady Macbeth, with the added perquisite of
the letter which, as in Shakespeare, she comes in reading. A vigorous
introduction at once contrasts her with the introspective Thane. The
letter-reading (an old operatic tradition obeyed by Verdi in *Un Giorno di
Regno* as later in *Traviata*) brings an immediate effect of creepiness, as
Shakespeare no doubt intended. But Verdi can underpin it with a long-
held chord. We may indulge in a special shiver as the singer ends her
reading to transfer her voice to the E that opens her sung recitative. It is a
step she must o'erleap (or else fall down). Once in singing gear, she is
away with her opening recitative and into her cavatina. Her theme is
Shakespeare's: she harps on her husband's lack of resolve. The
violoncellos drive along emphasizing the valour of her tongue. The
orchestra quickens excitedly as a servant enters to announce that the king
is on his way. In a striking passage she realizes the significance of the
tidings. The impact strikes her (see preceding page).

Although it stands in the commonplace position of bridge to the
cabaletta, it makes a portentous effect with its repeated 'Qui?' between
strings trembling with tension. This is Verdi's splendid equivalent of her

> He brings great newes.
> The Rauen himfelfe is hoarfe,
> That croakes the fatall entrance of *Duncan*
> Vnder my Battlements:

Then the invocation

> ,   Come you Spirits
> That tend on mortall thoughts vnfex me here . . .

is the cabaletta which, though it did not dare in a nineteenth-century
opera house to call the 'murth'ring Ministers' to

> Come to my Womans Brefts
> And take my Milke for Gall. . . . ,

does in the course of its two verses fill the auditorium with a musical
exclamation as powerful as

> Come, thick Night,
> And pall thee in the dunneſt ſmoake of Hell,
> That my keene Knife ſee not the wound it makes. . . .

The vigour of it, though quite conventional in style, is the vigour of Shakespeare's mounting climax to Macbeth's entry.

In the previous operas Macbeth would have appeared on cue to a tripping tune by the strings over a thrummed bass. But Verdi here sensed the solemnity of a murder-plot implied though unspoken. Without a vestige of Shakespeare's poetic imagery (that splendid exercise in simile and metaphor indulged in by the coaxing Lady), the composer puts his terse, pregnant dialogue over a handful of simple brass chords, the trombones curdling our anticipation. Verdi here, in compensation for the lengthy cuts he is about to make, cannot resist bringing forward the inevitable

> But ſcrew your courage to the ſticking-place,
> And wee'le not fayle.

At this point distant music is discerned. Macbeth recognizes that it accompanies the king. Lady Macbeth gives vent to one of her characteristic declamatory lines, bidding Macbeth join her joyfully in welcoming his arrival. No hoarse raven here, as she whips excitedly down from B in alt to middle C. They retire, and the distant music is heard closer.

The stage directions now refer to the music as 'rustic'. Presumably Verdi wanted to stress the unofficial character of Duncan's visit. This was no state ceremonial, with regal pomp and fanfares, but a local, domestic progress; Balmoral as opposed to Windsor. The *musica villareccia* lasts for 132 bars as it reaches the castle on its pleasant seat and then gradually dies away as the village band returns to the glen below. During this time the king arrives with Banquo, Macduff, Malcolm and his entourage, and in the company of the Macbeths they pass across the stage. This charade is based on Shakespeare's stage directions

> *Hautboys and torches. Enter, and pass over the stage, a Sewer, and divers Servants with dishes and service.*

But what can in performance provoke smiles (Wilson Knight cautions

producers here)³ is transformed by the composer into a stage routine of
uncanny foreboding. We may miss Duncan and Banquo making their
polite remarks, such as arriving guests are wont to do, and which critics
seize on as the only shaft of sunlight in this dark play. But we get instead
the unbearable sight of the old king, gracious and unsuspecting, being
silently shown to the apartments from which he will never emerge alive;
the very speechlessness of the principals, and the silence of the chorus,
speaking more volumes of foreboding to us than any hushed or *staccato*
ensemble could possibly have done. Meanwhile that curious village band
jigs on outside in the nimble and sweet martlet-haunted air. It always
seems to me that there is a touch of Thomas Hardy here in this sublime
juxtaposition of rustic simplicity and tragic doom.

The craftsmanship of this musical interlude blinds our senses to the fact
that no time-schedule is prepared for Duncan's dinner or post-prandial
recreation. The curtain does not fall, yet at once Macbeth is arranging
for his bed-time drink (as in Shakespeare—but several hours too soon).
We have in fact imperceptibly slipped into the play's second act. All the
great monologue from 'If it were done, when 'tis done' through the tense
conversation between the Macbeths that is one of Shakespeare's
highlights is missing from the opera, as is the restless intrusion of Banquo
and Fleance. Macbeth's conquest of his wavering, and his wife's
unspeakable viciousness are outside the text of the libretto; but they are
implied under the plaintive repetitions of the musical interlude, as the
innocent music trundles on with the murderous pair stalking across the
hall of their castle, the serpents under it.

Macbeth now has his first histrionic opportunity—'Mi s'affaccia un
pugnal?' ('Is this a dagger?') Clearly Verdi was at this point very much
concerned about giving his Macbeth a declamatory passage worthy of its
poetic original. He could introduce his Lady with all the trappings of a
full-blown aria; but his baritone must obtrude beyond the conventions.
It should be remarked that all through his operas Verdi gave his heroines
arias, but often experimented with his male parts, as Rigoletto, Paolo,
Iago and Otello, Falstaff and Ford. Macbeth's dagger speech is his first
such monologue, with its own nucleus of dramatic energy as opposed to
mere stop-gap recitative.

After his conventional address to the servant,

> Goe bid thy Miftreffe, when my drinke is ready,
> She ftrike vpon the Bell

there are three deliberate orchestral bars of *adagio* marked *ppp* into which
an *ff allegro* by the bass instruments suddenly bursts as Macbeth imagines
the dagger. In the score Verdi has written that 'This whole duet must be
performed by the singers *sotto voce, e cupa*, with the exception of some
phrases which will be marked *a voce spiegata.*' The instruction is therefore
to remain in force until the very end of the murder duet. Verdi sees the
scene as one, but it is not a duet, of course, until Lady Macbeth joins her
husband on his return from Duncan's bedchamber.

From his order to the servant to his departure to kill Duncan,
Macbeth's solo undergoes six time-changes: the two already referred to,
as his stealthy calm is broken into by the dagger's appearance and his
frantic words on seeing it come and vanish and return; a *largo* section—

> Thou marfhall'ft me the way that I was going,

allegro—

> I fee thee ftill,
> And on thy Blade, and Dudgeon, Gouts of Blood,

andante—

> Now o're the one halfe World
> Nature feemes dead,

allegro—

> Witchcraft celebrates
> Pale Heccats Offrings. . . .
> Thou, fowre and firme-set Earth,
> Heare not my fteps;

then, as the bell rings, the monologue ends *a voce spiegato* with a rhyming
couplet that anyone with small Latin and less Italian may recognize:

> Non udirlo, Duncano! È squillo eterno
> Che nel cielo ti chiama o nell'inferno!

The music is an honest attempt at matching the atmosphere. The vision
of the dagger is riveted with such deep brass growls that for a moment
one may think Hunding is on the prowl (and that is no bad dramatic

allusion). Then a stealthy motif creeps below his words 'A me precorri confuso cammin', a precursor of that tortuous theme that runs so tragically through Otello's 'Dio mi potevi scagliar'—more earth-bound by Verdi's 1847 roots, but conveying a suggestion of 'wither'd Murther'—

> thus with his ſtealthy pace,
> With *Tarquins* rauiſhing ſtrides, towards his deſigne
> Moues like a Ghost.

Here in fact we have a contrapuntal blending of two separate Shakespearean images, one in the vocal line, the other in the orchestra—no mean feat!

Then at 'Sulla meta del mondo' the cor anglais (not at this stage one of Verdi's usual instruments) creeps *ppp* upwards while the clarinet descends in answer. This time it is the voice that whispers *misterioso* of 'Murther's ftealthy pace,' while the orchestra tells of 'Curtain'd fleep' and its 'wicked Dreames'. Suddenly the music of the witches is echoed in galloping *allegro* snatches, while Macbeth bids 'the firme-fet Earth/Heare not my fteps', *grave ppp*. Then the bell, and the confident, almost boastful resolve of the man who has at last pulled himself together, the orchestra blaring out with the panache of a Beethoven finale.

Creepily different is Lady Macbeth's entry to seven perfectly simple yet eerie semibreve chords. Perhaps they portray her inner self-control.

Allegro (entra Lady Macbeth sola lentamente)

The cor anglais and bassoon drop a minor third ('it was the Owle that fhriek'd'): Macbeth (within) calls 'Who's there? what hoa?' and he comes in—'I haue done the deed.' Then begins the celebrated duet which Verdi rehearsed and rehearsed—never satisfied because he was dreaming of the unattainable, Italian Opera without Italian singing.

As soon as Macbeth shuffles up to his wife over the restless accompaniment and begins his 'Fatal mia donna' a new atmosphere is apparent, a restless desperation, a *perpetuum mobile* of terror, punctuated by his repeated cry as he beholds his hands:

Allegro

Oh   vista, oh vista or — ri — bi-le!

He goes on to tell what he heard in the bedchamber, and how *Amen* stuck in his throat—all to an urgent 'tune' where most composers would surely have fallen back on recitative. It is now Lady Macbeth's turn to punctuate, which she does by repeated comments of 'Follie'. Verdi set such store by this that when he offered his French version to Escudier he suggested the Italian word should remain. Her grace notes and triplets here are a mocking contrast to the earnestness of the transfixed Macbeth.

In a new *andantino* section he broods over the voices that addressed him in sleep, the trombones *ppp* adding their sinister touch of unreality. Lady Macbeth attempts to reason with him. There is a subtle change in the music with its hemi-demi-semiquaver quadruplets urging her argument. But it drives Macbeth to reply in a broad Verdian phrase

Co— m'an— ge— li   d'i— ra, ven-det—ta   tuo-nar— mi u—

drò di   Dun-ca——no le san—te vir—tù.

that however satisfying for both singer and audience seems a mistake. In Macbeth's emotional upset he should not be capable of rallying in a phrase so resolute as this; and furthermore the words are indefensible. For what he is singing is part of the earlier speech ('If 'twere done') which Verdi omitted. It was understandable that when he was vacillating before Duncan's murder he should have admitted

> that his Vertues
> Will pleade like Angels, Trumpet-tongu'd againft
> The deepe damnation of his taking off.

But now Duncan is killed, there is no room for so damaging an admission. No wonder Lady Macbeth quickly smothers its repetition with her spirited attempt to rally his spirits. The contrast between the two is excellent, as their parts intertwine and trail away *morendo*.

The pulses rise as 3/8 becomes 6/8 and Lady Macbeth suddenly realizes he has brought the dagger out instead of planting it as evidence of the grooms' guilt. The biting orchestral figure has the restlessness of *La Forza del Destino*'s fate theme, until she seizes the weapon and takes it back. Immediately there is the famous knocking, somewhat unnecessarily smothered by chords. Macbeth surveys his bloodstained hands. The lurid splash of Shakespeare's colour is missing, but the theatrical *coup* is as tense, as Lady Macbeth's return brings back her biting music to shame him. The knocking is repeated, breaking Macbeth's spirit in a superbly dramatic sequence.

Another change of time and key brings a pendant to the duet—by no means a cabaletta though just inside the convention of ending quickly. The music thrillingly expresses their mutual urgency brought on by the knocking; but still Lady Macbeth, as in Shakespeare, is more in control than her bemused husband, as the music so vividly tells us:

How fascinating is their exit, their combined *staccato* monosyllables receding into the castle shadows, the woodwind accompaniment lingering for a few bars *insensibilmente morendo ed allargando*. It is surely safe to suggest that Italian Opera never before threw up anything like these pages; and if Shakespeare's poetry is largely missing, its effect is uncannily reproduced. Whatever the omissions, we seem now to have caught up fair and square with the drama.

But now we have some adjustments. Firstly, the Porter is left out; and not surprisingly. Then Macduff is accompanied by Banquo instead of Lennox, for in this version we are short of Earls. So while Macduff goes to wake the king, Banquo gets Lennox's lines about the unruly night,

and his *arioso* with its sharp oboe commentary is all-of-a-piece with the
sinister uneasiness of the situation. Macduff's discovery and cry are as
electric as in Shakespeare. But from this point to the end of the act we are
fully under the opera's aegis; for now is the time of the ensemble-finale,
the conventional perplexity movement. As Macduff raises the alarm the
orchestra races like a passage from *Falstaff*, a gradual *crescendo* of bustling
excitement as the stage fills. To the general enquiries Banquo gives out
the terrible news in one desperate line. *Stupore universale*—and the finale
has begun.

In mid-nineteenth-century operatic music this long passage holds a
leading place. Dramatically, however, it does not bear very close
examination. Verdi had worked at white heat throughout the suspense
up to the climax. Now he sits back and lets the act run down-hill in a
welter of superb note-spinning. After the first *tutti* flush is over, with
telling effect there comes a soft, drum-tapped, unaccompanied phrase
for Macbeth, Madcuff, Lady Macbeth and her waiting-woman (here
elevated to sing in unison with her mistress). These alternate with a
phrase sung by Malcolm, Banquo and the chorus. This is a musical, but
not a dramatic, division of forces. When the brass ushers in the main
grandioso tune which everybody sings, the thing is quite basically divided
into treble and bass parts with no differentiation of character or outlook.
When there is any break-up, these simple musical considerations group
Macduff and Malcolm (both tenors) with Lady Macbeth, while Macbeth
and Banquo share the bass line. As an inner complication Malcolm (a
comprimario) is silent when the chorus is not singing, whereas the waiting-
woman shares almost the whole of Lady Macbeth's quite exacting part,
occasionally dropping a third or a sixth, but always singing. The
sensational faint (or feint?) of Lady Macbeth does not take place, for the
soprano top line must remain to the end. Nor can Malcolm give voice to
his private fears, for he has no Donalbain to discuss them with. When
the curtain falls we are very much back in the operatic world.

The second act of the opera opens parallel to Shakespeare's Act III,
Scene 2. Verdi has jumped the *locus classicus* of dramatic irony (*Macb.*
Faile not our feast. *Ban.* My Lord, I will not) and Macbeth's verbose
interview with the murderers. But he has salvaged some of his 'To be
thus, is nothing' speech, as we shall see. The opening may seem rather
tame at a casual hearing, for after a very few bars of introduction
Macbeth is discovered *pensoso*, followed by Lady Macbeth. They
exchange declamatory phrases that are not held together by any formal

shape; then Macbeth goes out *precipitoso*, leaving his Lady alone on the stage for a short concluding aria. But in this little scene there is plenty to consider.

The introduction starts with a brass semi-fanfare. It is in fact Macbeth's cry after the murder of Duncan. This brief trumpet call heralds his

Trumpets and Trombones

(MACBETH:Tutto è fi — ni — to!)

elevation to the throne, but at the same time it bitingly reminds us (and him) that he played most foully for it. The woodwind then echoes the opening bars of the murder duet. Thus we are quickly told what is uppermost in the minds of Scotland's new king and queen. (They are not so designated in the libretto. They are still Macbeth and Lady Macbeth as in Shakespeare, though the play does have *Enter Macbeth as King and Lady Macbeth as Queen*.) Lady Macbeth addresses her husband 'How now, my Lord, why doe you keepe alone?' One of her typical pronouncements—'what's done, is done'—shows her continued hold on

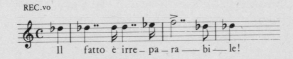

REC.vo

Il fatto è irre – pa – ra — bi — le!

her emotions. She reminds Macbeth that Duncan's son is 'ftolne away and fled, which puts vpon (him) Sufpition of the deed'. This adroitly borrowed from Macduff's conversation with Ross in a previous scene. The intelligent jig-sawing of Shakespeare's text for operatic needs was not entirely Boito's perquisite. The audience has somehow to learn of this important development, so its announcement is transferred to Lady Macbeth. Nor is this the end of the borrowing; for Macbeth's reply comes from his soliloquy while waiting for the murderers. His fears in Banquo are sticking deep.

They hayl'd him Father to a Line of Kings. . . .
For *Banquo's* Iffue haue I fil'd my Minde,
For them, the gracious *Duncan* haue I murther'd

The above borrowing is very neatly dove-tailed into Lady Macbeth's

But in them, Natures Coppie's not eterne.

Macbeth replies (in the play):

There's comfort yet, they are affaileable

The opera is more forthright:

Lady Macbeth echoing the droop of his words.

We have no crow making wing to the rooky wood, but we almost hear once again the 'Owle . . . the fatall Bell-man' in that pregnant echo. The poetry of Shakespeare at this point is not translatable into nineteenth-century Italian recitative; but there is a grimness in the dialogue as the orchestra deserts it, followed by the resolute Macbeth hurling his threat at Banquo almost exactly as he did before the killing of Duncan—a sinister repetition (see below and opposite).

Lady Macbeth is alone on the stage, for a solo scene she does not get in Shakespeare. Doubtless Verdi felt bound to give his prima donna a fling at this point, and in any case the music had to work up to an exciting

curtain. In the first version she sang a sort of cabaletta in which she defied the elements to shake the foundations of her secure throne, even though it had been obtained by evil means. In 1865 Verdi could write better arias and he replaced the original one with a new composition, far more skilfully imagined and scored, and with different words. The words in fact are an attempt to salvage some of Shakespeare's poetic thoughts and present them to the audience. In 'La luce langue' we can find verbal echoes of such fragments of the text as 'Light thickens', 'Come, feeling Night', 'A deed of dreadfull note', 'For't muft be done to Night', 'After Lifes fitfull feuer, he fleepes well . . . nothing can touch him further'.

All these are Macbeth's words, not hers. But the borrowing is admissible until the final lines. There she has a quick gloat at having gained the crown. This is most un-Shakespearean: her real comment was 'Nought's had, all's fpent', etc. She also expresses triumphant pleasure at the prospect of Banquo's death. This again is very un-Shakespearean—Macbeth never told her precisely what he was planning; he said, 'Be innocent of the knowledge, deareft Chuck.' This much admired aria is dressed in borrowed robes, ending right out of character.

Musically it goes *alle stelle*, a sure-fire show-stopper. It is in the vein of Verdi's newer concept of the dramatic solo, such as he gave to Mina, Amelia and Eboli. The first section, *legato e cupo*, is sombre, its prominent oboe preserving the sinister theme of murders past and future. Then the flow is stemmed while she muses on the new crime and its neccessity. Here she enters into a curious succession of repetitions (see p. 124).

It is hard to decide what Verdi had in mind. It may seem like the temporary drying-up of inspiration. It ought to be deliberate, and if so it must be the expression of her resolute nature—that which could address

her husband as 'Infirme of purpofe' and bid him 'be not loft/So poorely in your thoughts'. Another Verdi lady who indulges in these repetitions is Azucena. She too tried to impose her will on a man reluctant to accept it.

Four strange, powerful bars of *andante sostenuto* follow. They are marked *ppp*, and her voice climbs down below the stave ending on a low B. This really is sinister, but is prematurely dispelled by an *allegro* spurt which, even though it contains the instruction *con voce pianissima e un po' oscillante*, rushes on by way of a quotation from Beethoven's Second Symphony to a climax of emotional triumph as she repeats and repeats how Banquo, '*who was predicted King*, will fall'. The italics are mine. It was only Banquo's descendants who were predicted kings. Something has gone seriously wrong. It is this torrid and aggressive aria which has given most critics the impression that Verdi's Lady, unlike Shakespeare's, dominates the drama. But does she? Her part is artificially fed with plums. Prima donnas like to think they count more at the box office than their male opposites. But Verdi's Lady Macbeth only asserts herself by cheating. Here she sings words and thoughts that are really her husband's. At the end of the third act she comes on stage at a point where she has no business to be present. No wonder his mind is full of scorpions.

In an important passage Bradley discusses the development of Shakespearean Tragedy as it affects the audience:[4]

When the middle of the tragedy is reached, the audience is not what it was at the beginning. It has been attending for some time, and has been through a certain amount of agitation. . . . It is one thing to watch the scene of Duncan's assassination at the beginning of the Second Act, and another thing to watch the murder of Desdemona at the beginning of the Fifth. . . . We come [in *Othello*] to the great temptation-scene, where the conflict emerges into life, with nerves unshaken and feelings much fresher than those with which we greet the banquet-scene in *Macbeth*.

This aspect of audience-reaction has been insufficiently considered, and would make an interesting study. There is no doubt that the poetry of *Macbeth*, so brooding and bloody, conditions us to face the banquet-scene quite attuned to sup full of horrors. In the opera there is a relaxing of this grip at the very point at which it should not be so.

The murder of Banquo and the escape of Fleance is a crisis in the tragedy. Macbeth fails to learn by his mistakes and for the second time allows a son to survive when it would have been in his interest to make sure of a clean sweep. Malcolm, his enemy and successor, ran away to safety. Now Fleance, progenitor of the future kings of Scotland, has eluded the savage murderers Macbeth has so carefully and elaborately primed. Shakespeare's little scene with the three assassins, the sound of horses, Banquo's off-stage call for a light, Fleance leading him in with a torch, Banquo's casual prediction of rain followed at once by his murder, the extinguishing of the torch and the escape of Fleance—all this is concise and realistic. Verdi's version is not. Even at revision-time he passed as satisfactory his chorus of murderers. We can force ourselves into the delusion that it is dramatic, with its drum-taps and 'trema Banco!' But we cannot really help smiling. Banquo's aria, a fine piece of bass Verdi impressively curved and scored, seems artlessly introduced to ensure that the singer earns his evening's salary. For the murderers are in full force in the wings, with nothing to prevent them from carrying out their deed of dreadful note. If they did not feel inclined to interrupt Banquo's aria, they might have spent the time disposing of Fleance, who in any case has to stand idly for four minutes or so, listening to his father expressing his fears while doing nothing to avoid them. After the murder, the escape of Fleance 'crossing the stage followed by a murderer' cannot fail to amuse, when we consider how many men had gathered for his destruction.

So when the curtain rises on the banquet-scene, and the jolly music trips along reminding us of the *Traviata* we all knew long before we heard *Macbeth*, we are definitely not attuned as Bradley would have us. This above all is where Verdi's opera falls apart. It lacks central strength and its tension begins to disintegrate just when it should be building up.

The brindisi, as operatic and un-Shakespearean as the chorus of murderers, does succeed in rallying the drama even if it must be accounted an oddity. Brindisis are part of the stock-in-trade of opera and occur in some form or other from the earliest times right up to Benjamin Britten. It is also a tradition that the leading soprano may have a show-piece that obtrudes from her theatrical rôle into the realm of sheer virtuosity. In Verdi's operas we find Giselda's *polonaise*, Elena's *bolero*, Eboli's *canzone*. The brindisi of Lady Macbeth draws these two traditions together and combines them in one moment of musical occasion. Yet most of us have to use special pleading to convince ourselves that we can accept it in the theatre without misgivings.

To defend it we must decide how merry and ribald Macbeth's feast is likely to have been—or become, had it not been broken up. That the host, inviting Banquo, referred to it as a 'solemn supper' must not influence us to suppose it was a serious affair; for he means exactly the same as Lady Macbeth who calls it a 'great feast'. Later he disperses his guests-to-be

> Till feven at Night to make focietie
> The fweeter welcome.

Lady Macbeth coaxes him to

> Be bright and Iouiall among your Guefts to Night.

He retorts

> So fhall I Loue, and fo I pray be you.

At the start of the banquet Macbeth gives all his guests a 'hearty welcome' and adds

> Be large in mirth, anon wee'l drinke a Meafure
> The Table round.

Lady Macbeth observes he does not 'giue the Cheere' when he is closeted with the murderer. His reply

> Now good digeftion waite on Appetite

might be construed as a pleasantry: Later, when the ghost has faded for the first time, he drinks 'to th'generall ioy o'th'whole Table' and pledges a toast to the absent Banquo with the audacity of a Don Juan. After his second outburst Lady Macbeth says 'You haue difplac'd the mirth.'

Although Shakespeare does not specify 'musick' or anything tangibly related to a festive occasion, we can gather enough references that convey it was intended to be, and had begun to be, a convivial affair; not perhaps an Attila drinking-bout, but a high feast with all the appurtenances of revelry. There were bound to be drinking songs sooner or later. It is noteworthy that Shakespeare specifies only *Lords* at the table—no ladies. The operatic chorus is certainly mixed, and this is really a pity; for Lady Macbeth, alone in an all-male symposium, might the more naturally have felt the urge to show her undaunted mettle. But whatever the composition of the chorus, one may claim that the Macbeths would be doubly anxious to make their first royal party go with a swing. We can be sure it did not occur to her to sing a brindisi at dinner when she was hostess to King Duncan. But now she is queen there is no question of inhibitions. Besides, with Duncan's blood on her hands and Banquo biding safe in a ditch, she has all the more reason to impress her subject-guests with her gaiety. Verdi's decision to give her a drinking-song is not as naïve as some may think.

The opera scene is splendidly balanced between the soprano-led brindisi on the one hand, and Macbeth's colloquy with the murderer and his confrontation with the ghost on the other. Macbeth deliberately leaves his wife to do the entertaining and he takes no part in it whatever. She accepts so readily that we must surmise it has been well planned and rehearsed. The guests know the song well, for they join vigorously in the refrain. Very subtly planned is the crucial conversation with the murderer by the door, for the orchestra quietly plays the brindisi for a few bars, then twists its tune to an unobtrusive cadence. We presume the drinking-song is done with; for the jolly music strikes up again as Macbeth rejoins his guests, to be dramatically broken into by his sudden terror at the ghost's appearance.

Verdi was very particular about this. We read in his letters how he insisted on the ghost being impersonated by the singer of Banquo's rôle and not by stand-in. He was amazed when the bass argued that it was not professional for him to be the ghost. He had, perhaps, a point. His job was to sing. His part ended with the murder. Anyone else could have been made up as the ghost, for it was a silent appearance. It was undignified to come up through a trap-door with a veil over his head and gashes painted on his neck. (Verdi specified this. He had been told how it was done in London.) Be that as it may, Verdi always won arguments with singers, and the bass duly appeared at the banquet. Verdi even drew a plan of how the tables were to be arranged. He had determined on a real operatic novelty.

Macbeth's first fearful outburst reaches four high Fs, and is frenetic as it bursts out of the revelry theme. When he cries 'neuer fhake Thy goary lockes at me' his panic octave leap at the end is eloquent of his terror:

The exchange between him and his Lady is typical of Verdi's grip on terse, telling dialogue that we find throughout their scenes together. Macbeth's frantic hysteria reaches G flat. The ghost vanishes and the passions subside with quite uncanny effect.

Really moving is Macbeth's exhausted plea that the jolly drinking-song be resumed. Nothing sounds further away than the idea of merriment, yet he wearily asks for it.

Obediently the brindisi returns, its reprise now sounding automatic and mirthless. This is one of the wonders of inspired theatre. Verdi perhaps did not know what desperate anxiety we would experience at this point.

It may be just 'verse two' of the song; but it certainly creates an unnerving effect as she warbles her trills and grace notes all over again, and her guests join in the refrain like puppets in a ghastly game.

Ghastly: for out of its final chord emerges Macbeth's voice in a new key. The ghost has returned. His renewed terror is accentuated by the simple device of each bar starting with a crotchet, giving a sort of desperation to his cries. His outburst culminates in a frantic *tutta forza*; then as the phantom finally disappears, the string *tremolo* shivers alone, dying down in a perfect portrayal of returning calm. Over it comes a telling exchange:

We catch in these closing bars the collapse past breaking point with which Shakespeare so superbly ends his scene. But since this is opera we must have our ensemble-finale.

This is apportioned with some skill. Macbeth's verse is adapted from

> It will haue blood they fay: Blood will haue Blood. . . .
> I will to morrow
> (And betimes I will) to the weyard Sifters.
> More fhall they fpeake.

Lady Macbeth counters with

> O proper ftuffe:
> This is the very painting of your feare. . . .
> What's done, is done.

Macduff, who had so far sung with the chorus, now detaches himself and has a stanza of his own, in which he announces that Scotland is fallen on evil days and he must leave it. The waiting-woman and the chorus share his views about the state of affairs. Those who guard their Shakespeare jealously will raise their eyebrows on learning that Macduff has been present at the banquet. He made a point of staying away, and his absence had a powerful effect on Macbeth's subsequent actions. But Verdi has been working with a very limited cast. With no Ross or Lennox there must be at least one named guest, and music calls for the opera's *primo tenore*, Macduff. For the second time the composer has on his hands a concerted finale without sufficient characters on which to build it. This does at least give due prominence to Macbeth and his Lady, whose phrases pointedly alternate. Macduff's important statement and decision is quite obscured, since he sings most of his part with the chorus tenors.

Macbeth's opening, particularly when he sings of his intention to revisit the witches, seems to bring back the shape and curve of his first meditation when he met them at the beginning of the opera. Comparison between these passages will show the resemblance, another instance of the subconscious working of Verdi's mind when immersed in operatic creation:

al — le stre — ghe squarcierò, al — le stre-ghe squarcie — rò.

Al-la co — ro — na che m'offra il fa — to   la man ra-

—— pa — ce non al — ze-rò . . . non al — ze — rò.

Lady Macbeth meanwhile, continuing her relentless criticism of his weakness, reiterates the figure which she first used in her opening aria and later in her agreement to give her guests the brindisi (see opposite).

(This can still be traced near the end of the Sleepwalking Scene, and it is crystallized in those exasperated *Follie*s of the murder-duet which Verdi thought so important. It may express her impatience and intolerance. These related figures cannot be mere chance. Verdi had definite and

separate musical visions of the two Macbeths, and though he does not splash with the counterpoint of the symphonist, he etches concisely and sometimes with surprising clarity.)

The finale grows into a fine tune which swells and subsides as though building groundless hopes. One cannot help wishing, however, that Verdi could have seen his way to following Shakespeare more closely by letting Lady Macbeth send her guests home, so that the usurping king and queen could end this harrowing scene on that note of sheer moral and physical exhaustion that Shakespeare knew must be. It really is not the occasion for a conventional ensemble, however well written. But Verdi had not yet discovered the theatrical strength of a quiet ending (not yet—but nearly, for only four years after the revised *Macbeth* he re-wrote the wonderful trio-ending in *La Forza del Destino* to replace a crash-bang curtain).

We are now back with the witches and their peculiar mixture of outlandish extravagance and naïve nursery-rhyme that has tempted scholars to divide the text into genuine and spurious. Certainly two songs mentioned in Shakespeare are found to have existed also in *The Witch* by Middleton, who also gave Hecate a large part. Where Hecate intrudes into Shakespeare, her lines are clearly not by him; though perhaps not by Middleton either. It is the witch scenes that offer the greatest temptation to the producer with an eye to box-office. It seems that *Macbeth* suffered thus in performance even during Shakespeare's life-time; certainly at the Restoration. One conjectured reason for the striking brevity of the *Macbeth* text, as compared with the other great tragedies, is that it was understood that the performance would be lengthened by the elaboration of the witch scenes into a sort of masque.

Verdi naturally drew on the material to hand in whatever translated version came his way. When he revised the work for Paris and had to include the compulsory ballet in his new version, he followed the interpolated Hecate scene by bringing in the Queen of the Witches to mime her authority over the covens and convey her instructions about Macbeth's coming visit. All this is written into the score, and may have been explained in the theatre programme; but if we have no access to the key, it will be quite a problem to discover precisely what Hecate's unspoken gestures are indicating. One is reminded of Lord Burleigh's nod in Sheridan's *Critic*.

If the ballet is omitted, as is often the case, we do not have this problem; but we still get one of the songs from Middleton's play. This is

> Black spirits and white, red spirits and gray,
> Mingle, mingle, mingle, you that mingle may.

It is sung by Verdi's witches to a *ridda*, and in the Shakespeare Folio Hecate has brought in three more witches—six in all—the embryo of future multiplication and Verdi's tally of eighteen. There has been much scholarly argument about this passage; but Verdi cuts across all scholarship and has the choral *ridda* for no better or worse reason than that it would be expected by opera-goers. But he has changed the gray spirits into blue ones. This is neither error nor ignorance. Nicholas Rowe did this in his edition very early in the eighteenth century. All subsequent editions followed Rowe until Steevens, eighty years later, restored 'gray'. It is evident that the Italian version acquired by Verdi was at least sixty years behind the times, for it must have read 'blue'. Thus a bogus emendation, long since scrapped, lives on in the libretto of *Macbeth*. But for one thing we can be thankful. Although there are two versions of his opera, at least it is all by Verdi and demonstrably genuine, unlike the dramatist's text.

From 'Thrice the brinded cat hath mew'd' (whose theme introduced the Prelude to the opera) down to the thumping coda of the waltz, we are treated to a succession of theatrically ingenious, if technically transparent, music. It is really a period for suspension of disbelief. But to cut sections out of a performance does nothing to integrate the drama. These witches with their revolting cookery and disarming enthusiasm are there in the story. Perhaps some of the Elizabethans believed in them (they still occasionally burnt them alive). The fact that we are too clever today to take them seriously does not entitle us to leave them out. Shakespeare put them in; and Verdi kept them in. Who would remove the Norns or the Rhinemaidens, or the soup-brewing Mime? Spike Hughes remarks, not unjustly, that 'purists and pedants are sure to object to a waltz for eleventh-century Scottish witches. But what else should they dance? A minuet?'[5] Well, why not? Let his purists and pedants listen to the dance movements of Purcell's witches in *Dido and Aeneas*. Though its libretto calls for 'horrid music' the score gives us anything but this. Who knows what rhythms evil spirits danced to? Did Meyerbeer? or Berlioz? or Boito?

After the ballet, or instead of it, Macbeth arrives for the *Gran Scena delle Apparizioni*. Shakespeare is closely followed. The witches, their rituals and revels ended, now take on a far more sinister aspect, singing single-minded unison as though their occult powers are diabolically ranged together against him. The three apparitions deliver their messages over chilling brass chords. As in the play, Macbeth's courage waxes with each announcement. He makes a satisfied comment and an unsuccessful bid to hear more; then gives a cry of relief which quickly turns to a bloody resolve as he decides to destroy Macduff (a change of key in mid-phrase); finally exulting at the impossibility of a wood moving he sings almost an aria, but with four key changes denoting his restless excitement. As in Shakespeare he demands knowledge of Banquo's descendants, and when he is advised against asking, threatens the witches. In Shakespeare he does this with a curse, in the opera with a sword—each a vain threat.

The cauldron sinks. Shakespeare calls for hautboys and Macbeth says 'what noife is this?' Verdi stipulates a cornamusa under the stage, which equally arouses Macbeth's wonder. It is one of Verdi's most striking and carefully planned *coups de théâtre*, fully explained and detailed in his letters. The bagpipe effect is continued through the scene by means of two oboes and two bassoons, a contrabassoon and six clarinets. The result is weird, as Verdi intended; and to add to the sinister atmosphere the witches now divide themselves once more into three groups. While the show of kings is in progress (Verdi gives instructions and technical suggestions as to how best it should be produced) Macbeth comments in what is really an aria, but so broken by the apparitions as to seem far less formal. Gradually his self-control is torn apart, as his *legato* turns to *agitato* and his high notes multiply, with F natural as Banquo appears and, when he sees the mirrored progeny, three Fs and G. He approaches the apparitions with drawn sword, but desists when he realizes they are as yet unborn. His last expression of terror will be hauntingly paraphrased at the end of the Sleepwalking Scene, when Lady Macbeth's introvert fears echo his exasperation.

The remainder of the scene is full of curiosities. First of all, Macbeth faints. This is quite out of character and seems to be arranged to give a cue for yet more supernatural ballet. Spirits of the air are summoned to dance round him and revive him, which they come and do while the witches sing a chorus. In Shakespeare the stage direction reads *Music, the witches dance and vanish.* Macbeth stands amazedly, as well he might. But at least he stands. Verdi's fainting fit is an error of judgment; but worse is to follow. In the 1847 version, after the chorus and dance has brought him round, he ends the scene with a spirited cabaletta in which he threatens the destruction of Macduff's wife and children. This is in line with Shakespeare, but in the play Lennox has come to tell him that Macduff has fled to England. In the opera his sudden spite against Macduff is sprung on us all without particular explanation. The 1865 version has no cabaletta, but a short duet with Lady Macbeth, who arrives at the cavern with the lame words 'Vi trovo alfin!' How she found him at all, we cannot surmise. We are not sure, even in Shakespeare, how Macbeth himself discovered the cave, for his previous meeting with the witches had been on a heath. However, here is Lady Macbeth, introduced purely for the purpose of giving the soprano another turn. The resulting duet savours of patchwork. Firstly, Macbeth tells his wife what the three apparitions said. After each quotation she demands 'Segui'. It is dull and barren. But when Macbeth informs her about Banquo's descendants, she refuses to accept the prophecy in a chracteristic phrase:

Macbeth now expresses his intention of destroying the Macduffs. Lady Macbeth adds that Fleance must be hunted down and killed. This is tying up loose ends indeed. Shakespeare never thought of it. The two then join excitedly in a duet of vengeance. For a few bars this is excellent; but soon they are simply ranting 'vendetta!' In a passage marked with four *ps* they combine to contemplate the bloody plans they are hatching, and then their *vendettas* return. Why do they so work themselves up as avengers? *They* owe no revenge. *They* have not been wronged. Vengeance is Malcolm's and Macduff's, and they will repay. Thus the curtain falls on a development right outside Shakespeare. After the banquet the exhausted and disillusioned queen should not be seen again until she haunts the castle in her sleep. Her intrusion here is a pity, and it is unfortunate that the two should end this progressive act with the strains of Alfio and Santuzza just before the Intermezzo.

In Shakespeare there is a dramatic turning-point when, after the banquet has broken up. Macbeth is uneasy at Macduff's absence from the feast. His wife asks, 'Did you fend to him Sir?' After so many expressions of exasperation she suddenly addresses him as 'Sir'. This is the start of her submission, and we shall not see her again until she walks in her sleep. Her hectoring intrusion into the cavern, though giving the singer a welcome opportunity, disrupts her implied disintegration. Besides, she was not a party to the brutal Macduff murders; yet here in the opera she exults over their prospect. And when Macbeth acts entirely alone, he is bloody, bold and resolute. Malcolm was overlooked. Fleance escaped. But not Macduff's little ones. As Lady Macbeth sinks, he rises refreshed. But she must be *seen and heard* to sink.

The remainder of the opera is ingeniously contrived. Shakespeare's next eleven scenes are exchanged for four, yet the dénouement seems to lose very little. In both opera and play we are now given a respite from the Macbeths, and they in turn gain a breathing-space. Verdi's fourth act, opening with near-Shakespearean geographical carelessness in the border country with *Birnam Wood in the distance*, is as clever a remould as can be found in Italian libretti of its era. If we have lost the 'theatre' of the Fife murders and the breaking of the news to Macduff, we have also escaped the long, dull dialogue between him and Malcolm. What we gain, as only an opera can bring us, is the collective misery caused by the desperate Macbeth's 'dread exploits'. The scene is quite static, a kind of *requiem*:

O Nation miferable!
With an vntitled Tyrant, bloody Sceptred . . .

Indeed, the opening of the chorus does resemble that of Verdi's own *Requiem*, and Macduff's following aria may remind us in spirit of the *Ingemisco*. The long-delayed tenor aria here creates an impression as in no other opera—for where else has an audience to wait until the last act to hear one? The arrival of Malcolm with soldiers from England puts an end to the lamentations. Now at last the forces of liberation are united and mobilized.

> But gentle Heauens,
> Cut short all intermiffion: Front to Front,
> Bring thou this Fiend of Scotland, and my felfe
> Within my Swords length fet him.

The short, defiant chorus that ends the scene, made more spirited by the two tenor voices leading it, seems all the more pugnacious by reason of its brevity. As Shakespeare's Malcolm remarks, 'This tune goes manly.'

The Sleepwalking Scene now follows, just as in the play. But instead of Dunsinane Verdi transports us back to Inverness, which adds a dramatic savour to the somnambulism occurring at the very spot where the murder story began. But it will also present a problem to the liberating troops, under orders to carry boughs from Birnam Wood. Verdi has already moved the wood some hundred miles further south. Now he adds another hundred or so from Dunsinane to Inverness. Malcolm's army will be PBI indeed by the time they are given permission to throw down their leafy screens, somewhat shrivelled by now after their long march up from the Border. However, if Verdi can whisk the cast of *Aroldo* from Kent to Loch Lomond, he may be forgiven this more local indifference to geography. (Muzio, marvelling how some Americans arrived at Southampton one morning, telegraphed London and were in their seats at the opera the same evening, added 'From Southampton to London is 300 miles'!)[6]

The Prelude to the scene, much of which was played at the start of the opera, conjures up the right atmosphere at once, with its muted themes. What a contrast now with the surging confidence of the orchestra when Lady Macbeth first entered with her husband's letter! It is at this point in an opera, when the final drama is to be enacted, that an expressive orchestral movement can make an effect beyond the power of words. Verdi had done something of this sort with the funeral march in *Nabucco* and the violin prelude to the trio in *I Lombardi*, and was to do it again with consummate effect in *Traviata* and *Otello*. In Italy it thickened out into the *intermezzo*, an almost obligatory device of the *verismo* age. Wagner's uses of it are well known, his third act preludes evoking some of his profoundest music.

Here the dark and plaintive scoring, with the cor anglais wailing a kind of threnody, not only brings a poignant contrast after the martial *stretto-finale* of the massed warriors, but projects us forward into the nerve-racking demise that tragedy has prepared for the villainess. We remember Johnson's terse dictum: 'Lady Macbeth is merely detested.' The music of Verdi that steals through the dialogue and accompanies her last entrance contradicts Johnson and brings tears, if not of pity, then at least of despair that humanity can be so ravaged by nemesis. It is an aria, but so cunningly broken up that its form dissolves in the theatre. Shakespeare's scene is a prose one, but read aloud it is found to be spliced with pentameters in whole or part. Contrariwise Verdi's music is couched formally, yet seems to disintegrate into fragments. Did Verdi get nearer to Shakespeare anywhere in *Otello*? As near, of course—but perhaps not nearer. There are no reprise themes or echoes from her part, such as so many composers would have relied on. Yet there are subdued mannerisms that belong to her, and at the very end a weary borrowing from Macbeth's trembling cadence in the cavern when he was about to faint. In their weakest moments the two have this tenuous link.

Andante assai sostenuto

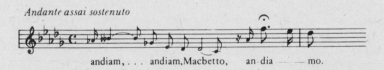

andiam, . . . andiam, Macbetto,   an-dia —— mo.

Andante quasi allegretto

oh ter-ror! . . . . oh mio ter-ror!   oh mio ter-ror!

And she fades away into the shadows, her *fil di voce* reaching D flat and dropping an octave with absolute finality.

The rest of the play consists of military intelligence, troop movements, and action in the field. Such scenes, second nature on the Elizabethan stage, have no part in opera. Verdi simply has 'a room in the castle' after which the backcloth is lifted to reveal a huge panorama. The treatment is straightforward. Macbeth at bay defies the world; then breaks into an aria which is in effect the equivalent of

> My way of life
> Is falne into the Seare, the yellow Leafe,
> And that which fhould accompany Old-Age,
> As Honor, Loue, Obedience, Troopes of Friends,
> I muft not looke to haue: but in their fteed,
> Curfes . . .

To steal this moment of tenderness from the general alarums he has a broad tune similar in type to that which took hold of him in the murder duet, when he thought of Duncan's virtues, pleading like angels. With this last flicker of humanity he faces the succession of blows which are to break him.

The *Cry within of Women* that tells of his wife's death brings only a few bars of rant—no attempt by Verdi here to match up with Shakespeare's famous lines, even though Piave had a brief shot at transferring some of them. Then comes news that Birnam Wood is on the move. Verdi has not bothered to work out that since he has opted for Birnam being down on the English Border, the castle defenders would have to be clairvoyant to identify the source of the branches now being carried towards them. Macbeth wastes no words, but calls for arms, echoed by his followers over twenty unaccompanied bars. The very lack of orchestral support makes them seem empty and bombastic, full of sound and fury, signifying nothing.

Then the scene opens to reveal the field of battle, with the advancing invaders carrying their branches from Birnam, 'the Englifh powre . . . led on by *Malcolm*, and the good *Macduff*'. At La Scala in a recent revival they carried Union Jacks, a gracious anachronism that not even James VI and I would have comprehended. The orchestral fugue, the conception of which so delighted Verdi, now spills its clashing fanfares over the theatre in a positively stirring little embryo of *Heldenleben*. It cleaves triumphantly through Shakespeare's usual jumble of short scenes and sweeps the action along to the confrontation of Macduff and his hell-hound.

The stage fills with victorious invaders and captured defenders, joined by 'Bards and People'. In the score Macbeth has been killed off-stage, and when Malcolm asks where he is, Macduff points to the wings and cries, 'Yonder, slain by me.' In Shakespeare Macduff comes in carrying Macbeth's severed head. But in Verdi's first version Macbeth dies on stage, after an aria in which he gasps out his disillusion, but without a vestige of repentance. (It is made clear by Shakespeare that neither of the Macbeths, although spiritually and physically broken, ever showed the slightest remorse for their career of butchery.) Now when Garrick produced the play he treated himself to eight lines of verse, written by himself, for the death scene. Piave's libretto has these lines, or a tolerably recognizable paraphrase of them. This, like the substitution of blue spirits for gray, points to Verdi's Italian version of *Macbeth* being quite an old one. Often today this abandoned aria is restored, thus giving Macbeth two solos in the last moments of the opera. And so, in this unpremeditated way, David Garrick lives on. . . .

The Bards open the choral finale with which Verdi closes the newer version. Who are these bards? It would appear that they derive from Rossini's *La Donna del Lago*. Verdi's division of the chorus into sections for Bards, Soldiers, and Women seems to have its roots in the quasi-barbaric exultation which Rossini had dreamed up for his first-act finale. The result is a satisfying paean of victory. *Macbeth* alone among Verdi's operas (save for *Falstaff*) ends in general rejoicing. But in *Falstaff* we have all the cast lined up, whereas now there are some notable absentees—to wit: the leading lady, the *primo baritono*, and the *basso* (all dead); the mutes Duncan and Fleance (one dead, one fled); and the witches (vanished). No wonder Verdi had to end with a chorus, and bring on Bards and Women to bolster it up. The nominal roll was too depleted for any other solution.

Spike Hughes delights in finding irreverent non-operatic echoes in Verdi's scores, and *Macbeth* provides him with at least two.[7] I feel tempted to add that whenever the thrummed chords that prelude this choral finale strike up, my mind irrepressibly harks away to *The Campbells are coming*. If Talbot's troops sang *Hearts of Oak*, why not this?*

As Verdi matured he grew out of his earlier work, and even referred contemptuously to some operas which we still enjoy very much. When discussing the revision of *Simon Boccanegra* with Boito, he called it a wobbly table but possible to mend. This was never his attitude to *Macbeth*. He wrote to Escudier in 1864:

* And in the panache of the very last phrase of all, is there not an uncanny whiff of Elgar?

To put it in a word, there are some bits either weak or uninspired, and some definitely not so good.

But he could never have alluded to it as a wobbly table; for when he dedicated it so touchingly to Barezzi he called it 'the opera which I like better than any of my others'. So although in fact its score presents us with some music written four years before *Rigoletto* and other music written four years before *Aida*, we should try to judge it as one; for it was as one that he offered it to Paris. There were no footnotes pointing out this or that to be unaltered from the original. He thought of it as homogeneous and worthy of his revered 'Shaspear'. Though his librettists were not capable of getting to grips with a masterpiece of English literature, his music has at least enshrined Macbeth and his Lady as operatic immortals, capable in the theatre of thrilling us with their doomed ambitions and the moral disintegration of their coveted royalty.

In *Bishop Bloughram's Apology* Browning wrote:

> Like Verdi when, at his worst opera's end
> (The thing they gave at Florence—what's its name?)
> While the mad houseful's plaudits near outbang
> His orchestra of salt-box, tongs and bones,
> He looks through all the roaring and the wreaths
> Where sits Rossini patient in his stall.

The thing they gave at Florence must have been *Macbeth*. Certainly *I Masnadieri* and *Stiffelio* were performed at Florence about the time Browning was writing that particular batch of poems; but it was not their première as it was *Macbeth*'s. Rossini had not yet left Bologna for Florence, but could well have been present. It seems that in singling out Rossini's apparent indifference, the poet himself was affecting a vague nonchalance, an intellectual superiority. Better not admit he had actually attended a Shakespeare Tragedy mutilated by an Italian composer! Better hide it under 'the thing they gave at Florence'. As for salt-box, tongs and bones—well, if we care to read thirty lines further on, we find

> Strauss is the next advance. All Strauss should be
> I might be also. But to what result?
> He looks upon no future.

Some music critic, our Robert Browning. . . .

NOTES

1 For details of these operas, see 'Shakespeare and Opera' by Winton Dean, in *Shakespeare in Music* (ed. Hartnoll).
2 *Bernard Shaw & Mrs Patrcik Campbell: their Correspondence* (Gollancz).
3 *Principles of Shakespearian Production*, ch. 4, p. 143 (Pelican edn).
4 Bradley, *Shakespearean Tragedy*, Lecture II—'Construction in Shakespeare's Tragedies', pp. 50–1 (St Martin's Library edn).
5 Hughes, *Famous Verdi Operas*, p. 65.
6 Garibaldi, op. cit. Muzio to Barezzi, 17 July 1847.
7 Hughes, op. cit., pp. 59 and 74–5.

6

THE MOORS

The picture of a great, misguided soul, furnished with every gift for excellence, and lost in spite of all its gifts: unchecked ardour and bad companionship contaminate his heart; hurry him from vice to vice, till at last he stands at the head of a gang of murderers, heaps horror upon horror, plunges from abyss to abyss into all the depths of desperation. Great and majestic in misfortune; and by misfortune improved, led back to virtue. Such a man in the Robber Moor you shall bewail and hate, abhor and love. A hypocritical, malicious deceiver, you shall likewise see unmasked, and blown to pieces in his own mines. A feeble, fond, and too indulgent father. The sorrows of enthusiastic love, and the torture of ungoverned passion. Here also, not without abhorrence, you shall cast a look into the interior economy of vice, and from the stage be taught how all the gilding of fortune cannot kill the inward worm; how terror, anguish, remorse, and despair follow close upon the heels of the wicked. Let the spectator weep today before our scene, and shudder, and learn to bend his passions under the laws of reason and religion. Let the youth behold with affright the end of unbridled extravagance; nor let the man depart from our theatre, without a feeling that Providence makes even villains instruments of His purposes and judgments, and can marvellously unravel the most intricate perplexities of fate.

THUS SCHILLER PRESENTED his *Die Räuber* to the annals of the Theatre! Only a very young dramatist could write of his own play in this strain, confident that it contained an imperishable lesson for the world. He had completed it while still a student at a very harsh, militarized academy when he was being forcibly trained for a career far from his own choice. *Die Räuber* was his youthful dream of revolt. It was the natural, exuberant rebellion of immaturity; but only in the mind of a literary genius could it be so luridly expressed. *Die Räuber* sprawls with unpruned verbosity and untrimmed imagery, outrageous at times, unactable even, but always exciting. It is a drama whose proscenium is the mind. It is a fantasy-play, roaming outside the unities and capable of taking any turn. When Schiller harnessed it for production he had to squeeze it into a mould into which it would not go.

Andrea Maffei, making a libretto for Verdi, was faced with the same problem. *Die Räuber* simply does not go into a libretto. It stalks the literary world like an uncaged monster, and the strictures of a conventional opera house could never contain it. Maffei was a translator of foreign books. He had already done Schiller into Italian, so he was quite familiar with the material he had undertaken to work on. Obviously much would have to be left out. Posterity has unanimously pilloried his result because of its omissions. But he could not have adapted it otherwise. To be served up in the musical world, *Die Räuber* demands a consortium of talents: Tchaikovsky for its tragic love, Berlioz for its apocalyptic visions, Liszt for its dramatic narration, and Smetana for local colour. Its canvas in fact is a great mural, fit substance for one of those rich symphonic poems which burst out of their orchestral confines with choral ecstasy. But it was to be an Italian Opera, for Lind and London.

Maffei, with self-explanatory caution, wrote a scholarly preface to his libretto as follows:

> This melodrama is adapted from Frederick Schiller's famous tragedy *Die Räuber*, the first dramatic work that came out of his divine intelligence before manhood and mature diligence cooled his over-zealous imagination. The violent contrasts which afflicted the poet's youth, and a mind instinctively sad, inspired this terrible drama which, as is known, led the ardent minds of many young men to hunt through the forests with the imagined intention of improving their habits with crimes and bloodshed. But if this fearful picture of society partly lacked truth and that wise understanding of the heart which we admire in *Stuart*, *Tell* and *Wallenstein*, it presents nevertheless a plot so lively and expansive, and a development of passions and actions so varied and effective, that one cannot be sure what other literary work is able to offer situations more suitable for music. . . .

Maffei then goes on to elaborate the problems of a librettist faced with such material, and admits that he must

reduce a huge concept to small dimensions without departing from the likeness of the original, as a concave lens reducing objects while absolutely preserving their appearance. . . . In this way my task is to circumscribe in a few verses the huge tragedy of *Die Räuber* without hoping or claiming for my effort the exalted title of literature. . . .

The critics have only too readily agreed with his renunciation of that claim.

The story is that of the Moor family, nobility of Franconia; an old father with two grown-up sons—bass, baritone and tenor. Their relationship forms the drama. The old man is credulous and feeble; the sons are rogues; one an adventurer without remorse or conscience, the other a villain much given to introspection. The lady of the piece, a cousin, is a pawn pushed around by their counter-moves.

Schiller opens with Franz the villain telling his old father how news has arrived of the younger son Karl's disgrace. Finding a price on his head for killing a rival in a duel, he has absconded (deep in debt) with several other ruffians, and has gone to ground. The illustrious name of Moor has been publicly contaminated. Franz can scarcely bear to hurt his father by telling him such damaging news. The father, whom we English must get used to calling 'Old Moor', is coaxed into agreeing that Karl must be told never to return to his ancestral home. Franz arranges to write the letter himself, since it would break the father's heart to do so. It is only when Old Moor has sadly departed that Franz reveals in a long monologue what Schiller has been trying to conceal from us by fairly transparent craftsmanship, that the dissolute absentee son is not the real black sheep of the Moor family. The villain is Franz himself, a professional, self-glorifying monster.

In the next scene we meet Karl in a Saxon tavern. He is with his band of 'drop-outs'. One of them brings him the letter which Franz has written on their father's behalf. When he reads its diabolical contents he works himself up to a frenzy. His cronies take advantage of this to elect him their leader, and they all depart bent on a life of organized banditry.

Maffei changes these scenes round, showing us Carlo and his friends in the tavern before introducing Francesco. If one wonders why he should have gone to this trouble, it can be explained simply enough. Tradition called for a chorus in the opening scene, so the story must open with the robbers to provide it. Schiller's arrangement was far better drama, because now we have Carlo receiving Francesco's letter before we in the audience know who Francesco is or why he sent it.

Before the destiny of the Moors is unfolded there is a short Prelude which, unlike the Verdi Overture and Prelude, has nothing musically to do with the opera. The reason is curious, and rather un-Verdian. The chief 'cellist in the orchestra at Her Majesty's Theatre was the celebrated Alfredo Piatti, well known in Europe and recently settled in London, where he was to charm more than a generation of Victorian concert-goers, ultimately receiving indulgent notices in *The World* from the pen of *Corno di Bassetto* thirty-five years later. So the Prelude to *I Masnadieri* is given over to a short 'cello solo, because the royal and distinguished audience would certainly want to hear something from Piatti. Muzio, who must have had a lovely time that evening, records that Piatti played it perfectly, that it was amply applauded, and that Verdi stood up several times to acknowledge the ovation.[2] It must be admitted that the music gives only the most elementary opportunities to an eminent 'cellist; but we English enjoy the habit of clapping regardless.

When the curtain rises Carlo is discovered alone, reading a book. He soliloquizes thus:

When I read Plutarch, I am sick and tired of these effeminate times. If only a spark of Hermann's spirit still lived in the cold ashes of my forefathers! We should then see all Germany free!

In an operatic quiz this would be a good question: What opera opens with the words 'When I read Plutarch'? It is a curious attempt by Maffei at establishing some kind of intellectual flavour at the very start, as a sop to the shade of Schiller. But in the play Karl is holding a discussion with his friend Spiegel, who recommends Josephus rather than Plutarch. For a lone tenor Maffei's is a strange utterance, yet in it we may sense a sort of pre-echo of the opening of Gounod's *Faust* (also derived from the philosophical stable of German *Kultur*).

Some voices outside interrupt Carlo. 'There go my shameless, drunken partners in crime,' he comments. Their short chorus is quite negative and gives us no immediate awareness of being in the company of desperadoes. He then sings a cavatina in which he recalls the beauty of his ancestral home and the pleasure of Amalia's company—all now denied him until his father allows him to return. When his friends come in with the letter, he thinks it contains his father's pardon. On finding its true contents he flings it down and rushes out. One of his cronies picks it

up and reads it. His beloved brother has warned him that his father does
not wish him to return and if he does so he will be put in solitary
confinement and fed on bread and water. This amuses the chorus, but
Carlo comes in again and is now in a vindictive mood. They decide on a
life of crime, elect him Captain, and send him off into a cabaletta of
defiance. This absolutely conventional tenor-and-male chorus opening
contains an agreeable cavatina and a rousing cabaletta which
unfortunately develops into an echo of *Attila*. But it is hard to equate the
unanimous chorus with Schiller's brigands, of whom no less than eight
are named and have distinct traits and foibles. No doubt Verdi could not
have coped with them separately, any more than Wagner could manage
to interest us in his individual Valkyries even though he gave them all
splendid names.

We are now introduced to the terrible Francesco. Like his brother he
is shown alone, meditating. No Plutarch for him, but a long recitative
expressing his malignity. Maffei's verse is vivid—one can tell a literary
hand is at work:

> Späuracchi egregi
> Per le fiacche animucce. Osa, Francesco!
> Spácciati del vecchiardo . . . È vivo a stento
> Questo logoro ossame.

His cavatina, in contrast to that of Carlo, is darker, and its broad, 'cello-
supported tune more insistent, repeating its phrases with a sort of nasty
relish. At the end Maffei has hopefully written in the instruction

Returns to his meditations—then goes on:

but Verdi eagerly brushes aside the meditations without pause, as he
pushes the tale of villainy forward. Arminio is called in and given his
orders to disguise himself and tell Old Moor he has just left Carlo dead
on a battlefield near Prague. Arminio is Schiller's Hermann, an
ineffective suitor of Amalia, another poor dupe in Franz's diabolical
game.

We are already into Schiller's second act, for Maffei has brought
forward the plot to tell Old Moor the lie about Karl's death. This is not
an unreasonable alteration; but it has resulted in two scenes in succession

consisting of a solo cavatina-cabaletta, first a tenor then a baritone. There
is not much dramatic conflict in separate portraits of rival brothers,
though in a cabaletta contest between them we might not be sure which
headed the charts. In the theatre, of course, and at Her Majesty's on that
July evening in 1847, Queen Victoria, the Prince Consort, Adelaide the
Queen Mother, Edward Prince of Wales, Prince Louis Napoleon, the
Duke of Wellington, Princess Augusta Duchess of Cambridge, and 'una
infinità di Lord e Duchi'[3]—all were only there for la Lind. Tenor and
baritone trifles were but padding, artificially postponing the awaited
entry.

And now, in Scene Three, here is Amalia at last, seated beside old
Massimiliano Moor who is (just as in Schiller) fast asleep. An eye-witness
report in the Parisian *Gazette Musicale*:

> Jenny Lind appears in her turn, preceded by a little symphony for
> wind instruments, which is of more value than the air which
> follows.

Such dilettante sarcasm can be swallowed for what it is worth, but then
the writer sums up the aria thus:

> Jenny Lind is really to be pitied for being condemned to sing such an
> air, which suits neither her voice nor the voice of any one.[4]

Sheer prejudice could scarcely go further. It is comforting to read in
Muzio's account (also prejudiced of course):

> . . . of a lightness beyond compare . . . gentle and light as a
> feather. . . . Verdi has invented a new way of writing the cavatina.
> The applause was terrific.[5]

No doubt the applause was indeed terrific; but for Lind, not Verdi.
Truth to tell, the aria is not exactly graceful or charming, being
composed perhaps as a display for the illustrious soprano rather than a
faithful expression of Amalia's character. Charles Osborne may well be
right in suggesting a simpler passage was specially adorned for Lind's
benefit.[6]

But we must transfer our attentions to Massimiliano Moor. He is about to stir and give expression to his dreams. They are of Carlo, but when he recognizes Amalia he greets her in a phrase that (to me) is the most moving moment in this turgid tale of blood and hate and terror:

Andante

O po—ve—ra fan—ciul——la! l'a—

—— pril del—le tue gioie io di—sfio—ra——i.

Their duet, admired in all the commentaries, contrasts musically the ailing old nobleman and the tender young niece. Francesco and the disguised Arminio come in, the latter to tell his fictitious tale of Carlo's death. Not at all like an operatic messenger does he do this, but with an aplomb that marks his individual delinquency. Francesco shows Amalia what purports to be Carlo's sword, on which there is an unlikely message written in blood absolving her from her vows and bidding her to be Francesco's bride. But Verdi has forgotten to make his villain dissemble. He reads out the message with such savage relish that one really cannot suppose it will be believed. However, it reduces Amalia to sheer misery, foreshadowing for a moment the anguish of the deserted Aida by the banks of the Nile.

The quartet is confidently written, with each part musically distinctive and impressive—Massimiliano broken and abject; Amalia lyrically prayerful; Arminio remorseful at his brazen deception; the evil Francesco pounding out his hate. At the end Old Moor collapses. Amalia, believing him dead, rushes out. Francesco gloats over the completion of his plan. We seem suddenly to have arrived at the end of *I Due Foscari*. Maffei has adapted Schiller very freely indeed, but not without skill. What he has left out is purely the stuff of imaginative literature and not fodder for an operatic horse. The malevolent gloating of Francesco over his father's apparent death could have become a final cabaletta, if the baritone had not already enjoyed a good one to bring down the previous curtain.

Now in Act II Maffei goes all Gothic and brings us whither Schiller assuredly did not—to the graveyard of the Moors. A new tomb is prominently inscribed with the name of Massimiliano Moor; for Francesco has immured his feeble old father in a dungeon and mounted a mock funeral. Amalia does not know this, as she kneels before the tomb. Nor does the audience. It is the scene of her big aria, Jenny Lind's showpiece, so much admired and in particular because of the superb cabaletta that springs from her lips on learning that Carlo is not really dead. Preceded, like most of the arias in this opera, by a confident orchestral prelude, it seems to foreshadow a noble musical treat almost before it starts. Unfortunately Maffei has inserted behind the recitative an off-stage chorus, the sound of a macabre banquet celebrating Francesco's acquisition of his father's stolen estates and titles. This is not necessary to the plot, nor can we tell who these unseen revellers are. Amalia's opening line does declare that she has absented herself from a wicked feast, but we are apt to overlook the first line of a recitative when the curtain has just risen and we are having a look at the scenery (and deciphering inscriptions on tombs). Furthermore, Verdi has quite failed to give a shred of interest to their music. In fact, if there was one thing Verdi consistently failed to do, it was to cope with off-stage revels and carousals. We find a similar failure in *Alzira*, another in *Aroldo*, and even in *Traviata*, where the carnival chorus beneath Violetta's bedroom window cannot really be applauded as a musical feature.

In the cavatina Amalia is invoking the spirit of Carlo. Then a repentant Arminio tells her he is alive. Her heavy mood springs at once into an ecstatic cabaletta. The whole *scena* has a built-in strength as though Verdi had measured up to the challenge of introducing himself in person to London and at the same time gratifying the artistic intensity of Lind. The audience at Her Majesty's duly applauded. It took Muzio to comment that the applause was loud enough to bring down the theatre. Muzio incidentally wrote that he found Lind 'very good, attractive, well educated and refined (*garbo*)'.[7] What a prophetic epithet for a Swedish star!

We are pretty well halfway through the opera by now, and out of the six musical numbers so far there have been four arias, three with pendent cabaletta. This is unusual, and did not go unnoticed by Chorley, who wrote in the *Athenaeum*:[8]

There is not one grand concerted piece—a condition hard upon a composer whose only originality has been shown in his concerted music.

The critics of the 1840s still linked true Italian melody with the limpid solos of Bellini and the simple tunefulness of Donizetti and Rossini. Verdi's arias, expressive as they were intended to be of the dramatic emotions of their performers, sounded crude by comparison. They did not relax, nor could the listener. So this opera, with as yet no conspicuous chorus, a quartet and a short duet, and no less than four solos, was unfolding to the ears of the experts with a notable lack of balance.

But now comes a duet, for Francesco has left his infamous party to seek out the truant Amalia. He protests his love to her in affectedly simple phrases, recalling Richard Crookback's villainous wooing. She spurns him, though Verdi plays with some rather emptily ornamented voice-blending at a point when he should have been expressing contrast. Francesco begins to insult her grossly. Though the music is of average quality, it becomes noticeably tender as she pretends to ask his pardon and makes as if to embrace him. But the orchestra suddenly snaps out of this mood as Odabella-like she snatches his sword and holds him at bay. The quick movement that concludes the duet is spirited if ordinary. But its words merit examination. Maffei has written into his libretto some meaty invective (true to Schiller) of a sort not usually uttered before such as Queen Victoria, herself no novice at Italian. A paraphrase may be worth giving:

FRA: Insolent woman! Prison walls will behold the bending of your neck.

AMA: Filthy tyrant! I am only happy out of your sight.

FRA: What a hope! Oh no, you arrogant one, you stay here, my whore and slave!

AMA: Ah!

FRA: My whore! Your very name will make everyone blush. It will be a pleasure to drag you by the hair (*Attempts to drag her*.)

AMA: I have offended you. Forgive me. (*Pretends to embrace him and snatches his sword*.) Get out, rude fellow, unless you want to be stabbed in the heart with your own sword. The spirit of your father is here to guide the deadly weapon.

FRA: O despicable little woman, you don't know whom you are provoking. You deserve to pay for this outrage with your blood. My vengeance will be worked out on you with chains, whips and novel tortures.

All this vicious, horror-comic sadism was doubtless obliterated by the artless innocence of Verdi's unexceptional music. It could in more sophisticated hands have degenerated into a sort of *Tosca*. Mercifully the curtain falls abruptly on the cabaletta, and the interval prepares us for the Bohemian woods and forests with glimpses of Prague through the trees. The librettist heads the text simply: THE GANG. We are of course back at last with the *masnadieri* whose existence we may be excused for having forgotten.

Schiller's robber scenes are animated, involved, outspoken, crude and turgid. He thought up some adventurous rapscallions. Verdi merely has a chorus of anonymous ruffians, save for one, Rolla, whom we now hear is a prisoner although as yet we have not met him. We are told that the Chief has threatened to make a bonfire of Prague in revenge. Sure enough there is an immediate glow in the background. The Chief has punctually kept his word. Women and children fleeing in panic rush through the trees shouting that the end of the world has come.

Another section of the gang arrives with Rolla, who has been rescued by Carlo. A chorus describes the exploit. Carlo himself sings an aria in which remorse troubles his conscience; but news of a counter-attack is brought, and the Robbers arm themselves for action. This little scene is Maffei's drastic précis of a passage in Schiller which is so full of reported horrors that only the film industry could cope with its literal presentation. To snatch Rolla from torture and execution Karl Moor has ordered the burning of Prague. But his delinquent followers have indulged in a looting spree, and have blown up a powder magazine involving the deaths of over sixty people including the aged and infirm, pregnant women, new-born infants—all the ingredients of total war. In the play the remorse of Karl is brief, soon to be turned to defiance by the intrusion of a fire-eating priest, who arrives ahead of the troops to dictate drastic terms. Karl and his *Räuber* hear him out contemptuously and spurn him. Maffei has not been tempted to introduce this colourful priest.

Nor has Verdi mastered the choral effects that this scene requires. The restless excitement, the drive forward which he would one day manage in *Don Carlo*, is lacking at this stage. The narrative with its sturdy brass unison backbone is adequate, but only superficial, routine stuff. However, when Carlo contrasts the glory of the sunset with his own abject circumstances, there creeps in a breath of emotion, all the more welcome for being somewhat rare.

Adagio

Na – tu — ra! oh sei pur bel — la! sei pur

bel — la! . . . . . . e   stu – penda;

The *romanza* starts tenderly, and when it turns to memories of Amalia its rippling accompaniment brings a suggestion of poetry to a scene mainly concerned with violence. If Maffei and Verdi could not paint Carlo with the romantic hues of a Dick Turpin or a Robin Hood or a Captain MacHeath, they have at least shown him as a man with a free soul struggling to break out of the cage in which his lawless activities have caught it. Musically we appreciate this when the choral finale engulfs him after his reverie. It is on a lower plane. It is robust, but trivial like all that the Robbers stand for. But it is not the music of dedicated demons. Verdi might just as well have been writing for crusaders about to liberate the Holy City. Indeed, the weakest part of this opera is the chorus. Its very title implies their importance, yet their music is either negligible or worse. The colourful rogues of Schiller, unbelievable as they may be, deserve more than relegation to a static chorus. Even Rolla, after a few solo bars, reverts to obscurity after what may well be Verdi's shortest tenor part. Yet Prague has been set on fire for him.

At the beginning of Act III Carlo and Amalia meet at last, in the forest near the Moor castle. Amalia opens the act with a dramatic cry powerful enough for Elisabetta. For a few bars her stature is that of a tragic heroine. Then the Robbers are heard in the wood, singing tunelessly of burglary, arson, rape and murder. But it is Carlo who emerges from the thickets and all is set for the love scene. Schiller imagined extravagant refinements of mistaken identity. Maffei gives Verdi an uncomplicated duet; but he has written the bulk of it in stichomythia instead of the usual exchange of stanzas. This has forced Verdi into a few moments of careful and tender writing, before the inevitable cabaletta with its trills and leaps.

The scene changes to another part of the forest, showing the ruined tower in which Francesco has immured Massimiliano Moor. The Robbers are gathered, and sing Maffei's long paraphrase of Schiller's

song full of revolting images of satanic cruelty and sadism. One recalls
Francis Toye's amusing translation of a murderers' chorus in *I Lombardi*.[9]
This is its monstrous offspring, and as in the case of its sire, Verdi simply
did not have in his genius the freak tinder for setting it alight. Mercifully
it ends with the chorus going to sleep, giving their leader Carlo the
chance for a reverie in which he admits he can never be united with
Amalia; observes that, while his wicked gang can find repose, it eludes
him; draws his pistol, cocks it, and then throws it down with the decision
that pride should conquer grief. This recitative brings us a stage nearer
committing ourselves to sympathy for the wretched criminal who has
created for himself a despicable world to be lonely in. No aria develops.
Curiously there are to be no more recognizable arias in this opera. The
remaining solos will be labelled *racconto*, *sogno* and *giuramento*. If it were
not for the *Coro di Masnadieri* and the cabaletta of the love duet, one
might say that the score moves to a higher plane in the last two acts,
despite the notice in the *Gazette Musicale*:[10]

> After this act [the 2nd] there is a third, and after the third a fourth; but I
> will ask your permission to tell you nothing about them, for the
> constant decrescendo seemed to me to make itself felt.

Now Verdi had written quite a large proportion of *I Masnadieri* when
casting limitations caused him to drop it and switch to *Macbeth*. On 13
August 1846 Muzio mentioned that the next opera would be *L'Avola*, *I
Masnadieri* or *Macbeth* but the choice depended on what singers would be
available at Florence.[11] A fortnight later *L'Avola* seems to have been
scratched.[12] *Macbeth* would be ready for Lent if the baritone Varesi were
on hand. Next week Muzio was writing 'It will either be Fraschini and
so *Masnadieri* or if not it will be *Macbeth* with Varesi.'[13] On 24 September
he notes that *Macbeth* with Varesi is certain, and Verdi would then write
Masnadieri for London in the spring of 1847.[14] On 4 October Lumley
visited Verdi at Milan and we read that one clause in their agreement was
'To write *I Masnadieri* of which he had already finished two acts.'[15] On 3
December Verdi himself wrote to Lucca mentioning that he had 'a new
libretto: *I Masnadieri*, of which I have done about a third of the music'.[16]
Next day in a letter to Lumley he claimed to have composed 'about half
of *Masnadieri*'.[17] But at the same time he was discussing the libretto of
Macbeth with Piave, and it was *Macbeth* that reached the stage first. At
some time in the late autumn of 1846 Verdi must have put the score of

Masnadieri away, to begin the composition of *Macbeth*. When he took it up again, *Macbeth* was going the rounds of Italy.

It is possible to detect a new post-*Macbeth* flavour in *I Masnadieri* as soon as Amalia sings her opening phrase at the very start of Act III:

The whole of her recitative down to the entry of Carlo possesses a firmness, an eloquence not so far discernible in her part. In the love duet, before the pretty, Bellini-like passage, there is an *andantino* section in which they address each other in turn with the measured phrases of the Macbeths:

And to come back to the recitative of Carlo which we reached before this digression, we can once again hear the contemplative accents of the soliloquizing Thane of Cawdor (see opposite). This is surely a novel tenor passage for Verdi. From now onwards the score abounds in passages that cannot fail to impress. *Macbeth* is now behind, and the experience of its composition is oozing out through the latter half of the *Masnadieri* score.

Arminio comes to feed the starving Massimiliano in his tower dungeon, and brings the old man out for Carlo to see. Carlo's phrase 'Ombra del Moor' was singled out by Toye who both quoted it and found it 'decidedly Wagnerian'.[18] It *is* decidedly like *Macbeth*, together with the passage that flows from it on the strings down to Carlo's cry 'Oh caos eterno!' The old father's *racconto* too is built dramatically as he begins to recover something of his former dignity, but breaks down under the strain and finally faints after indicting his villainous son.

When Carlo rouses his gang by means of a pistol shot, he harangues them in yet another passage quite devoid of the old rum-ti-tum, Verdi here striving to be expressive and declamatory without hint of a tune, yet with selective scoring. The act ends Meyerbeer-fashion, the Robbers

suddenly joining like political conspirators in a great oath of support for Carlo's vengeance on Francesco. It lies half way between the *Ernani giuramento* and that of *La Battaglia di Legnano*. But had Verdi given it to Macduff and Malcolm, Macbeth would indeed have been ripe for shaking. The gangsters of Saxony have suddenly assumed a new stature, and have ranged their big battalions on the side of God.

As Schiller approaches the end of his sprawling play, the floodgates of melodrama are opened. Maffei gives us the last two scenes in his fourth act, both severely truncated. First it is Francesco's turn. These Moors always come by turns. Amalia has a duet with each of them, but they seldom meet one another. Carlo and Francesco do not meet at all, either in the play or the opera. Francesco now enacts a précis of Franz's appalling nightmare Vision of Judgment, in which he finds himself face to face with the descent into Hell. He summons a pastor. Moser, bass as all operatic priests, brings the villain no comfort. The situation reflects Faust and Don Juan, with Damnation poised for the knock-out. There is, however, one important difference between play and opera. Maffei has chosen to let his villain escape, just as Boito would do with Iago forty years on. This is not altogether presumptuous of Maffei, for Schiller himself could not make up his mind about Franz's demise. In his original work Franz, at bay in the castle with the robber gang smashing the windows and setting it on fire, rips off his hat-cord and strangles himself with it. In the later arrangement for the theatre this macabre realism is exchanged for a more refined exercise of violence. The robbers take him alive to Karl, who forgives him contemptuously and hands him over to the gang's justice. This justice turns out to be starvation to death in the tower where he had immured his old father. You can take your choice. Maffei chose neither. But he did avoid the temptation of arranging a tenor-baritone duet. Schiller's original conception, in which the 'white' villain and the 'black' villain never actually confront one another on the stage, is more subtle.

Verdi's final act starts without a prelude as Francesco rushes in terrified by the dream from which he has just awoken. The music is suitably agitated and sonorous. Arminio, now transferred from Schiller's Hermann to his Daniel, in a handful of lucid comments reminds us that he was once the tenor lead in a first-rate quartet but is now sadly relegated to the rôle of operatic stooge. To him Francesco relates the vision—a mixture of *Ezekiel* and *Revelation*. For this Maffei has given Verdi thirty-two dodecasyllabic lines—twice the length of Macbeth's

dagger monologue and almost certainly the longest solo passage in any
of Verdi's libretti. He has tackled it splendidly, always at declamatory
yet lyrical level, with no temptation to slip into an aria. As he moves
from one section to the next, Verdi's changing accompaniment
underlines the verbal picture now with hollow, muted brass, now with a
staccato tread of haunting terror, now with drum-rolls that lead into the
fanfares of the Day of Judgment and the crack of doom.

Muzio called this[19]

The most dramatic part of the opera. The music is descriptive and
with each section of the narrative the form of the music changes. This
wonderfully written piece has to be heard several times for all its
beauty to be appreciated.

Soffredini in his analysis found[20]

Good and weak passages alternating in it, and a sense of strain as it
proceeds to its end.

The sense of strain may perhaps be detected in the performer, but surely
not in Verdi's structure. Certainly it is the music of a composer who has
but recently tackled Banquo's ghost and the Apparitions, and is
confident he can deal with supernatural terrors and the hysteria they
induce in their victim's mind. Francesco's 'Sogno' lasts for 90 bars. 'Pari
siamo' is only 70, and Iago's 'Credo' less than 80. The favoured Muzio,
who was always able to be 'in on' the actual composition of Verdi's
operas, was right enough when he wrote that it must be heard several
times for full appreciation. How many times, alas, are we able to hear it?

The arrival of Moser the pastor brings a new twist to Francesco's
terror, for he receives none of the hoped-for spiritual comfort. As
troubled baritone and inflexible priest exchange phrases we find
ourselves at a tentative rehearsal of *Don Carlo*—Philip and the Inquisitor.
The musical means are more slender, but the chilling impact is there.
Moser is a compact little study of the Church Malevolent. As their voices
unite above the brass the apocalyptic vision seems to have become a
reality in the person of Moser, while beyond can be heard the
triumphant shouts of the destroying Robbers. Brief and stormy is the
finale, as priest and impenitent part their several ways off the stage and
out of the opera.

The last scene takes us back to the forest for the reconciliation between Carlo and his father. Its quiet, lyrical opening makes an effective contrast with the previous scene, developing with dignity into the tenor-bass duet 'Come il bacio' which was once the opera's sole representative in the gramophone world, recorded for Columbia in 1903 by Mieli and Brancaleoni—a record long since vanished into the mists of junk shop and waste disposal.* It is a fitting musical climax to the sufferings of each, both now finding a moment of peace in their last hour, with Verdi at his choicest level.

Some excitement pulses along as the Robbers bring in the captured Amalia and Carlo has to confess his liberating force is composed of murderous thugs and he is their leader. Out of this dramatic revelation is born the trio that ends the opera so splendidly in a steady flow of inspired melody, no stranger to those who know their *Lady and the Fool*. The Robbers themselves, having throughout the opera followed their Captain loyally if often banally, now turn on him with a vigorous unison, with trombones barking their determination to uphold his sworn command. Here suddenly one feels the potential menace of a unanimous mob. Old Massimiliano relapses into the oblivion which has dogged him throughout the story; Amalia, after her joyous upsurge of devotion turns on Carlo and bids him, if he must remain a criminal, kill her before he leaves her; which he, rousing himself from his dejection, suddenly does. Too swiftly the curtain is down. We have been swept along on a mounting tide of passionate music, only to see the leading lady savagely slain. What could they have thought that night in the royal box when, expecting the Swedish Nightingale to go off warbling a vaporous threnody full of 'muoio', 'gioia', and 'Iddio', they suddenly beheld her down and out without so much as a B flat?

Certainly this happens in Schiller's play, but with some explanation. Maffei's Carlo simply cries 'Now for the gallows!' He was heading there anyway without the murder of his cousin and bride-to-be. In the play Schiller presents us with a final romantic twist. There is a huge reward for anyone who can capture Karl alive. He has seen a poor man toiling by the road to support eleven children. To him he will surrender—a last gesture of charity. With which superbly bent logic he goes complacently to his doom. Maffei could hardly have incorporated this. It would have severely taxed the comprehension of operatic audiences, who in any case

* Not unique, however, for two more acoustically recorded versions have since come to my notice.

could not often hear the final words, drowned as they usually were by *tutti* exclamations of *Morto! Orrore! Dio! Sei vendicata!* and the like.

One of the features at Her Majesty's Theatre which gave the critics their opportunity was the sight of Lablache emerging at the point of starvation from the tower in which he had been imprisoned. Lablache was enormous. Chorley wrote:[21]

> His shoe was a big as a child's boat.—One could have clad the child in one of his gloves; and the child could almost have walked (though no Blondin) on his belt.

The odd thing was that only eleven years previously Mercadante had written an opera on the same subject, *I Briganti*. This was produced in Paris in 1836, with Lablache in the same part. According to Pougin, nothing could be remembered of Mercadante's opera, save the delirious laughter that greeted the entry of stout Lablache, emaciated by his solitary confinement.[22] Nevertheless the same tun of man was cast for Verdi's version. As Lumley wrote:[23]

> Lablache, as the imprisoned father, had to do about the only thing he could not do to perfection—having to represent a man nearly starved to death.

Lablache for a time taught Queen Victoria singing, but that was fifteen years earlier, and before she was Queen. According to the Countess of Longford 'at first she trembled so much that no sound came out'.[24] One wonders if now she had her revenge by indulging in a royal smile when her vast quondam instructor was greeted by Carlo with the words 'Ombra del Moor!' and replied 'Ombra non son'. But let the loyal Muzio have the final quip: 'Lablache is great in this opera, *even greater than his paunch.*'[25]

Muzio's account of the première of *I Masnadieri*, sent from London next day to Antonio Barezzi, is perhaps the longest existing account of the opera, which does not (except for Charles Osborne's recent contribution) get many pages in the Verdi books.* Muzio's analysis has little critical value, as it is simply a cavalcade of superlatives. For instance, when he comes to the final trio, he writes:[26]

* Charles Osborne gave it eleven pages. Now we have twenty-three from Julian Budden.

In all his operas the Maestro has some trio which is a chef d'œuvre, but this is the chef d'œuvre of all chefs d'œuvre.

As for the orchestra, it was 'marvellous, it couldn't have been otherwise, with Verdi conducting'. And the stolid, unemotional English are credited with having made the unanimous comment—'Bientifol'. Yet public support warranted only three performances—not enough, if we agree with Muzio, for the English to discover how 'bietifol' it really was.

And what of opinion in the Royal Box? Queen Victoria, on her return to Buckingham Palace, wrote thus in her Journal:[27]

. . . went to the Opera, where we saw the production of Verdi's 'I Masnadieri' in 4 acts, which is the same subject as 'I Briganti' by Mercadante. In this new Opera by Verdi based on Schiller's 'Die Rauber' the music is very inferior & commonplace. Lablache acted the part of Maximilian Moor, in which he looked fine, but too fat for the starved old man. Gardoni acted the part of Carlo Moor & was beautifully dressed. Lind sang & acted most exquisitely as Amelia & looked very well & attractive in her several dresses. She was immensely applauded.

Exactly a week later she was at Osborne House, and bathing in the sea for the first time in her life.[28] Perhaps the cool Solent, lapping around her with unaccustomed liberality, soothed away any lingering memories of the very inferior and commonplace music to which she had been subjected by her own Royal Command.

NOTES

1 *Die Räuber*—'Avertissement an das Publikum' in programme at Mannheim Theatre, 13 January 1782 (tr. Carlyle—*Life of Schiller*).
2 Garibaldi, op. cit. Muzio to Barezzi, 23 July 1847.
3 Ibid., 23 July 1847.
4 *Gazette Musicale*, 1 August 1847, quoted by Pougin in his *Verdi*, p. 113 (tr. J. E. Matthew).
5 Garibaldi, op. cit. Muzio to Barezzi, 23 July 1847. Muzio's words (. . . *gentile, e leggera come una piuma* . . .) unconsciously anticipate the text of 'La donna è mobile' and of 'Quand'ero paggio'.
6 Osborne, op. cit., p. 173.

7 Garibaldi, op. cit. Muzio to Barezzi, 29 June 1847.
8 *Athenaeum*, 24 July 1847.
9 Toye, op. cit., p. 240.
10 Pougin, op. cit., p. 114.
11 Garibaldi, op. cit., Muzio to Barezzi, 13 August 1846.
12 Ibid., 27 August 1846.
13 Ibid., 3 September 1846.
14 Ibid., 24 September 1846.
15 Ibid., 4 October 1846.
16 *Copialettere*, XL, p. 32.
17 Ibid., XLI, p. 33.
18 Toye, op. cit., p. 281.
19 Garibaldi, op. cit. Muzio to Barezzi, 23 July 1847.
20 Soffredini, A., *Le Opere di Verdi*, p. 104.
21 Chorley, op. cit., p. 19.
22 Pougin, op. cit., p. 111.
23 Lumley, B., *Reminiscences of the Opera*, p. 192.
24 Longford, E., *Victoria R.I.*, ch. 3, p. 45.
25 Garibaldi, op. cit. Muzio to Barezzi, 19 July 1847.
26 Ibid., 23 July 1847.
27 *Journal*, Buckingham Palace—22 July 1847.
28 Longford, op. cit., ch. 16, p. 211.

7

THE MILLERS AND THE WALTERS

Ah if only you knew what memories and excitements that heavenly song arouses in an Italian's heart—and above all in the heart of one who has sung it from his tenderest years! If only you knew! They say that once upon a time the Swiss mercenary troops were forbidden on pain of death to play the *ranz des vaches* because it reduced them to tears and brought desertion or death to its hearers, so ardently did it arouse in them the desire to see their homeland. Youth, patriotism, love—those were the days!

So Boito wrote to Camille Bellaigue,[1] and the heavenly song was Rodolfo's aria 'Quando le sere al placido'. What better diploma could a song achieve? Verdi's choruses and defiant duets had roused patriotic fervour in the theatres, particularly those policed by Austrian troops. But this little lyric, capturing in a few bars the yearning sadness of a Silver Latin elegy, had beaten them all; for it really had played on the tranquil emotions of an Italian too young to be caught up in the glamour of the *Risorgimento*. Imitating a *Puritani* cantilena in its simple musical mesh (and later copied more cloyingly by Thomas for the tenor in his *Mignon*), it hangs like a lustrous pendant just at the point when Verdi had grown out of being the 'musicien qui a une casque' and had slipped into the liaison with Guiseppina Strepponi which would become a fifty-year bond. It is only when one is on a crest of confidence that one can write a song like this. He had done nothing approaching its type before, nor ever would again.

Until the Verdi revival we only knew *Luisa Miller* through gramophone records of this aria; and they were very few. Caruso's version was never published; but we had Bonci, Anselmi and De Lucia; later Schipa and Pertile. All seem to be hushed into their best behaviour when singing it into the recording machine, Pertile alone breaking out *spiegato* as though he were Des Grieux or Cavaradossi. Yet only Bonci sang the music as Verdi wrote it (though in one phrase he muffed the words), with no attempt at showmanship, however tentative. In the first fully-recorded version Lauri-Volpi blotted his copy-book with a bravado finish. In the next Bergonzi, as one would expect, took Bonci as his model and Verdi as his idol. If ever an Italian aria demands perfection, it is this; and Cammarano's contribution is no bad little poem in its own right.

Indeed, Cammarano's share in the making of *Luisa Miller* is worth examining. Cammarano was adept at pouring famous literature down the operatic funnel. His *Lucia di Lammermoor* is typical—workmanlike and quite lyrical in a stilted, formal way. For Verdi he had done *Alzira* and *La Battaglia di Legnano*, the one poorish, the other distinctly ingenious. Schiller's *Kabale und Liebe* was quite a challenge, for it provides little enough of that heroic strain of *noblesse* which had gone all along into the making of the Verdian canon. The characters have no inner glow of idealism, lofty or crooked. Most of them are nasty or stupid. The theme is that which has sold countless women's magazines—the love of an aristocrat incognito for a working-class girl, but with no romantic solution to sugar the day-dream. It is a domestic tragedy, reminiscent of those sub-Shakespearean plays by Heywood, Dekker and the like; strong in subject but with lowered sights. It is in fact a good play, if one can overlook the occasional extravagances of language or expression which the young Schiller indulged in. But it seems remote from the operatic world. It does not contain, for instance, a single song. The nearest approach to music is at the beginning of the second act, when the rise of the curtain reveals Lady Milford (elegantly swathed in a loose negligée) running her fingers along the piano keyboard. But the opening words of her attendant take her away from the instrument and she shows no further interest in it. Louisa's father, however, is a retired musician. But apart from some of his remarks and allusions there is but one excursion into his quondam world, when the petulant Ferdinand, exasperated at Louisa's sudden coldness, grabs a violin belonging to him, plucks at the strings, then rips them, throws the instrument down and stamps on it with a loud laugh. (What the old music teacher said when he found this out, Schiller has omitted to tell us.)

One usual problem, however, Cammarano did not have to face—that of reducing a large cast. In *Die Jungfrau* and *Die Räuber*, as also in *Macbeth* and Werner's *Attila*, some twenty or more performers are required. *Kabale und Liebe* demands precisely ten. Yet Cammarano jettisoned four of these before adding two of his own; and he made all sorts of internal changes. His discussions with Verdi over the fashioning of the libretto are those of an experienced collaborator fully aware that he has already written with success for composers such as Mercadante and Donizetti before Verdi came along. A remarkable passage opens one letter:[2]

> If I did not fear the charge of being a Utopian, I would be tempted to say that in order to get absolute perfection in an opera one single mind ought to supply both words and music. This leads straight to my conclusion that when there are two writers they must at least be on the closest terms, and that if the verse must not be the music's servant, nor should it be its boss. I am convinced of this maxim and have always worked in obedience to it. I have always put my views to the composers with whom I have collaborated.

This makes fascinating reading for the opera student and sets up a fine motion for a debate. Although many lesser operas have had their lack of success ascribed to feeble libretti, some have managed to triumph in spite of this handicap; while there is surely no evidence that composers who have written their own libretti have stolen an artistic march on those who have relied on partnership. Without citing instances it could be argued that most composers who thought they were the best librettists for their own music had to work extra hard at their composition to accompany all those splendid word-passages which collaboration would have whittled down. Their literary aspirations have proved a rod for their own musical backs.

Cammarano felt that, however interesting their mutual planning, it was somehow frustrating for two intellects to be harnessed over a project that one might carry out alone. He was no amenable Piave, ready to insert a cabaletta behind Verdi's back for an importunate prima donna. He worried about failing to do justice to the play he was adapting. In *Luisa Miller* he worried particularly about his treatment of Lady Milford, the second lady of the drama. This Lady Milford has a large and important part. She is the mistress of the German prince who lurks behind and above the plot. She has just been discarded, and President von Walter sees in her a social match for his son Ferdinand, who is wasting his eligible youth on the *bürgerliche* Luisa. Ferdinand is outraged at this unsuitable suggestion, but finds that the English Lady is, although a *Favoritin*, a philanthropist who actually loves him. This introduces a dramatic complication, though we have to believe Lady Milford when she says she has only exchanged the favours of her bed for concessions to the poor and oppressed in her lover's Principality. This may extenuate, but does not annul, the circumstances of her immoral conduct. However, she is English; and Schiller seems to have considered this to be her salvation. In fact, she turns out to be, in reality, Johanna Norfolk. She leaves Germany nobly (?for Arundel). Schiller confessed that he had developed a special interest in her. She matured in the moulding, as later did the Feldmarschallin Fürstin Werdenberg.

This picturesque lady, Luisa's rival, could have played a powerful part in Verdi's opera. It was Cammarano who could not see how to retain her. In acknowledgment of his synopsis Verdi wrote to him,[3]

> I admit I should have liked two leading ladies. The mistress of the Prince in all the fullness of her character would have pleased me, just as Schiller portrayed her. She would have been a contrast with Eloisa, so that the love of Rodolfo for Eloisa would have been the more beautiful. But in the end I realize I can't have exactly what I want, and I must accept it as it is.

Cammarano admitted,[4]

> Schiller's dramatic conception of the part of Milady is sublime. I am not at all happy about leaving her out, but I find it quite unavoidable. For if she were retained, and her role enlarged, we still wouldn't find a second prima donna to take on her part; since it would be impossible to make it dramatically as important as the part of Luisa. . . .

As it turned out, Lady Milford became the Duchess of Ostheim, losing her English pedigree and her scarlet reputation in exchange for the position of President Walter's widowed (and presumably respectable) niece. Her entire part consists of a duet with Rodolfo and a dialogue *scena* leading into an unaccompanied quartet. She is quite static—a mezzo voice and nothing more—and Verdi even asked Cammarano what kind of voice she should have.[5] It seems odd that neither librettist nor composer could establish her right to a full dramatic rôle in musical contrast to Luisa. But the two-soprano opera was out of fashion since the castrati had been reprieved and trained as tenors. Secondary rôles such as Enrichetta, Lisa, Fenena and Medora were more or less episodic; and Verdi never attempted genuine travesti of the stature of Arsace or Maffio

Orsini. It seems that, having decided to call the opera *Luisa Miller* after its heroine (whether or not they knew that this had originally been Schiller's intention too), the name-part must prevail in both musical and dramatic importance. In this respect *Sonnambula* and *Linda* spring to mind, and the ballet *Giselle*. These must have been models, with their simple heroines adulated by peasants in the rustic setting of Theatreland's Tyrol. *Luisa* hangs in this gallery; and in the passages that lead from it are to be found many a sentimental operetta with an absurd plot and music that refuses to die. In such idyllic surroundings there may be broken hearts, misunderstandings, suicides and the like; but never a dynamic, passionate contralto to steal the show from the leading lady. So the Duchess of Ostheim, who in Schiller's play gets only a mention, takes over delicately from the soiled adventuress Lady Milford in a part that will never earn much personal triumph for the mezzo-soprano who agrees to sing it.

The other characters to be jettisoned were Frau Miller and Hofmarschall von Kalb. Luisa's mother is certainly no loss. She is delineated by Schiller as feather-brained and garrulous, but with her weather-eye firmly on her daughter's social chances. We have all come across Mrs Millers, but in the theatre they belong to the Comedy of Manners and are not for heroic opera. Von Kalb also is in this category. Congreve or Sheridan could have done something with him. Schiller makes him the addressee of Luisa's dictated letter, which Wurm forces her to write in exchange for her father's liberty. In cutting out Von Kalb Cammarano had to think again about this letter. He decided that Wurm, who had designs on Luisa, should compel her to write it to himself. Verdi did not agree with this absurdity.[6] Cammarano, however, stuck to it and justified himself by pointing out that there was no one else to write the letter to, and if addressed to Wurm it would work powerfully on Rodolfo's jealousy. As usual Cammarano got his way, but by means of intelligent discussion.[7] In one respect only can we regret the exclusion of Hofmarschall von Kalb: Schiller's stage direction at his first entry insists that '*he exudes a musky smell over the whole parterre*'. Here indeed is a new dimension; a lost opportunity for a Dali or a Wanamaker!

The remaining alterations are minor ones. The Präsident becomes Il Conte, a title more likely to be understood by Italians. Ferdinand was altered to Rodolfo; for this opera was being presented at Naples where the king, widely and disrespectfully known as Bomba, was named Ferdinand, and was a very touchy monarch indeed. Rodolfo may have been suggested by *La Sonnambula*, at the same time unconsciously paving the way for one of opera's most celebrated lovers. By contrast Wurm was retained, un-Italianized. What a splendid patronymic! If ever a scaly reptile trod the stage, it was Wurm. Only Sadler's Wells could have had the nerve to re-christen him *Franz*! Were they afraid of their patrons' all-too-certain capacity for giggling in the auditorium?

The overture to *Luisa Miller*, with its wistful phrase that recalls *Zampa*,

tells us that we are about to witness an opera in the course of which romantic delicacy will be disrupted by life's brutal realities. The little prelude to the first act with its pastoral lilt and woodwind reminds us at once of the Bellini of *La Sonnambula*; but one can also detect the loose scattering of seeds that will one day be tightened up in the harvest bundles of *Falstaff*. The birthday chorus of villagers with the solo of Laura, a charming creation, is a further exercise in Bellini-Donizetti—tuneful, graceful, ephemeral. Cammarano could be relied on to open each act with a traditional chorus, just as he always provided a sub-title, in this case 'L'Amore'.

In this airy and pleasant scene we meet the Millers and know them at once. The father embraces Luisa with a tender, mellifluous phrase, and she is soon off in raptures about her lover Carlo (for Cammarano has added his own piquant contribution to the story by having Rodolfo court her under a false name to hide his aristocratic identity). Her aria 'Io vidi e'il primo palpito' is contrived, artificially preluded, and full of decorative figures which may be passed as illustrating her 'primo palpito' but which are a bit sophisticated for so demure a young lady (Schiller gives her age as sixteen—the same as Strauss' Salome). But her enthusiasm is infectious and when Rodolfo appears the two are soon singing together in sixths a theme that sets us forward in our seats expecting the 'Verrano a te' of Lucia and Edgardo to break out. But instead they indulge joyously in an *allegro brillante*, against which the voice of the father is later heard expressing his doubts as to the young man's intentions and suitability—expressing them in the nicest possible way and entirely without malice. The ensemble works out happily with Luisa twice holding a long B flat over the dotted quavers of the others until at the climax, with an added romantic touch, the church bell is heard and all goes *ppp* as Luisa, Rodolfo, Laura and the villagers gradually file into the church, leaving old Miller alone.

To him at once comes Wurm. None too enthusiastically Miller greets him by name—a lone quaver amid rests. The effect is slightly sinister. His is the only monosyllabic name in Verdi (with the exception of the very minor Jorg in *Stiffelio*) until Ford and Meg. This is not to overlook Sam and Tom who are never addressed as such. Verdi insisted to his librettist that there should be something comic about Wurm;[8] but there is no trace of this on his first appearance. The singer may portray it, but not through his notes. In fact his opening phrases are punctuated by an orchestral figure bearing a hint of menace. Miller's aria rejecting Wurm's claim to Luisa is straightforward and dignified. He insists on being his daughter's father and not her dictator, and he concludes with a cadenza which, though musically unnecessary, serves to throw into contrast the next dry remarks of Wurm who prepares the ground for telling him that Luisa's lover is Count Walter's son. Whereupon he departs prudently, having lit the fuse of his petard, leaving Miller to a cabaletta of dismay on finding that his suspicions were not without foundation. Confidently he proceeds, with a purposeful build-up to a long-held top G flat. But we are conscious that this is a personal cabaletta, an emotional outburst—not at all the fiery explosion of a frantic or vengeful man of action. Verdi, his helmet doffed, is scaling down his tones without sacrificing his tunes. Although he opted for Miller to be a retired soldier instead of a music teacher, this was only to satisfy himself that he would be working with familiar material, a Banquo rather than a Bartolo. The first scene passes without a hint of tragedy to come. We have not yet met Count Walter.

But we do now, in the next scene. It is his turn for an aria. He is in his castle with Wurm lurking behind him. It is essential in this opera for the producer to make the most of the difference in social levels between the Walters in their stately home and the Millers in their cottage. Like the Capulets and the Montagues they are opposites; but they are divided by class, not feud. It may be thought that Verdi has not himself troubled to make a musical distinction; but surely he has. One need only listen carefully to Walter's aria 'Il mio sangue' to notice a more authoritarian theme than those given to the Millers. Count Walter sings with a sort of inbred superiority. He might be a Silva or a Foscari. He is certainly no homespun peasant. His growling bass accompaniment is broken by strenuous chordal phrases. Even his cadenza is less florid and more purposeful than Miller's. At the end of his recitative a short and conventional orchestral comment may pass unnoticed, but it is the die-stamp of a motif which will recur throughout the opera warning us that *liebe* is doomed by *kabale*:

When he speaks to Rodolfo of Federica's old affection for him, there is a noticeably aristocratic restraint in his phrases with their steady accompaniment. Then, according to the directions, 'Joyful sounds are heard'. These sounds herald and accompany the arrival of the Duchess and her retinue. A 3/4 *allegretto* full of dotted semi-quaver figures has a courtly dignity as it leads through twenty bars to a chorus of ladies-in-waiting, pages, servants and bodyguards. Verdi has clearly tried to give this retinue some august flavour not to be found when the simple villagers are fêting Luisa. The duet for Rodolfo and Federica, marked *andantino affetuoso*, is certainly couched in the cultured accents of aristocratic restraint, as the voices exchange, then blend in sixths, then break again, while the orchestra becomes more insistent as Federica realizes her wooing is to no purpose. Up to the point where she repeats 'Ad altra' four times and he four times responds with 'pietà' the scene has gone well. But now the old cabaletta convention intrudes and the remainder of the duet does not compel the same attention. Not that Verdi fails here. The music is still loftily designed; but it jerks, and we would rather it did not. At any rate it contrives to remain far less impassioned than the words they are singing. So it may be passed off as symbolical of that well-bred 'stiff upper lip' we are not so likely to encounter *chez* Miller.

Which is where we next find ourselves. Distant horns lead off an unaccompanied hunting chorus above which Miller informs Luisa that Carlo is in fact the Count's son and is betrothed to a lady who has already arrived at the castle. The warning motif (page 176) is heard again. Rodolfo enters and declares his love. He and Luisa kneel before Miller. The clarinet plays a solo declaration of troth in which the part bracketed [a] is an echo of the example on page 176. When Miller expresses his fear

of what the Count will do, the strings send a shiver down Luisa's spine as she gasps 'Io gelo'.

Rodolfo then confides in them that he has secret information which will deflate the Count his father. A sinister underlying theme played by the bassoons seems to be related to the example on page 174 from the Overture, but the approach of the Count is heralded by the little phrase of warning (see the example on page 176) which recurs in the orchestra at intervals throughout the ensuing scene, unobtrusively but obsessively.

At Count Walter's entry the dialogue is underpinned by a nimble orchestral tune reminiscent of *Lucia*. Miller defends his daughter with just that spirit asked for by Cammarano when he turned him from a music teacher into a soldier. But Verdi is careful to restrain him even when sorely provoked by Walter's insult to Luisa ('mercenary whore', he calls her). Everything now works up to a finale which Verdi and Cammarano had discussed in their letters. Verdi had asked for verses giving him a concerted passage without a stretta or cabaletta. He had his eye on a dramatic curtain and sketched his own dialogue for Cammarano to work on 'exactly like Schiller'. Cammarano in his turn warned Verdi that if there were to be no stretta he must speed up the music and make it exciting towards the end, otherwise there might be an anti-climax. He even went on to tell the composer that the peasants would be tenors and the archers basses. This was indeed collaboration![9]

The finale does not emerge 'exactly like Schiller'; but the gist is preserved, with the Count implacable in the face of his taunting son, until the latter utters his blackmailing threat and the Count at once releases Luisa. Here Verdi, after building up an ensemble in which all the principals are well delineated, snaps off the summit for the brief Rodolfo/Walter confrontation that so dramatically turns the story. We have a fascinating instance of thoughtful operatic construction.

The second act, headed INTRIGO (or *Kabale*), starts with a Cammarano chorus, a narrative by the villagers telling Luisa that her father has been hauled off in chains to the castle. Verdi is back in his Donizetti-style tunefulness, but when the chorus suddenly switches to pious observation there is a vivid foreshadowing of the prayer in the *Otello* storm. Luisa's despair is beautifully depicted in her isolated phrases above the chorus. But equally fascinating is the sudden unanimous cry of 'Wurm!' as that objectionable creature appears in their midst and they melt away at his abrupt command. The dictation by Wurm and the letter-writing by Luisa are handled with the sublime simplicity of genius. Alternate tension and despair are portrayed by a bare reiteration of dotted quavers dropping an octave and bouncing back again while he reads, and a clarinet phrase as she writes. *Traviata*-lovers will have to admit that Luisa set the pattern for Violetta's pen. But the notes that punctuate Wurm's dictation have all the grim persistence of a turning thumbscrew, particularly when they reach down to G below the bass stave as the infamous exercise comes to an end. With further subtlety Verdi now works into the score a cavatina and cabaletta for his soprano so indelibly embedded into the *scena* that they pass as frantic dialogue and do not seem to reach the stature of solo set pieces, so etched are they into the scheme of Wurm's villainy. We get a taste of Tosca's desperation before Scarpia, but the sheer economy of Wurm's evil casts a spell more chilling than Puccini's lavish chords. Wurm's triumphs come in short orchestral outbursts, as when she tells him the letter is finished and he takes it, and again when she capitulates to his infamous demand. 'A devilish smile spreads over the lips of Wurm' say the stage directions—and if the orchestra depicts this smile accurately it is indeed a vicious sneer. Verdi may seem to have forgotten his stipulation that Wurm should be in some way 'comico'. Yet perhaps not quite; for when he replies to Luisa's cabaletta he really does slip into the jargon of a *buffo* bass:

His words may be the language of a suitor, but his music is strictly for the suitor doomed to rejection; the patterning of a Di Luna whose humour is revealed only to those who can be amused by the sheer audacity of stage villainy. Verdi could hardly have dreamed up an Ochs or a Beckmesser; but he may have had in mind something of the sort we are familiar with in the Hoffmann stories—the Lindorf incarnations. But when it came to writing the music, he appears to have plumped for discretion. Schiller's Luisa says to Wurm, 'I would strangle you on our bridal night and then give myself with pleasure to be broken on the wheel.' Even the Bride of Lammermoor did not thus openly announce her intentions.

The next scene starts with the strings playing the beginning of Walter's first-act aria, as he is revealed soliloquizing about his wayward son. To him comes the inevitable Wurm to report on the success of his interview with Luisa. As they converse, a suggestion of the fateful theme (page 176) repeats itself insinuatingly in the orchestra, reminding us that out of their conference only misery can come. Something of the atmosphere of a Fiesco-Boccanegra duet creeps into this sinister interview, as Walter recalls the murder that gave him the title and claims he did it solely to secure an inheritance for his son. As Wurm begins to describe their ancient crime the memory of it overwhelms Walter, and there rises up in the music that turbulent horror which seized him in his first aria—a most effectively used echo. Wurm then takes up Walter's tune, but this time over a throbbing and slithering orchestra that deepens the mutual uneasiness of the two villains. Walter tells Wurm that Rodolfo knows about the murder. The orchestra, splendidly handled, gallops apace with Wurm's growing terror until at last they combine in a duet marked *meno mosso* working up through a dramatic climax, *più vive* then *più mosso*, to the final fling *sempre incalzando sino alla fine*—a fine piece of opera for two wicked basses.

Wurm goes and Federica enters for her arranged interview with Luisa. The recitative section is marked by repeated octave drops. Each utterance contains, or consists of, this interval. It happens eight times, and it has the effect of reminding us of Wurm's evil dictation of the letter, as though his departure has left behind a clammy shadow. The very artificiality of it seems as contrived as a carefully set trap. When Wurm returns with Luisa Verdi writes another Donizetti-type tune to trip glibly beneath the conversation. We might suppose this to be the run-up to a big duet between the Duchess and the peasant girl; but Verdi has a surprise for us. As the rippling tune seems to be pursuing its conventional course, with Luisa obediently admitting she is in love with someone, the Duchess asks who it is, and she replies, on a flattened crotchet, 'Wurm!' Once again that monosyllable jumps like a nerve. Instead of a battery of brass chords with timpani the orchestra trips away with a new tune while Wurm 'bows humbly'—a brief flash of *comico* palely foreshadowing Falstaff's self-satisfied acknowledgment of Master Brook's compliments. As the Duchess insists on knowing the truth, Luisa, pointing to Wurm, reiterates falsely her 'immenso, ardente amor' for him. Verdi's accompaniment to this rapturous confession gives it the lie. There is passion in her words, but lead in her heart.

Then she starts the unaccompanied quartet which Toye described as 'a truly remarkable piece of music, worthy to rank among the best examples of its kind in operatic literature'.[10] Soffredini called it a madrigal and praised it extravagantly.[11] The Cetra 'Complete' Recording cut it out. It is surely a *tour de force* of singing. Here are a soprano, a mezzo-soprano and two basses, all performing without a supporting note in the orchestra for 65 bars. Verdi had planned this from the start. In a letter to Cammarano he wrote, 'After the Walter-Wurm duet, a quartet? I'd like it if you could do one for unaccompanied voices.'[12] One might ask how it would affect the librettist to know whether his lines were to be sung with or without the orchestra. What Verdi was asking for was a very strictly metrical set of stanzas. Cammarano, with his great experience of operatic formulae, could and did understand. The result is this superb, if unexpected, *coup de théâtre*. Although Verdi often used a short unaccompanied ensemble to denote a moment of repose or perplexity, it seldom lasted as far as the twentieth bar and never actually brought down the curtain as does this surprising quartet. It possesses some unique character hard to identify. There can be no comparison with the one in *Rigoletto*, which is dynamic dialogue moving along dramatically. This one is quite static, artificial and, one might argue, unnecessary. Yet it has an inescapable effect. The voice of Luisa clear above the other three, often more than an octave above, gives the impression of a caged songster warbling its heart out in solitary confinement. And that is precisely the situation. Luisa *is* trapped. There is no romantic tenor to accompany her or give her support and hope. Surrounded by a mezzo and two basses—all evilly disposed towards her, she is pinioned in captivity. This quartet is a harmonic tableau, a mezzotint of sustained cruelty. We should feel at the end of those nearly 70 bars that the performers have earned their evening's fee. Federica will not appear again. Wurm will sing only nine more notes. For Walter there is very little to come. Luisa alone has musical glories ahead. But in spite of this hers is not the crowning glory; for in the next scene comes Rodolfo's 'Quando le sere al placido'.

It is set in the castle gardens, a welcome change after four successive indoor scenes. Verdi insisted on the placing of this aria, and it comes at exactly the right moment, lamenting the passing of love beneath the maze of intrigue, the point of no return for the ill-fated pair. Cammarano feared anti-climax after it and suggested it should precede the quartet.[13] Verdi too felt doubts, thinking the second act, like its predecessor, ought to end with the usual ensemble. As a compromise the soldiers and servants were brought in to swell Rodolfo's cabaletta and bring down the curtain with a full-throated stretta. Cammarano had entertained his own doubts about the chorus in this opera. It seemed to intrude without dramatic necessity, simply to fill the stage and build up finales. The drama, so personal in its intimacies, could have been worked out with the very minimum of choral addition. He was right. The idyllic and rustic openings are charming; the aggressive finales overweighted.

Rodolfo's famous aria is preceded by a recitative of some power, not over-accompanied by any means, but with its vocal phrases punctuated significantly by extensions, inversions or variations of that motif (page 176) which denotes the doom of his romance. One passage at least has the audacity to rival Otello's 'Dio! mi potevi' as its emotion mounts towards the outburst of lost control.

The aria is preluded by a descending wail on the violins, only a single bar, but eloquent of misery. Entirely captivating is the very last phrase of all, when he cries of his betrayal first *ff* then *pp* (the point at which so

Allegro

Ma dun—que i giu-ri, le speran-ze, la gioja, le la—grime, l'af—

fan—no? Tut—to è men-zo——gna

many famous tenors have tried to show they knew better than the composer, and always with the most unhappy results.) This aria, as Verdi knew and Cammarano anticipated, would have made a moving curtain; but the story demanded a continuation with Wurm at bay discharging his pistol into the air to avoid a duel and bring on the chorus to his aid. The rushing orchestral music, Donizetti-like once more, is feverishly excellent, until Rodolfo plunges into his cabaletta in defiance of his father and the gratuitous advice of the soldiers and servants who have rushed in on hearing the pistol shot. It is this hurly-burly which prompted a reporter for *Opera* to write,[14]

> The second finale is full of violent and senseless noise, with pistols being fired off into the air in terrifying fashion, and an enormous troop of soldiers and flunkeys swarming on to the stage in the middle of the most intimate discussion between their commander and his son, simply in order that the obligatory operatic chorus can take place.

This comment, fair enough in all conscience, is eloquent of just what Cammarano must have feared and Verdi must have failed to envisage. But the simplest galleryite could tell any librettist or composer that, however tense his opera, the discharge of an explosive will always bring down the house.

The third act, headed IL VELENO, unlike its two predecessors consists only of one scene. We are back in Miller's cottage. The short prelude contains the theme on which the Overture is so succinctly built (page 174), and it runs liltingly through Laura's colloquy with the peasants, but we also hear the ominous mutterings of fate. Laura has a delectable little part, quite a miniature portrait aglow with freshness. When Miller is left alone with his daughter the orchestra, suspecting the unnatural calm before the storm, warns us of trouble. As he reads Luisa's letter to Rodolfo there is a tangible darkening, with the prelude theme under a long string tremolo. In contrast Luisa's hint that she has suicide in mind comes starkly unaccompanied, to be followed by Miller's desperate outburst up to the pinnacle of the baritone range, the orchestra pounding in a Verdian chordal crescendo. Luisa then expands her theme of death and the grave in a passage full of dotted triplets, marked *delicatissimo*—quite an exercise in controlled singing and carrying a sort of near-delirium as though one who discusses such a morbid subject must be slightly unbalanced. Morbidly her old father replies, moved to tears at his daughter's state, claiming a prior right to occupy her tomb—fanciful stuff on the edge of melodrama, but reverently composed by the single-minded Verdi who never doubted he could think up the right music for any emotional situation. It causes Luisa to change her mind as with a two-octave run down from top C she tears her letter up. Immediately a new lilt comes into the music. A load has been lifted. Verdi here writes a passage which he was to borrow for *Traviata*. Father and daughter decide to flee; but this will be no spirited adventure, only a life of vagrant poverty. In a tune that pours out a sense of weary dejection the old man *con molta passione* describes the lonely fate in store for them. At first hearing it will remind us of Boccanegra's lovely stanza in his duet with his daughter. But a careful comparison reveals the manner in which Verdi has spun a ducal dignity into the one and a plebeian pathos into the other. Miller sings to a conventional tonic/dominant-type accompaniment; the Doge has a staccato four-in-a-bar thrum such as we find in Otello's 'Ora e per sempre addio'. As simple as this is the musical difference between heroism and humility.

The organ is heard playing in the village church, the lights of which are visible through the cottage window. It is the nuptial music of Rodolfo and Federica; but the bridegroom arrives with other plans. He will not marry the Duchess, he will instead poison Luisa and himself. Luisa prays, while he stands and watches her. This is the sort of situation much liked by Verdi, who draws on Giselda's prayer in *I Lombardi* for his model. In Schiller Lady Milford (Johanna Norfolk) has returned to England and Ferdinand is not betrothed to anyone. In fact, his frightened father has accepted Luisa as his future daughter-in-law. But with her dictated letter (to Hofmarschall von Kalb) in his pocket Ferdinand sees no future. So he goes to the Miller cottage to taunt and kill.

Opera-wise it is always popular to have music off-stage; and what

better than a chilly organ impersonally preluding a hated marriage? So
we have this theatrical tableau, with Rodolfo introduced in the stage
directions as 'a man swathed in a long cloak'. He comments as she prays
that it is a good moment for prayer. Like Otello, he would not kill her
unpreparèd soul, and he pours poison into the cup on the table. Beneath a
high tremolo the doom motif coils downwards and upwards, Wurm-
like. Rodolfo asks if she indeed wrote the letter and she admits it. All the
orchestral comments here are dramatic—heavy descending thumps for
his menacing queries; woodwind sighs for her admission. Then he asks
for a drink to cool his anger and she hands him the cup. When he bids her
drink after him there are four dark repetitions of that fateful phrase
followed by an ominous drum-roll. As he taunts her with 'Another
woman awaits me at the altar' he practically repeats the opening line of
the recitative to 'Quando sere al placido'.

They exchange phrases dramatically, Rodolfo tending to the poetical,
as

Allegro agitato
largo

que — gl'oc – chi in cui splen-de   de — gl'astri rag— gio più vi— vo e ter-so. . .

Predictably a long duet develops, but the desperation of the words is
somewhat overridden by the ecstasy of the music (which very much
resembles a movement in the *Sicilian Vespers* ballet). Pathetically the
andante section ends with the frustrated lovers singing a unison G; but
while Rodolfo holds his, Luisa drops an octave, as though her doomed
pulse is giving out.

When the castle clock is heard striking, a new turn comes over the
scene. The lovers, exhausted by their emotion, face each other for the
revelation. Again Rodolfo taxes her with her love for Wurm. Once
more that nasty name is coldly emphasized, this time by its separation
from the verb 'amasti' by being in the next bar, so giving Rodolfo a
chance to pause slightly before uttering it. But she will not reply. As he
threatens her, fate shudders twice more deep under a tremolo. When
Luisa at last tells the truth her *allegro agitato* carries a memory of the
Macbeths' desperate conclusion to their murder duet. Then there is a
plunge into a further agitated passage through which *Nabucco* persists in

obtruding; and with Rodolfo's horror at the tragic mistake he has made
we glimpse fleeting flashes of *Otello*'s final pages.

With Miller's arrival the lovers are a stage nearer death. Woodwind
arpeggios sketch the ebb of life and when Luisa asks for her father's
blessing we hear the 'poison slither' in the strings (page 177). The last act
of *Trovatore* begins to take premature shape. It is a short trio, and *Trovatore*
comes nearer to parturition until, as Walter, Wurm and the chorus come
in, the swift events—Luisa's death, Walter's cry, the chorus' invocation,
the murder of Wurm before he has time to sing one note, Rodolfo's
dying fling at his father—all these anticipate very closely indeed the final
pages in Di Luna's dungeon. When we listen to *Trovatore* we do not
realize that Verdi tried out its terse, tumbling catastrophe in *Luisa Miller*.

The sudden end, dramatically swift, was rather better done by Schiller.
In the play, with Luisa dead and Ferdinand dying, his father invokes
heaven to blame Wurm, not himself. Wurm is astonished. The Präsident
insists. Wurm, under arrest, claims exemption from responsibility and
assures the Präsident he will divulge such secrets as will bring him to the
gallows. Miller flings back to the dying Ferdinand a bag of gold which he
had given him earlier; whereupon Ferdinand dies beside Luisa before
giving his father the satisfaction of a last filial gesture. The officers arrest
the Präsident and march him away. All this, except the return of the gold
(which gift Cammarano sensibly omitted), could have made an excellent
operatic finale. But it seems traditional to alter the end of a play on
which an opera is to be based. One item at least we may be thankful
Cammarano did not retain—the *lemonade*. Ferdinand and Luisa were
poisoned, not with wine as the Borgias, not with water as Boccanegra,
not with a bouquet as Adriana Lecouvrer, not with leaves as Lakmé, but
with lemonade. Did Schiller suppose the humble Millers never aspired to
a bottle of wine? How the Italians would have laughed!

NOTES

1 Bellaigue, C, *Verdi*, ch. II, pp. 27–8 (*Les Musiciens Célèbres*—Librairie
  Renouard).
2 *Copialettere*, LXXX—Appendix, Cammarano to Verdi, 11 June 1849.
3 Ibid., Verdi to Cammarano, 17 May 1849.
4 Ibid., Cammarano to Verdi, 11 June 1849.
5 Ibid., Verdi to Cammarano, 23 July 1849.
6 Ibid., Verdi to Cammarano, 17 May 1849.

7 Ibid., Cammarano to Verdi, 11 June 1849.
8 Ibid., Verdi to Cammarano, 17 May 1849.
9 Ibid., Cammarano to Verdi, 4 June 1849.
10 Toye, op. cit., p. 296.
11 Soffredini, op. cit., p. 132.
12 *Copialettere*. Verdi to Cammarano, 17 May 1849.
13 Ibid., Cammarano to Verdi, 11 June 1849.
14 *Opera*, vol. 20., no. 12, December 1969, p. 1050.

8

TRIBOLETTO

Is the play indecent? What do you think? Is it because of the theme? Listen to the plot. Triboulet is a hunchback, mentally sick, and the court jester. These three burdens corrupt him. He hates the king for being the king and the nobility for being the nobility. He hates men in general because they are not crippled. His only pastime is making endless trouble between the nobles and their king, playing the strong against the weak. He absolutely depraves the king, enticing him to every kind of viciousness. He introduces him to respectable families, all the while pointing out which wife to seduce, which sister to entice, which daughter to debauch. In Triboulet's hands the king is just a puppet who upsets the very existence of those among whom he is being operated.

One day in the middle of a gala, at the moment when Triboulet is egging the king on to have an affair with the wife of M. de Cossé, M. de Saint-Vallier pushes his way in, goes right up to the king, and violently rebukes him for having dishonoured Diane de Poitiers. Triboulet mocks and insults this father whose daughter the king has seduced. The father raises his arms and curses Triboulet. On this depends the whole play. Its real theme is *the curse of M. de Saint-Vallier.*

Look at the second act, for instance. Who is the victim of this curse? Triboulet the king's jester? Not at all: Triboulet the human being, the father of a daughter. For Triboulet has a daughter, that's the point. She is all he has in the world, and he keeps her hidden away in a lonely house in an unfrequented part of the city. In direct contrast to his debauched and vicious goings-on in public, he cocoons and isolates her. He keeps her innocent, pious and pure. His greatest fear is that she may be led astray; for being himself wicked he knows what this would lead to. So of course the old man's curse is going to hit Triboulet through his one and only cherished possession—his daughter. The very king whose sexual excesses he has been encouraging will ravish his own child. The identical fate which struck M. de Saint-Vallier will descend on the jester. And then, with his daughter assaulted and seduced, he will set a trap for the king and his daughter will be caught in it. Triboulet has two pupils, the king and his daughter. He has trained the king in vice, but has brought up his daughter in virtue. The one destroys the other. He plans to abduct Madame de Cossé for the king, but it is his daughter he hands over. He plans to avenge his daughter by killing the king, but it is his daughter he kills. Nemesis does not stop halfway. The curse of Diane's father works itself out on the father of Blanche.

Thus Victor Hugo set down in his *Preface* the synopsis of his controversial and ill-starred play, and nobody else has ever improved on it. This was the plot that so scandalized Paris and so captivated Verdi. For the composer it was an 'absolute must'. But although he found the drama instantly translatable into music, it could not be transferred from the world of literature to that of the opera house without a series of obstacles, some reasonable and some curious, being erected across its path. The censorship's attack on Verdi and his librettist is well known. Banned in Paris, the play stood little chance of acceptance in Venice even with Verdi's music and the title *La Maledizione*. Il Re Francesco was the first casualty; he had to be uncrowned and reduced to a provincial duke—Burgundy and Normandy came up as suggestions, but in the end the plot settled down in Italy, Mantua being the choice. So Francesco became Gonzaga (the illustrious family name of the Dukes of Mantua), Saint-Vallier emerged as Castiglione, de Cosse as Cepriano, Bianca as Gilda, Triboletto as Rigoletto, Magellona as Maddalena, etc. Even then it was objected that there were existing families named Cepriano and Castiglione. The one was easily altered to Ceprano, the other more drastically to Monterone. Gonzaga, it goes without saying, had to be struck out, but he was still allowed to remain under his title of Duke of Mantua. (As well permit the Dukes of Norfolk or Bedford while disallowing Howard or Russell.) Even the title *La Maledizione* joined the list of casualties, *Rigoletto* at last emerging. Whatever the real derivation of this name (its dictionary meaning is a 'round dance'), it was new, intriguing, and euphonious.

There is no need to dwell on the opera's lasting popularity in this country, or to jeer at the inaccurate forecasts of failure and oblivion pronounced by the critics to whom it was new (in more than one sense). A Covent Garden season has seldom been without it since the war. It has been recorded in full (or thereabouts) some twenty times—far more than any other Verdi opera. An acoustic version was made in 1917; it was the first opera to be recorded electrically and the first of Verdi's to be issued on LP in the English market. Today, when a recording company wants to keep abreast of the times, out comes a new set of *Rigoletto*.

But however familiar we are with it as score or spectacle, we must always be aware of the intriguing origins. We must recognize that the libertine Duke is not really a Gonzaga, but François I. We are in fact brushing with French history and the scandals of the Valois as Hugo had raked them up and Verdi was happy to repeat them. Hugo did not rewrite history as shamelessly as Schiller; but he elevated gossip to the status of fact in the manner of the old historians of the Roman Empire. The roots are embedded in truth, but the plant luxuriates. Of François Valois Francis Hackett wrote, 'Had his head opened on a hinge, the first thing to pop out would have been a woman. . . . One glance from him was enough to skewer a pretty girl.'[1] His own sister Marguerite delighted in telling stories about him in her *Heptameron*. She related how her royal brother, in pursuit of a young married lady he fancied, found that he had to scale a monastery wall *en route* to her bedroom; so after spending the night with her he would join the monks at prayer in their chapel on his way back to the palace, which greatly impressed the abbot and intrigued Marguerite.[2] Jeanne le Coq was the lady's name. In her elderly, cuckolded husband we may find the original of Hugo's de Cossé (Verdi's Ceprano), and in the nocturnal prowl that led him to her may be the origin of his tryst with Blanche (Verdi's Gilda). His attendance at the chapel after leaving her bed gives just that mingling of *lubrique* with *religieux* which is the essence of French Romance, and is preserved by Hugo in the King's admission at the very start of the play that he is in pursuit of a *femme bourgeoise* whom he sees every Sunday in the congregation of St Germain-des-Près. The opera faithfully copies this opening. (A television producer went so far as to exhibit his flirtation at the communion rail while the prelude was being played—one of the most tasteless aberrations imaginable.)

Among Hugo's courtiers are several whose names were closely linked with the amorous escapades of their King, and yet who later occupied important positions in the state—notably Anne de Montmorency, Constable-to-be, and Chabot de Brion who was to become an admiral. But the best known was Clément Marot the poet, who had been a valet to Marguerite. All three were to be prisoners-of-war at Pavia. Clément

Marot (Verdi's Marullo) is of particular interest. His court poetry, even when composed with artificial adulation, breathes colour and life into the ghosts of the Louvre. Of Diane de Poitiers he wrote:

> Dont le nom gracieux
> N'est ja besoing d'escrire
> Il est escript aux cieulx
> Et de nuyct se peult lire.

And Diane was the cause of Hugo's dramatic intrusion by Saint-Vallier into the royal gala; for she was his daughter and the King had added her to his enormous catalogue of conquests; later she was to become the celebrated mistress of his son Henri II. Though never Queen, she was (like Banquo) ancestor of four future kings. And all the palaver of the curse which drew laughter from François and brought disaster to Triboulet stemmed from her adventure. When Monterone comes in and chills the festivities it is Saint-Vallier we are listening to, and the cause of his fury is the beautiful Diane, preserved to this day on canvas or in marble among the great collections of France, by no means always dressed.

As to the gathering of the courtiers by night for the abduction of Triboulet's daughter, the suspicion of zany improbability that may possess us is largely dispelled when we read:[3]

> While Francis remained in Paris he and his favourite companions went about every day in disguise, besides mumming in masks at night. . . . All honest citizens, when compelled to be out after dark, carried with them, as decreed by the law, small hand-lanterns. Generally the first efforts of their assailants were to possess themselves of the lanterns and extinguish the light. In the scuffle that ensued hard blows were often given and received, while a falling mask or two would reveal to the affrighted bourgeois some well-known faces amongst the brawling party of aristocratic and royal practical jokers.

In such an atmosphere and amid such habits the most cynical opera-goer may accept the probability of the open-air night scenes in Rigoletto; for they are indeed glimpses of old Paris.

The contrast between the fine figure of a King, protected by heaven, and the mis-shapen jester, entangled in his own hell, is brought home in this note:[4]

A man of five feet ten inches, or eleven at most, which the armour of Francis I in the Louvre shows the height of that monarch to have been, was regarded, apparently, as gigantic in that age of humpbacked, stunted growth, and deformed royalty. Deformity was then very general in France. Infants and young children were so tightly swathed and bound up that their muscles became contracted, their limbs crooked, and rarely did any grow up without some bodily defect more or less developed. Francis may therefore have well been looked on as a wonder.

And later on, by the same authoress:[5]

The king was readily recognized, from his large oval face and very bold features. He is said to have had the largest nose of any man in France, except Triboulet, the Court jester, which would seem rather to impugn his claim to that large share of manly beauty with which his flatterers have credited him. The royal nose was, of course, a more shapely one than poor Triboulet could boast of. He, who said so many wise and witty things, and to whom so many more he did not say are attributed, was a sad object to look upon; his appearance being that of a sort of deformed man-monkey.

Triboulet, though Hugo sets him up as a paterfamilias and man of property, does not seem to have enjoyed much independence, for when France went to war he was compelled to travel to the front line. The bombardment of an Italian town so alarmed him that he hid under a bed. Jean Marot, father of Clément, tells this story and describes the jester thus:[6]

Triboulet was a fool, with no strength in his horn,
At thirty as wise as the day he was born;
Little forehead, great eyes, a big nose, figure bent,
Long, flat stomach, hunched back, to bear weight as he went;
He mimicked all people, could sing, dance, and preach,
Always pleasant, none ever resented his speech.

It is only the last line which will surprise us, for that by no means describes Hugo's Triboulet or Verdi's Rigoletto. But this was written before Francis became king. He has had time to become bitter. For one thing, he has lost his adored wife. We can never be absolutely in sympathy with the exaggeratedly sentimental references made by Rigoletto to his deceased wife and by the dying Gilda to her assumpted mother. But we must accept that it was her death that made the jester so possessive a father. Blanche in the play is only sixteen. Not many Gildas realize this. She is little more than a Juliet in age, but obviously several years younger when her father, in Jean Marot's verses, was thirty. So sufficient years have elapsed for Triboulet to wax bitter and poison-tongued in the court of François.

His real literary canonization, of course, is by way of his brief intrusion into the immortal Rabelais. In Book 3, chapter 37, Pantagruel persuaded Panurge to take counsel of a Fool, telling him,

> I have often heard it said in a vulgar Proverb, *The wise may be instructed by a Fool*. Seeing the answers and responses of sage and judicious men have in no manner of way satisfied you, take advice of some fool, and possibly, by so doing, you may come to get that counsel which will be agreeable to your own heart's desire and contentment. [tr. Sir Thomas Urquhart]

So in the next chapter they discuss the merits of Triboulet, and Rabelais launches into one of his characteristic catalogues of properties and virtues, some of which we could have thought of but most of which we would not. Hidden among them, much to Rabelais' credit as a prophet, is 'A *baritone* fool'. The upshot is that they decide France should celebrate a Triboulet-Day in the manner of the All Fools' Day of Ancient Rome; and they send to Blois to have him fetched. When Triboulet arrives they present him with an inflated bladder, some toys, apples and wine. He eats some of the apples and drinks all the wine; then delivers an oracular warning and retires to play with the balloon. Pantagruel and Panurge dispute as to the meaning of the warning, which broadly suggests monastic cuckoldry. Triboulet takes no further part, save to strike out with his toy sword and his bladder. They decide he is an honest and good-natured fool, not exactly *Der reine Tor* of Parsifal, and a long way from the *bien méchant, bien cruel et bien lâche* of Hugo's

Triboulet; so they present him with a splendid new coat and send him back whence he came.

Thus Triboulet is good-naturedly bowed out of Rabelais, to make a much metamorphosed re-appearance in Hugo as the evil genius of a King who, born under Virgo, needed none. But it is the essence of *Le Roi s'amuse* that we have a first-class story which itself is fiction, but with historical embroidery that makes it starkly possible. Quite apart from the curse of Saint-Vallier and its insecticide-like effect on Triboulet, the real kernel of the drama is its Royal Court setting and the off-beat repercussions that so overwhelm those caught up in them, yet leave the divinely-protected monarch not only unscathed, but unaware. Hugo puts this in a nutshell:

MAROT: Que savez-vous ce soir?
M. DE GORDES: Rien, que la fête est belle,
  Et que le roi s'amuse.
MAROT: Ah! c'est une nouvelle!
  Le roi s'amuse? Ah! diable!
M. DE COSSÉ: Et c'est très malheureux!
  Car un roi qui s'amuse est un roi dangereux.

And it was Marot who, in the prevailing fashion of dilettante word-play, discovered that he could make an anagram of François de Valois.[7] It worked out *De façon svis royal* (I am every inch a king.) And so he was!

We do well, when listening to *Rigoletto*, to be aware of the reality which an intelligible if not intelligent censorship succeeded in veiling from contemporary and future audiences. The sting in the story lies in its proximity to the highway of history. It may be but a *cul-de-sac*, but the heavy traffic of monarchy, politics, warfare, renaissance, reformation audibly rumbles by to those who care to listen. This idle tenor Duke, so debonair and carefree, is really the King who at the Field of the Cloth of Gold was challenged by our own Henry VIII and threw him. And if Mantua seems to be far away from Paris, it may be as well to remember that Charles de Bourbon, Constable of France, who saved François at Marignano but fought against him at Pavia, his mighty political rival in fact, was through his mother a cousin of the Duke of Mantua. So in their determination to preserve the sanctity of the French King, the Venetian authorities doubly insulted him, first by turning him into an Italian

Duke, then by selecting a Duke who was closely related to his greatest enemy.

Yet, as Victor Hugo said, 'The real theme of the play is Saint-Vallier's curse.' Verdi, knowing this, was happy for his opera to be called *La Maledizione*. But in the end, *Rigoletto* is more select and memorable.

Piave, however, compelled to relegate his plot from *Le Roi* to *Le Duc s'amuse*, did not altogether lose by the change from a Valois to a Gonzaga. The period was exactly contemporary. Federigo Gonzaga,[8] the first Duke of Mantua, was honoured by the title when he entertained Charles V in 1530. François I, having been defeated and captured by Charles at Pavia, had been released from detention and was back in France, consorting with Anne de Heilly and planning a splendid renovation of the Louvre. The Gonzagas, if they had no Louvre for Piave's opening scene, were busy bringing such glamour and colour to Mantua that the opera could still open in a theatrical glare of Renaissance glory. For the Duke of Mantua's mother, the famous Isabella d'Este, had enriched the city with her art collection, with buildings to contain it, with her *Grotta and her Paradiso* and her *Giardino Pensile*, and the commissioned paintings of Andrea Mantegna. Her son the Duke was no less enthusiastic. He built the glittering Palazzo del Te, and brought Giulio Romano to decorate it specially for the reception of the Emperor Charles. So amid the frescoes and murals of Mantegna and Romano strolled and conversed the baritone of *Ernani* and the tenor of *Rigoletto*.

But besides this Piave-Verdi link there is another strange one. Federigo had a cousin, Vespasiano Gonzaga, who married Diana de Cardona. After her death, he took a second wife, Anna of Aragon, sister of the Duke of Segorbia. It will be recalled that Ernani, on revealing to Charles V that he is no bandit but a nobleman, addresses him thus:

> Io son conte, duca sono
> Di Segorbia, di Cardona . . .
> Don Giovanni d'Aragona
> Riconosca ognuno in me.

So Ernani was closely related to the two wives of the Duke of Mantua's cousin.

While caught up in this intriguing digression, it is irresistible to note the lurid fate of Vespasiano's first wife, Diana de Cardona. She took a lover and he caught them together. Whereupon he is said to have killed him in her presence, locked her up for three days with his corpse, and then brought her a cup of poison, standing over her while she drank it. What an operatic finale for Verdi! But one feels that if only Ernani had survived, this vindictive Gonzaga would never have got away with it. . . .

The first Duke of Mantua may occupy no great place in history, but he and Isabella d'Este founded a resplendent Duchy. The Reggia and the Palazzo del Te were fabulous galleries of Renaissance art. Ceilings and walls glowed with classical mythology; for Giulio Romano was a pupil of Raffaele himself. Here such subjects as the *Marriage of Cupid and Psyche*, the *Bath of Venus and Mars*, *Apollo and the Muses*, the *Judgment of Paris*, the *Rape of Helen*, *Venus and Adonis*. various *Amours of Jupiter* must have delighted the Duke. Well may he have mused, as he wandered before and beneath his rapturous collection of nudes and gazed at their 'opulent, unfettered, and often highly imaginative beauty':

> Questa o quella per me pari sono
> A quant'altre d'intorno mi vedo,
> Del mio core l'impero non cedo
> Meglio ad una che ad altra belta. . . .

Here too in the Reggia was the miniature house where Isabella d'Este kept her troupe of performing dwarfs. These were no doubt the origin of and inspiration for Zeffirelli's dwarfs in his kaleidoscopic opening scene of *Rigoletto*, by no means the extraneous feature they may have seemed to some. For the historically minded this opening scene can carry a richness of architecture and art, of wardrobe and masquerade, without overplaying sixteenth-century Mantua and the zenith of the Gonzagas. For

> The Gonzaghi, after their elevation to the Ducal dignity, abandoned themselves to splendour and luxury; and, corrupted by the flattery of courtiers and the ease of Court life, indulged freely in vices of which the record lives in their history.

They sowed recklessly the seeds of their own destruction; and our operatic Duca di Mantova, though no dramatically acceptable substitute for François Premier, survives immortal in Verdi's musical rogues' gallery, his honour rooted in dishonour.[9]

Verdi opens *Rigoletto* in the simplest possible manner with a trumpet and a trombone repeating the note C eight times, the first five unaccompanied, the last three shrouded in gloomy and foreboding chords of brass and bassoon. This is the motif of the buffoon's brooding soliloquy as he pores over the curse of old Monterone. Rigoletto's craven belief in this curse is the hinge on which the plot opens and closes. It becomes an obsession which preys on his mind and destroys him. The same curse is pronounced on the Duke, but the extrovert nobleman laughs it off and survives unscathed. The invulnerability of the master sets in terrible relief the pathos-prone helplessness of the man. The prelude is wholly occupied with his complex. We hear the awful hold that superstition has on him, followed by the mental anguish which it brings in its train, whether to himself or his ensnared daughter. When the violins and woodwind wail pathetically in rising and falling semitones, we get a foretaste of the shame, disgust, remorse, disillusion and despair that will pursue father and daughter to their ultimate disaster. These sobbing semitones will recur enough to form a sort of identity-disc for the opera. As they now die away, the curse is re-echoed brokenly, punctuated four times by drum-rolls, the effect catching a wisp of *Tuba mirum* and *Mors stupebit*.

Even more gripping is the deliberately sudden switch as the curtain rises to plunge us into a glittering kaleidoscope of Renaissance gaiety. It should be, of course, a *fête de nuit au Louvre*, and Hugo makes sure of an animated impact. Piave, relegated to Mantua, had not this incentive to recreate history and demanded no more than an operatic *festa*. Donizetti and Bellini would no doubt have opened with a bright chorus of introduction; but Verdi, wanting to get on with the business, has insisted on following Hugo by plunging straight into a dialogue. We are to understand that the party is in full spate; but our experience of the warning prelude reminds us that, despite the *festa da ballo*, the *banda interna* belting away *brillante*, and the *Cavalieri e Dame in gran costume*, something is rotten in the state of Mantua.

To start an opera by breaking into a dialogue was a novel experiment, but it was a device used again by Verdi in *Simon Boccanegra*, *La Forza del Destino*, and *Aida*. Its very informality commands instant attention, in contrast to the conventional opening chorus which gave operas a comfortable send-off. Before and behind the conversation the dance music alternately pounds and trips, introducing some four distinct tunes (none likely to have graced the Louvre of François Premier or the

Gonzaga Palace). However, their rapid succession brings a restless mobility, a fluid shallowness to the scene, capturing the worthless gallivanting of an amoral society. The Duke snatches a lull in the proceedings to throw off his *ballata* with its irresistible appeal over an outrageously basic accompaniment; to be followed by a string band on the stage playing first a minuet then a *perigordino*. Over the former the Duke flirts with Ceprano's Countess. In a few minutes Verdi has painted for us, musically, a rake and a gallant—careless and dissolute, meticulous and artful. The all-too-short minuet has the classical grace of Lully or Gluck bringing a moment of stylized courtliness quite at home in the Versailles of Louis if not in the Louvre of François. It is suddenly demolished by the interruption of Rigoletto, obtruding himself out of nowhere to throw an insult at Ceprano. This entry of Rigoletto is subtle. He is the protagonist; but in this brilliant gathering of the nobility he is a cipher, lumbering with a bitter heart in a twisted body. No red carpet is laid for his arrival. He is not there, and suddenly he is there—like Alberich at the beginning of *Rheingold*. But when he breaks in upon the delicious minuet to taunt the near-cuckolded Ceprano, he sings the very notes with which he will brood over the curse—the reiterated Cs—and when he sings Piave's stanza about the Duke and his pleasures, instead of the tune Piave no doubt thought Verdi would write, Rigoletto has forty-six notes of which only six are not C. His ironical spite pre-echoes his deflation. Having thus delivered himself of a string of observations which may have failed to arrest the attention of an audience wrapped up in the orgiastic goings-on of the *festa*, he goes out as suddenly as he arrived. And the *banda interna*, which had taken the minuet's place, now gives way for the string consort to play the *perigordino* for those who have opted to dance it. But their particular pleasure is short-lived. Soon the band is at it again, while the courtiers, apparently tired of the official proceedings and desirous of escaping from their partners, gather round for some gossip, the subject being the discovery that Rigoletto (of all people) has a mistress. As Clément Marot says in the play,

Quoi! Triboulet la nuit se change en Cupido !

And the obedient Piave has put into his libretto

Il gobbo in Cupido or s'è trasformato.

There is of course an infinite variety of repartee and allusion in Hugo which cannot be served up in the opera. As with the individual robbers of Schiller we cannot expect to be able to identify and listen to each courtier. Marot has become Marullo and Borsa may be derived from De la Tour-Landry, as Ceprano is certainly De Cossé. But as for the other seven, they are relegated to the chorus where, though sacrificing their personalities, they have at least preserved their idle superficiality. Only we do miss Hugo's sub-acid Triboulet. For he took some pains to show us why the courtiers all hated him. A little touch like

> LE ROI (chantant): Vivent les gais dimanches
> Du peuple de Paris!
> Quand les femmes sont blanches . . .
> TRIBOULET (chantant): Quand les hommes sont gris!

might well have been worked into the libretto.

While the dance music continues in the background the courtiers are joined by the Duke and Rigoletto. The latter is making witless but provocative suggestions as to how Ceprano should be dealt with, all in Ceprano's hearing. Hugo informs us that De Cossé was the fourth fattest man in France; so Ceprano, if the producer is faithful to his original, can be made a ridiculous butt as exasperation leads him to draw his sword. Rigoletto's ascending phrase of mockery may pass quickly here, but the tables will be turned in the last act when Sparafucile cheats him over the body of his victim and uses a similar phrase for his deceit.

Allegro con brio

È ben na—tu—ra—le! Che far di tal te—sta? A co—sa el-la va—le?

Verdi now fills his stage for an ensemble which builds up as the courtiers are joined by the corps de ballet from the ballroom for a *tutta forza* climax; but it is a climax well-engineered by the composer for a dramatic *coup de théâtre* quite beyond the scope of Hugo. For out of the typical tonic-dominant cadence emerges the lone voice of Monterone, demanding an audience with the Duke. His intrusion extinguishes the orgiastic fires at once. The *banda interna* packs up, to be heard no more. The dancers are immobilized; the Court dumbfounded. Only Rigoletto has the audacity to face the Count, just as in Hugo, but with music's added advantage of echoing mimicry.

Monterone is of course Jehan de Poytiers, Seigneur de Saint-Vallier; and though his part in Hugo is a short one, the dramatist exalted him purposely, giving him the stature of a classical, almost Biblical mouthpiece of moral indictment. He is introduced as an old man, all in black, with white hair and beard—a chilling contrast to the gold-robed king, his colourful courtiers and their glamorous ladies. Saint-Vallier was in fact under fifty at this point in his life; but it is recorded that during the night before the date fixed for his execution his hair did turn white. Victor Hugo has made important use of the tradition that the king pardoned him on the scaffold in exchange for his daughter Diane's virginity. His Saint-Vallier upbraids the king's lechery and disowns his raped offspring, and it is deliberately introduced for Triboulet the mocker to listen to; for his own cherished daughter is about to be seduced along the very same primrose path. Hugo set great store by this parallel, but he avoids the temptation to incorporate Saint-Vallier's alleged comment on descending, reprieved, from the scaffold:[10]

Dieu sauve le bon con de ma fille, qui m'a si bien sauvé.

(Even in these permissive times it is better left in the original French.)

Rigoletto, playing to the gallery, advances towards him *con ridicola gravità*, his tasteless deportment accurately depicted by the strings, which swagger defiantly as he moves, aping his insolent gestures and hollow heroics. The idea is symphonically perfected by Strauss in *Till Eulenspiegel*, but the naked embryo is here. Verdi has chosen the strings for several comments on Rigoletto's behaviour and emotions, as we shall see. Having taken up his position, the buffoon taunts the old nobleman about his daughter's dishonour, though the libretto does not clarify the reference for us. A twisting figure in the orchestra succinctly portrays the bent mind and body of the clown, whose very next phrase with its mocking trill was appropriated by Leoncavallo for Taddeo in his *Pagliacci* Harlequinade.

As in Hugo, the proud aristocrat ignores the vulgar abuse of the hunchback and addresses himself to the Duke. His reply is in splendid contrast to Rigoletto's viciousness. His firm declamatory tones are incisively welded by a biting *tremolando* for violins and violas, heavily punctuated by uprushes of the whole orchestra and accented by regular comments on bassoon, tuba and double bass. This defiance by Monterone is quite one of the best things in the opera and dramatically conveys the importance of Saint-Vallier, whose real predicament the libretto somewhat glosses over. At the climax he curses the Duke and Rigoletto. The latter cringes, but his master is unmoved. Verdi then colours the shocked reactions of the nasty courtiers by a *sottovoce* ensemble with a *pppp* marking at the start, gradually following the traditional crescendo to bring the curtain down. But before it ends we seem to catch an echo of the blustering dance music broken down into 3/4 time and suggesting the complete collapse of the festivities. Like Belshazzar's Feast, the *fête en Louvre* has disintegrated; and the cowardly buffoon has been unmasked. Dramatist and composer must now work to make us sorry for him. His contribution to the stretto-finale has been seventeen repetitions of 'orrore!'. In spite of the universal hatred in which he is held, nobody seems to have thought of cursing him before. He cannot take it; and when the curtain rises again he is still smarting.

Hugo places Triboulet's home across the Seine, for he stipulates that the tower of Saint-Severin is visible, and the church in which the king has first set eyes on Blanche is St Germain-des-Près. Both these churches are south of the river. In the opera, of course, it is Mantua and there are no landmarks. But *l'hôtel de Cossé* becomes *il palazzo di Ceprano*, in whose shadows nestles the home of the hunchback; no hovel, for Hugo and Piave after him stress its respectability. The corrupt Court Jester, once free of the licentious Louvre, is a man of principles and property, brings up his daughter with puritanical strictness, keeps a servant and enjoys a private garden with patio and terrace. All the more terrible is his tragedy, for he is fundamentally the superior of his betters, and only debased by his contact with them.

Now he stands in the road outside his home, stripped of his professional garishness, wrapped in a plain cloak, as dismal as the cul-de-sac outside his gate. This contrast with the previous scene is important. He must be seen to belong to two worlds; but they are now inexorably linked by the memory of the curse to which he has just been subjected. His opening words—'Quel vecchio maledivami'—are an exact repetition of those eight Cs on which the trombones started the opera. They will never leave his head for long. Then a muted 'cello and bass play a mournful tune above pizzicato strings, a tune full of patterned rises and falls such as portray emotion over and over again in this work. Above it the buffoon and the assassin conduct their duologue *con mistero*, the orchestra being cautioned to play *ppp. estremamente piano*. Whence did Verdi conjure up this atmospheric *tour de force*? Nothing like it can be found in his previous operas. Possibly its seeds are in the meeting of Ernani and De Silva before the tomb of Charlemagne—another Hugo borrowing. Perhaps it is quite new. So much in *Rigoletto* is quite new. One notes the contrast between the would-be-talkative Sparafucile and the tongue-tied buffoon, who can only contribute single words or short interruptions to the dialogue, and who, when Sparafucile expansively repeats his memorable name for future reference, can only reply 'Va, va, va, va.' Evil repels evil. The Burgundian cut-throat, who has not shed his original nationality on being transferred from Paris to Mantua, departs into the ill-lit shadows as Alberich fades from Hagen's vision, leaving Rigoletto alone with plenty to think about.

At once he changes. He is voluble now, and rhetorical. He senses common ground with the assassin but he has his wit for rapier. The strings which delineated his swaggering posture in front of Monterone now play a more disjointed and uncertain variation—a subtle deviant—and again he recalls the curse. Then he is off, crying out his detestation of mankind. The strings interpolate yet a new comment as he works himself up. He is a hunchback. He is a fool. He has to laugh and may not, as other men, indulge in tears. The curve of his phrasing

Adagio

Il re—tag—gio d'o-gni uom m'è tol—to . . . il pian———to!

should be noted, for in the last act, about to commit his victim to the river, he sings a similar one, but in triumph instead of despair. Mock-triumph, it turns out. Verdi's musical repetition may have been sub-conscious but it is dramatically telling.

Over plucked strings he muses about his fortunate and gifted lord and master, who can so carelessly demand to be amused. Oh dannazione!' he cries, as the violins rush up and start a *tremolando* above which he declaims his hatred of the courtiers. Three chords *tutta forza* seem to work up his defiance, but suddenly a solo flute *dolce* drops liquid semitones of pathos and he takes up the theme as though he is starting an aria. But it is no aria. Once again there is a restless change of mood. He remembers old Monterone's curse. Pulling himself together, he shakes it off with his usual declamatory curve. On his final note strings and wind rip out a gay tune, and he enters his shadowy courtyard. The spell is broken. Piave and Verdi may have improved on Hugo at this juncture; for Triboulet, having rid himself of Saltabadil (or *L'Homme* as the text darkly calls him), goes through the door into his courtyard and there speaks his long soliloquy. Rigoletto, however, remains in the street when Sparafucile has departed; sings 'Pari siamo' outside his gate; then slips into his little private world to be greeted by Gilda and the C Major *allegro vivo* which momentarily dispels his dark mood. It is a transition at once neater and more profound than in the play.

The tripping music is certainly refreshing, but the vivacity is all on Gilda's side, for it is not very long before her father is voicing his suspicions and generally behaving with mistrust. To her curiosity about their family background he is curt and uninformative, and the jolly music gives way at once to rapid chords. But when she mentions her mother he melts into his first real tune in the opera—'Deh non parlare al misero', with a disarming modulation. Verdi is back to his consummate craft of pouring out the right melody to embody the singer's emotion. The anguish and inner tenderness of this hard-boiled creature, expressed in such a manner, seduce us into realms of pity. Gilda joins him *con agitazione*, and another Verdian father-daughter duet is under way. From *Nabucco* to *Aida* they unfold; a juxtaposed relationship much favoured by the composer. But here is no mutual understanding. All is restless, frenetic. The father is on edge; the daughter importunate. She ingenuous; he suspicious. As in the preceding monologue, themes break off, moods change, a climax is reached with crashing chords (*Ernani*-type), and then Rigoletto begins 'Ah! veglia o donna', his second tune and still in character with his penchant for sentimental self-worry. Even this duet is interrupted by his sudden suspicion that someone is lurking in the street. He actually breaks off in the middle of a word, and the orchestra rushes along as the Duke sneaks into the courtyard. Rigoletto, not observing him, resumes and completes the grand tune—with some nervous embroidery by Gilda—with the full orchestra rounding it off as Rigoletto departs. This structural weakness is taken over from Hugo. We are left to wonder why the hunchback, after so carefully letting himself into his courtyard, should be obliged to go out again so soon, without even entering his house. If he had pressing business elsewhere, why come home at all? Of course he has to be out of the way when Gilda's (or Blanche's) girlish dreams come true with a declaration of love, just as he has to be back again for the dramatic finale devised by Hugo. But we cannot help feeling that Triboulet's necessary absence is not well accounted for. True, he does remark that it is time for him to go back to his degrading duty. But this cannot be true, for we all know (if *he* does not) that his royal master is not just now in the Louvre, and all the remaining courtiers (as we shall soon see for ourselves) are having time off. Piave's Rigoletto makes no sort of excuse. He just sings 'Addio' and departs.

Gilda is now alone with Giovanna—alone save for the lurking Duke, who has so far contributed but two bare interpolations—'Rigoletto!' and 'Sua figlia!'; whereas Hugo's King Francis indulged in much by-play over the bribery of Dame Berarde. His comment on discovering that the girl is the jester's daughter—'l'histoire est impayable!' gives an insolent bravado to his escapade. But Verdi's skill does not flag in Rigoletto's absence. First, in Gilda's simple phrases we sense her cocooned loneliness, immured in this cul-de-sac with the bustling city beyond. Her simple musings are interrupted by the Duke—right in the middle of a word (as in Hugo)—and the measured woodwind notes are replaced by a palpitating violin figure which races along as it unnerves Gilda, until the Duke embarks on his cantabile 'È il sol dell'anima'. This is right in character; hypocritical, stylized, artificial. It is akin to 'La donna è mobile' but without the exuberance. It is a calculated ploy to which the simple Gilda naturally responds, though she so lacks personality that her contribution adds nothing individual. Indeed right through the pendent *vivacissimo* she merely repeats his phrases. In both her duets the men take precedence, for she lacks the maturity and confidence to hold her own.

But after the Duke's departure she really captures our interest. It is her moment for 'Caro nome'. Familiarity has taken this aria out of its context. Yet how deft and true a delineation of her character it is! With a disarming descent of the E major scale over a basic accompaniment it exactly paints her fragility, her cloistered prudery, her tentative yearning. In this instance Piave should not be forgotten. He wrote this stanza as a professional librettist, knowing that here was the moment for an aria, but not knowing just what Verdi would provide. Hugo's

Blanche speaks two lines and that is all. Piave's Gilda has these two lines as recitative. The aria follows, a fortunate interpolation if ever there was one. Gaucher Mahiet, the crafty King has called himself. 'Gaucher Mahiet . . .', she repeats dreamily. In Mantua this becomes Gualtier Maldè. At least the King had the wit to give a false name that meant 'left-handed'. As for the Duke's alias—Verdi had old friends called Demaldé, including Margherita Barezzi's mother.[11] One of them may have been carelessly or even deliberately enshrined in operatic literature. To confuse the issue Edouard Duprez' French version prefers Carlo Baldi, while one English translation of Hugo's play quite inexplicably plumps for Godfrey Melune! But whatever the variation, they all lead to *caro nome*. . . .

The flute's trills and the solo violin's figure (which will recur at a later dramatic moment in Gilda's story), the divided violins muted and *pppp*—all these breathe maidenly delicacy; and there is no cabaletta. In its place is a piece of unashamed 'theatre', for as Gilda goes indoors and her voice *si perde poco a poco*, the courtiers gather outside for their planned abduction of the buffoon's supposed mistress. In hushed wonder at her beauty they whisper their admiration, in-filling beneath her receding operatic trill. The music, simple though it may be, induces an emotion wholly missing from the corresponding moment in Hugo's play. Anyone who has heard this aria only in recitals or on single gramophone records, be they by Melba, Tetrazzini, Hempel, Boronat, Sembrich, Kurz, Galli-Curci, Barrientos or dal Monte, can have little conception of its sheer captivating effect in its true, uncut stage setting even when sung by a provincial soprano whose name will never go *alle stelle*. It is one of the best examples of Verdi conjuring a masterpiece out of the most basic material.

We must follow indulgently the proceedings with which the act ends. The courtiers prepare to carry out their kidnapping 'rag'. Rigoletto returns home and in spite of being outside his own house is not only persuaded they are there to abduct the Contessa Ceprano but in addition can be blindfolded without even discovering that the darkness is not just that of a murky night, and can hold a ladder while the courtiers scale his own wall and make away with his daughter. We never found out exactly why he left home so suddenly in the first place. Hugo discloses his own doubt by giving Triboulet the curious line

Je reviens . . . a quoi bon? Ah! je ne sais pourquoi!

Rigoletto reduces this to 'Riedo! . . . perchè?' He is not the only one in doubt over this point. But here he is, and almost at once brooding anew over the curse, and then he bumps into the courtiers. The strings give a jaunty foundation to the ensuing dialogue as they lie to the buffoon about their intentions and craftily co-opt his help. Then the bassoons add a dark and sinister aspect and the 'cellos close the scene with a nagging urgency. All this stage business, though invented by Hugo, fairly taxes credulity. No Shakespearean fool could have been so easily gulled. The King of France's jester may sting others with his wit, but has little left for his own defence when cornered. All through the play at crucial moments he is slow in the uptake. He *must* be, or he would have found a worthier niche in society. But Verdi takes it seriously enough, and tackles it with his usual confidence.

The courtiers embark on their *sottovoce* chorus 'Zitti, zitti moviamo a vendetta', a Donizetti-like movement very much Made in Italy. It is a perfectly good operatic device, and one should not begrudge it to the members of the chorus, who in this work do not exactly receive their expected quota. For they are not only confined to males, but in the middle of the second act they leave the stage for good. But *Rigoletto* approaches so close to the standards of music drama that one cannot exclude a passing regret that one has to listen with a stiff upper lip to 'Zitti, zitti', and not only to listen, but to watch the chorus bumbling aimlessly about in the dark and the buffoon, who does not take part in the singing, standing there even more bewildered than they.

But when the chorus is over, the action and the music are well on the move. We may think, when the courtiers have grabbed Gilda, that their cry 'Vittoria!' has strayed from *La Battaglia di Legnano*, but Hugo's *gentilhommes* at this point exclaim 'Victoire!'—so Piave is in the clear. Rigoletto, left alone, the dirty work accomplished, finds at last that he is blindfolded. He tears off the mask and scarf, rushes into his house and drags out the faithless Giovanna. Meanwhile the strings, so loyal to the buffoon in his moments of triumph or terror, reiterate a motif *crescendo* through nineteen bars to end on a full chord, and he lets out a final cry in remembrance of the fatal curse. His life crashes and tumbles, but in the music there is no shred of pathos or pity. This emotion is carefully and tellingly reserved up Verdi's sleeve.

The second act, which is Hugo's third, opens on a conventional note, the Duke lamenting the disappearance of Gilda; for apparently he has returned to Rigoletto's house later, only to find it empty. He does not know, of course, that his courtiers have stolen her for him. This is not in the play, and replaces a more faithful transcript which was banned by the Venetian authorities on moral grounds. In the play Blanche evades the King's advances and takes refuge in a room, only to be followed by her seducer brandishing the key, for it is his bedroom. This seemed, understandably, a crude impropriety. So Verdi had to be content with an aria of reflection the music of which betrays a sort of weary exercise. The opening is marked *agitato* and the Duke enters *agitatissimo*, but we are not in the least emotionally caught up. His repeated cry 'Ella mi fu rapita' does not move us, nor even amuse us. His pseudo-sentimental *cantabile* is shallow, and his aria 'Parmi veder le lagrime' is colourless. Verdi, who could so well paint his tenor as a gay devil, was out of sympathy with his tantrums.

The courtiers arrive with their news that they have secured the buffoon's mistress. They embark on yet another operatic chorus. This is perhaps a lapse from taste, particularly when the tune is reinforced by trumpets in unison, as though these miserable toadies were Verdian soldiers. But one phrase is noticeable, for it will be echoed pathetically by Rigoletto when he appears. Before this moment, however, we have to sit through the Duke's cabaletta, if it can so be called, in which he expresses a lively anticipation of pleasures to come. This is usually omitted in obedience to some tradition or other. If it is not musically valuable it does add one more objectionable facet to the Duke's emotional range and one more example of the insensibility of the courtiers; and since Verdi took pains to include it, there seems no justification at all for a cut.

When the Duke goes *frettoloso* in pursuit of Gilda's virginity, Rigoletto wanders in. That he has been hanging around we can surmise from the violins, which echo a phrase from the courtiers' chorus ('restò scornato ad imprecar, restò scornato ad imprecar'). But now, instead of sounding complacently triumphant, it exudes sheer pathos. Rigoletto takes it up, la-ra-ing with a show of indifference. Here again are the drooping sobs we have already met in the Prelude and in 'Pari siamo'. As in Hugo the courtiers mock him. Ceprano takes special delight in accosting him. Rigoletto echoes his sarcasm by repeating his exact notes, a trick to be remembered nearly forty years later by Iago. It is eloquent of his lack of real wit that the buffoon should rely on cheap repartee. He has already used this negative device on Monterone. It is sour and ineffective and the courtiers laugh outright. This passage, with the broken and suspicious jester at bay amid the mocking courtiers, is a classic example of dramatic opera at its most memorable and moving. If we dislike Rigoletto in the first scene, and are indifferent to him in the second, we must feel for him now. Verdi, without an aria, has seen to that.

A page comes to look for the Duke, with a sudden burst of buoyant music that may remind us of Falstaff's 'Ehi, paggio!' though Oscar is nearer in time. Rigoletto is on his guard; the courtiers are confused; the truth tumbles out. All this is elaborately worked in by Hugo, but Piave preserves the essentials and provides Verdi with the opportunity for a great dramatic solo outburst. Hugo gave his Triboulet full rein at this point. He addresses each courtier in turn, but meeting only with cold silence lashes at them with:

> Vos mères aux laquais se sont prostituées!
> Vous êtes tous bâtards!

As he had just named several illustrious French families this line produced a fine uproar at the play's one and only performance. Piave is more careful!

Verdi's great monologue opens with yet another passage for strings—nervously tense this time. Over them Rigoletto works himself up until with the full orchestra in support he hurls himself at the door beyond which his daughter is being raped. When he fails the strings take over again, descending as his spirit breaks. He turns to Marullo, just as Triboulet finally (and to no avail) appealed to Clément Marot—'mon bon Marot . . .'. The cor anglais joins in here, adding pathos to his plea as he sings a simple melody in the calm after the emotional storm. The cor anglais is an instance of Verdi's care, for this instrument has little else to do in the course of the opera and for that reason sounds all the more compelling. Rigoletto ends his solo with the melodic simplicity later to be given to the distraught Aida, pleading with her tribal gods. Marullo is indifferent. The courtiers are silent. The baffled loneliness of the buffoon is underlined by a 'cello's tortuous accompaniment, and suddenly the full orchestra blazes up as Gilda emerges. Hugo here is more explicit than Piave. His Blanche is *éperdue, égarée, en désordre*. A dramatic reading of the play would give the athletic King Francis about fifteen minutes over-all for what the French call his *gymnastique*. Verdi, bound by his metronome settings, gives the Duke of Mantua approximately eight minutes with Gilda. One can have some innocent fun with a gramophone and a stopwatch; for instance, Bergonzi is twenty-five seconds quicker with Scotto than Cioni with Sutherland. Berger yields to Roswaenge forty-five seconds sooner than she does to Peerce. *L'auditeur s'amuse.**

What we are really doing, of course, is timing the conductor's individual reading of Rigoletto's *Scena ed Aria*. No one in the theatre can be thinking of the goings-on in the next room while listening to the baritone on-stage and watching how subtly and skilfully he faces up to his tormentors. But while he sings and moves us to pity, the orchestra is playing the double role of accompanying him and at the same time commenting on his daughter's experience beyond the locked door. Put Rigoletto out of your mind and just concentrate on the orchestra and you will hear the rape of Gilda. It starts at the *allegro vivo*, when he cries 'La giovin che stanotte al mio tetto rapiste.' At that moment the Duke has moved on from 'chatting up' to physical seduction. With the *andante mosso agitato* (Rigoletto's 'Cortigiani, vil razza dannata') the point of no return is past and it is a matter of seconds to the climax (the six bars from 26 in the score). Then the *meno mosso* is the aftermath. In the post-Havelock Ellis age this sort of thing has been done in the opera house with far more advanced and realistic orchestral technique. Instances that spring to mind are in *Rosenkavalier* and *Arabella*, *Lady Macbeth of Mtsensk*, *The Rape of Lucretia* and *Troilus and Cressida*. Verdi, forbidden by censorship even to allude to the shocking fact that the Duke had a key with which he could lock himself and Gilda in, used the orchestra to tell us far more than theatrical convention would allow. He employed the simplest means, veiling his commentary under the guise of an accompaniment; and no doubt the majority of listeners never give it a thought, so that when Gilda emerges dishevelled, they suddenly realize what has been going on—though Verdi has been telling them all the time.

Triboulet in the play, his ravaged daughter beside him, assumes a spurious grandeur as he faces up to the courtiers and orders them to leave him, adding a warning that the King too had better keep out of his way. The courtiers are superciliously amused, but obey him; though he has a little trouble in getting his message across to De Cossé (the one who has most enjoyed his discomfiture). In the opera this moment is finely managed. Rigoletto, reiterating the C on which he broods over the curse, now twists it into a defiant command stretched over nine bars and ending with a distinct echo of Monterone. He mocked the Count once,

* These calculations are as inexact as they are ungallant.

but now he is smarting under the same outrage. The Duke has raped both their daughters. Rigoletto does not at the moment see that this is the working-out of the curse. He is suffering as Monterone did, and he ironically rants like him. The courtiers (without Ceprano holding back, unless the producer likes to have him imitate De Cossé) sing a quatrain *ppp* and retire in mock obedience. This tiny chorus is a somewhat refined version of the crude music of the murderers in *I Lombardi*. The courtiers are, indeed, murderers of a sort.

It is in very different circumstances from before that father and daughter now face each other. Previously the father hectored and bullied. Now the very thing he has most feared has happened, and he is deflated. The pathetic oboe sets the atmosphere. Gilda sings her near-aria 'Tutte le feste al tempio', telling how she first met her seducer in church. One recalls Théophile Gautier's Madelaine de Maupin—'We, as usual with girls of our age, talked of love, suitors, marriage, and of the handsome men we had seen at Mass.' Gilda works herself up as she pours out her confession. Rigoletto, his faithful strings throbbing in support, gives his consolation, blaming himself on yet another repeated C before expanding into a fine tune, upon which follows the sad duet 'Piangi, fanciulla' with its characteristic semitone wailing. This phrase, given to the violins,

is typical of the opera. But it is a pathetic extension of a phrase for solo violin that punctuated the opening bars of 'Caro nome'. At the nadir of Gilda's fortunes we get this tiny reminder of her lost romantic zenith.

The ensuing duet is among the gems of baritone-soprano music. Rigoletto once more has a tune marvellously in character, a tune unheroic, self-pitying, but undeniably moving. It bears a curious affinity with 'Ah veglia, o donna', which anxiously expressed a warning. But now 'Piangi fanciulla' expresses his broken acceptance that the warning was unheeded. Verdi has this way of indefinably relating tunes without actual repetition. At its close, in dramatic contrast, Monterone is brought across the stage on his way to prison. This comes straight from Hugo, who introduces Saint-Vallier to effect a stinging curtain. Saint-Vallier halts before the private door of the King's apartment and comments bitterly that his curse has quite failed. He ends with the line,

Je n'espère plus rien. Ce roi prospérera.

Triboulet caps it,

Comte! vous vous trompez.—Quelqu'un vous vengera!

Whereupon Saint-Vallier is dragged off to the Bastille without another word, leaving the smouldering buffoon to plan his revenge. But the curtain falls at once. It is only in the opera that we hear him revelling in the prospect of vengeance. Rigoletto has Triboulet's final line (and sings it as usual mostly on his favourite C); but he then at once plunges into the quick movement of the duet, 'Si, vendetta, tremenda vendetta', with Gilda pleading in an extension of Blanche's

O Dieu! n'écoutez pas, car je l'aime toujours!

This makes a sound dramatic finish to the scene. Rigoletto rails at the Duke's portrait, before which Monterone had paused on his way to prison. Hugo does not introduce the portrait. Triboulet and Saint-Vallier face the bedroom door beyond which the King has bedded both their daughters. Yet one wishes that Rigoletto could stand menacingly beneath that Louvre portrait by Titian—the one specified as a model by Hugo—with its profile the absolute embodiment of lecherous preoccupation!

As for Verdi's duet, many commentators have placed it on a lower musical plane than what has gone before. Certainly it sounds like a conscious harking-back to Bellini's 'Suona la tromba', particularly when the brass takes a hand. But it brings down the curtain on an exciting note, fairly belting out the overtones of Hugo's Triboulet—

Quelqu'un vous vengera!

Act III opens in quiet, stark contrast, with eight bars given to a solemn theme on the strings, followed by a barren, virtually unaccompanied dialogue between Rigoletto and Gilda. We see the dingy, dilapidated outskirts of Mantua on the bank of the river Mincio. In reality the

Mincio is the Seine, and this is the sinister Place de la Grève, the very spot where Saint-Vallier mounted the scaffold and placed his head on the block, only to be reprieved by King Francis in exchange for his daughter Diane's honour, and sentenced instead to *une prison perpetuelle*. Near at hand is the palace of la Tournelle where the Royal Family lived when in Paris, and where the stench of the adjacent open sewer was so offensive that Francis rebuilt the old Louvre into a new and more salubrious abode. Such is the real setting for the hovel of Saltabadil and his sister Maguelonne.

Verdi has not gone out of his way to provide any sort of link. We are left to conclude that this is the start of Rigoletto's revenge plot. Hugo takes rather more care, and reveals that a month has elapsed since the previous act, during which time the jester's daughter would appear to have overcome her scruples and taken naturally to the King's bed, Triboulet smouldering the while and casting his net carefully for the ultimate catch. But even Hugo does not tell us exactly how the King was tempted to visit this ramshackle and unsavoury *auberge*. We can assume, however, that just as the courtiers brought Blanche to François, so now he has steered François to Maguelonne. It is one of the aspects of the 'Fool's Revenge'. But we miss Triboulet's sneer when François appears in the tavern, that a divinely anointed King can so demean himself as to seek wine and women in such low surroundings. We too easily forget, in the opera, that the man who *s'amuse* is *le Roi*.

While we are still collecting our wits and sizing up the situation the orchestra suddenly pumps out the tune of 'La donna è mobile', stopping abruptly a bar short of completion to let the Duke start *con brio*. This historic ditty can compete for 'top tune' in any musical company. It simply flares up out of nowhere and burns out with its own incandescence. It is indeed historic, for its words were engraved by François himself on a window-pane at his other new palace of Chambord, inspired, some say, by his witty and literary sister Marguerite. Hugo borrowed them, Piave translated them, Verdi clothed them in a tune that has bounced around the world in endless orbit.

The tune owes some of its effectiveness to the explosive contrast with the music that precedes it. Practically every phrase sung by Gilda and Rigoletto in their colloquy, and the few remarks of the Duke and Sparafucile, have a downward droop, descending so monotonously as to presage disaster. Into this atmosphere bursts 'La donna è mobile' as though a champagne cork has been suddenly released. It is an outstanding example of musical ingenuity. First and foremost it is a tune, and a tune that uninhibitedly depicts the Duke's sexual recklessness. It emerges from his throat as though he has sung it all his life. If François scratched the words on a Chambord window, no doubt he had a ready tune for them. But it is an earthy song for an earthy situation. It was not sung in front of the courtiers at the Louvre or the Mantua palace. There he was his own arbiter of elegance, and gave them 'Questa o quella', rhythmic, mercurial, gallant. Now, in the *auberge* by the river, with peasant Maddalena as his clandestine date, our Gualtier Maldè sheds his refinement. Rigoletto knows the song well, we can be sure. 'Osserva dunque,' he tells Gilda. 'Per poco attendi.'

One must admire 'La donna è mobile' for this reason—it is a tune set inside a musical score and complying with the necessity of transcending its setting. In the spoken play a sudden song must have some effect. But in an opera which is already wholly vocal, how much more striking must this ditty be! Verdi has achieved it, and within a tuneful score the Duke's song sticks out a mile. It is the right tune in the right place; and how cunningly Verdi has given it an orchestral postlude, diminishing from full orchestra gradually down to oboe and clarinet and then bassoon. In this *diminuendo—ppp—più piano* there is a curious sense of foreboding, as though the clockwork of a sprightly musical-box is running down, while Sparafucile moves about in sinister preoccupation with his loaded hospitality.

Hard on this comes the Quartet, that illustrious, timeless masterpiece that made Hugo envious. It is triggered off by the entry of Maddalena, who takes the Duke's fancy at once. Readers of the late Frank Walker's mammoth excavation into Verdi's private life will have discovered that he knew a Maddalena.[12] She was Barezzi's maid, and later caused a scandal by marrying him after the death of his wife, her mistress. Though this was later than *Rigoletto*, we may if we like imagine that Maddalena was already eye-catching at least to Barezzi. His first wife had been a Demaldé, and now in the operatic Maddalena we may have found a second borrowing from the family album. The Duke loses no time in addressing her in affectionate terms. His easy-going melodic line is all-of-a-piece with his character. But under his opening words 'Un di, se ben rammentomi' we hear once more that violin figure of dotted semi-quavers that accompanied the start of 'Caro nome' (and see page 211), which must surely be linked with the watching Gilda, who now sees her seducer in action and cannot but recall her first heart-throbs in her

father's courtyard. But the Duke goes gaily on, the orchestra blithely
borrowing the trills of his Court Band. 'Iniquo traditor!' cries Gilda
jealously. 'E non ti basta ancor?' comments her father, viciously relishing
the situation he has contrived for her enlightenment.

With the *andante* section the Duke begins his love-song to Maddalena.
Like his previous 'È il sol dell 'anima' and his brief exchange with the
Contessa di Ceprano it is stylized and gracefully artificial—the
calculated phrasing of an experienced lady-killer. The orchestra
accompanies and punctuates, but no instrument carries his tune. But
when Maddalena replies she has flute and clarinet in unison; and Gilda's
comments have oboe and violin. Rigoletto is unaccompanied. So the
Quartet develops, carefully planned. Gilda soars in broken anguish; the
Duke is debonair and lyrical; Maddalena coquettishly plays hard-to-get;
Rigoletto remains sober and sombre, impassive as one who has survived
the onslaught of emotions. It is a perfect example of what genius can do
with a dramatic situation which is itself first-class. Verdi cannot be
accused of skilled note-spinning. Each of the four pursues an individual
rôle. They blend and are contrasted, and the result is one of the best
known passages in all opera. A contributor to the *Record Collector*[13] once
listed all the recordings of the Quartet known to him. There were
ninety-three! Later correspondents added eleven more, so it has
comfortably achieved its century without taking into account Liszt's
Paraphrase.

The Quartet works itself out *ppp* and Rigoletto quietly tells Gilda to
go home, dress as a man, take a horse, and ride to Verona. A pretty tall
order for so sheltered a young miss; but she goes obediently. So the
lyrical bonanza is over, and we are for the dark.

The music takes a new turn at once, new not only within this opera,
but to Italian Opera in general. There has been nothing quite like this
before. Verdi has suddenly eschewed the rippling tune and rum-ti-tum
accompaniment. Instead, as though himself overawed by the tense
situation, he has resorted to the starkest methods, taking the old *recitativo
secco* and re-framing it so that, whereas it used to fill in, it now carries the
drama and achieves equal importance with the set-piece. We are
suddenly very close to a more sophisticated operatic era; but the basic
simplicity of the scoring has an effect more telling than the sumptuous
symphonics of later days. The immediate atmosphere is created by deep
semibreve chords on the lower strings, punctuated by a solo oboe
repeating a single note two octaves higher, with an eerie, almost

electronic effect. Rigoletto confers with Sparafucile and makes his down payment, fifty per cent in advance. So careful is Verdi to insist on the accuracy of his tone-picture that he annotates the score with a demand that 'this recitative must be performed without the accustomed *appoggiature*'. He means that the singers must be right inside their parts and not thinking how they may impress the audience. For twelve bars the oboe and 'cellos hold a chord while buffoon and cut-throat do their sinister business. When Sparafucile asks the identity of his victim, Rigoletto follows Triboulet with fine theatrical effect:

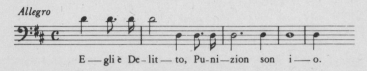

E —gli è De–lit— to, Pu-ni—zion son i—o.

If this is compared with that moment in 'Pari siamo' when he deplored his miserable rôle of the Duke's entertainer,

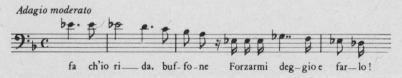

fa ch'io ri—da, buf-fo-ne   Forzarmi deg–gio e   far—lo!

we will see with what subtlety his present mood of vengeance derives from his former bitterness. As he departs, the violins tremble, followed by a flute will-o'-the-wisping downwards and a piccolo ribboning up. It is the first indication of a storm, as Sparafucile grimly observes to himself. Immediately a clarinet repeats the theme of 'Bella figlia dell'amore' to draw our attention to the interior of the building and the Duke's gambit to break Maddalena's resistance. Again we hear the orchestral pointers to the coming storm, and this time the bass drum behind the scene indicates the first thunder, and the tenors and basses of the chorus *vocalizando a bocca chiusa* follow the drum with a very fair representation of wind moaning before reaching gale force. Such eerie soughing Verdi must often have heard in the trees of Sant'Agata. Busseto and Mantua lie in the same great plain. The voices of the chorus humming off-stage to imitate the wind was very *avant-garde* indeed. One wonders if the gentlemen of the chorus thought as Banquo did about appearing as his own ghost. For but for this they could have gone home in the middle of Act II. Yet here they are, retained to make a dozen wordless entries without being seen.

So Verdi parades and repeats his devices while the clipped dialogue goes on between the Duke, Maddalena and Sparafucile. First the deep strings return, a fourth higher with flute instead of oboe impingeing high above; then the tremolo, the wind and the lightning. 'Povero giovin! grazioso tanto!' sighs Maddalena, softening after another clarinet wisp of the Duke's 'Bella figlia'. Then he goes upstairs and sings 'La donna è mobile', but drowses away into sleep, the clarinet carrying on where his voice fails, until right in the middle of a word he is gone. (It was in the middle of a word that he first appeared to Gilda.)

The manifestations of the growing storm continue. Gilda returns breeched, booted and spurred as ordered by her father; but she has abandoned her horse and the road to Verona. The trio which is to culminate in her murder begins to work up in intensity, like the storm. Sparafucile gets his only tune, a short but resolute one. Maddalena pleads eloquently. Gilda, still outside, seems to be singing a piece of *Aida*. Verdi has contrived it all to be tremendously exciting and theatrical, as the trio pauses for a clock to strike the half-hour before midnight (when Rigoletto is due to arrive for his prize), for Gilda to knock and knock again between peals of thunder, for the humming chorus to add an extended curve of moaning backed by bassoons, and the trio to start up again. At its second climax Gilda, knowing now she is at the point of death and about to save her faithless but magnetic lover, knocks for the last time and is admitted.

At this point Hugo has a quick curtain, with an interval which enables him to preserve the unity of time; for when his last act begins, the scene is exactly the same and Triboulet has come for the King's corpse. Piave and Verdi keep the entire action in one uninterrupted act, which is very much more satisfactory. It is true that there is now a great deal less than half an hour between the clock striking 11.30 and midnight; but in between, the storm bursts overhead with such violence that time is quite secondary. Verdi lets all hell loose for sixty-three bars with the whole orchestra pouring down torrents together with drummage and cymbalclature and a thunder machine. Woodwind depicts the pattering rain, 'cellos and basses rumble, violins race, the chorus adds its weirdly gothic moaning. Then oboes, flutes and violins flicker fitfully as the storm abates its fury; and Rigoletto appears.

In the annals of opera this storm hardly receives its due, partly because, being such an integral element of the drama, it cannot be detached for separate performance. The old-time 'orchestral selections' would not include it; nor was it ever recorded for the gramophone as a separate item. One had to go to the theatre to hear it, or buy a complete recording. Between its first mutterings and its last lightning flash lie nearly sixty pages of the full score. Unlike many musical storms, it is meteorologically feasible. Unlike many operatic storms, its fury is not aided by a cowering chorus on stage. Each flash, each rumble, is bound into the stage directions, into the music, into the dialogue. Rossini loved storms. He introduced them into *Guillaume Tell* (exciting), *Le Comte Ory* (amusing), *Otello* (superfluous). Verdi followed him and had storms of a sort in several of his operas, but they are of short duration and not in themselves memorable. Yet here in *Rigoletto* he conjures up a tempest with such restraint, such control, such balance, that it must be acknowledged as a true work of art. Norman Del Mar has named as 'the great storms of music' the Pastoral Symphony, *Die Walküre, Otello*, and *Peter Grimes*. Three of these are operatic and certainly make more noise than the one in *Rigoletto*. But none is so uncannily true to nature, so meticulously worked through. Two are sea hurricanes and one a forest gale. For all their power and intensity none has the pitiless nagging of the *Rigoletto tempesta* as it passes overhead from one horizon to another, relentlessly scheduled like a bombing raid, and as accurately timed.

So Rigoletto comes on for the last time. In steady, measured recitative he anticipates his triumph, so firm of purpose after the wild storm, whose dying cadences still flicker fitfully. No instrument supports his vocal line. His opening phrase, so self-satisfied,

Del—la ven–det–ta al—fin giun–ge l'i— stan— te!

is a sardonic reflection of Maddalena's softening attitude towards the Duke,

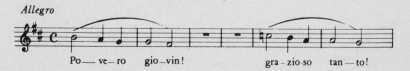

Po— ve—ro gio–vin! gra - zio-so tan—to!

upon which was based her successful plea that he should be spared. Now
Rigoletto comes to claim the victim, and the phrase of his triumph is
derived from the one which led to the change of victims. Long-held
string chords give a taut effect made more ominous as they stop for the
clock to strike midnight followed by his knocking on the door, and
resume as Sparafucile comes out with the fatal sack. Before the clock
strikes Rigoletto repeats his opening phrase in anticipation. There is
another grim twist in the cut-throat's pointing to the deepest part of the
river, for he sings a drawn-out imitation of Rigoletto's own mockery of
Ceprano in the first scene of the opera; as though the heartless cruelty of
the jester in prosperity is now being bent against him in defeat. There is
lightning and a receding peal of thunder as Sparafucile goes back indoors,
leaving Rigoletto alone with the sack. This in Hugo's play is the supreme
moment of dramatic suspense. Triboulet gloats over the corpse of the
hated King. Only the audience knows the truth, while Triboulet's
vindictive triumph waxes unbearable. Sixty-six lines he declaims over
what he supposes to be the body of

> François de Valois, ce prince au coeur de feu,
> Rival de Charles-Quint, un roi de France, un dieu,
> —A l'éternité près,—un gagneur de batailles
> Dont le pas ébranlait les bases des murailles,
> L'homme de Marignan. . . .

We feel as we listen that the wretched, ill-used hunchback well deserves
his bloodthirsty triumph, while all along we know that he is in for a
shattering revelation.

In the place of Triboulet's long speech Rigoletto has twenty-eight
bars, but absolutely in character. Instinctively they are moulded like the
soliloquy 'Pari siamo', but freed from the sense of introspection and
anguish. This is the point where an operatic cabaletta would be
permissible, but Verdi was not cabaletta-minded when he worked out
the destinies of these people. How right he was, with the famous *coup de
théâtre* looming, to precede the break-in of the Duke's ditty by recitative,
so that the contrasting song will make extra impact. We are denied the
immense, pregnant exultation of Triboulet:

> A l'eau François premier!

But the sudden impingement of 'La donna è mobile' on Rigoletto's peroration is guaranteed to catch the emotions of the most experienced operatic audience. Here, in some fifty bars of disarming musical simplicity, is unfolded all the pity and terror of the ancient drama (see opposite).

The throbbing strings that pound out the hunchback's heart-beats; the lightning flash that reveals his daughter's face; the two-octave shudder-down of the violins that rends his credulity; the next flash of lightning that mocks his words 'fu vision!'; the *tutti* reinforcement of his desperate bangs on Sparafucile's bolted door—all these are searing cracks of the tragic whip. And it is all so simple that, if there is nothing that a music scholar may admire, it may well incite the envy of a composer. His fruitless battering on the door recalls his frantic and equally futile attempts to break into the Duke's bedroom during Gilda's rape. The poor, deluded creature is never more helpless than when he springs into action. Eight blows he delivers, each backed by a full orchestral crash. But there is no answer. Sparafucile and Maddalena have slunk out of the story. The music works up to Rigoletto's cry of realization:

which once again, seems to carry an echo of the past—this time the 'culto, famiglia, la patria, il mio universo' of his first duet with Gilda in his own courtyard (and each is backed by the bassoons).

So we reach the final duet. Verdi once (acknowledging that this opera has no conventional ensemble-finales and hardly any arias) claimed it to consist of a succession of duets.[14] If not literally accurate, it is a pointer; for all along the drama is concerned with pairs of people: the Duke and Contessa Ceprano; Rigoletto and Monterone; Rigoletto and Sparafucile; Rigoletto and Gilda; the Duke and Gilda; the Duke and Maddalena. This last, quite short, duet is a worthy successor. Gilda sings brokenly; her dying tune has an appealing lilt beneath its flute arpeggios; Rigoletto's urgent phrases break in characteristically, with the redoubled mental passion of a distorted and helpless body. Gilda dies in the middle of a word (this trick once more). Rigoletto recalls the curse of Monterone. Its evil forces are worked out to the full. In Hugo's play there is a curious end. Triboulet in desperation rings a ferry bell by the Seine. Various people appear, including a surgeon. Triboulet's downfall is thus underlined and emphasized; for he who but recently ruled the roost amid the revels at the Louvre is now abject and quite unrecognized by the passers-by of Paris. He made King Francis laugh, but having lost all, he is a cipher. Verdi's crisp ending is more forthright and catastrophic. 'Ah! la maledizione!' is a strong ending: 'J'ai tué mon enfant!' decidedly less so.

The sack was, of course, one of the items objected to by the authorities; why, it is not clear, except that it was an unheard-of innovation. Verdi pointed out that the end would be absurd without it, and achieved its retention by agreeing, as a *quid pro quo*, to omit the brandishing by the Duke of the bedroom key. But the sack may well have brought its trail of minor troubles to producers. Bernard Shaw records[15] that the Ancona-Melba performance at Covent Garden in 1894 included the final duet. He adds, 'As far as I know, it has never been done on the stage since its excision immediately after the opera was first produced.' To modern audiences this may seem surprising; but Covent Garden must have cut it out again, for Dyneley Hussey tells us that it was re-introduced in 1924 by Maria Ivogun, having been previously omitted—'whether because the *prime donne* thought it beneath their dignity to sing in a sack, or because the Rigolettos found dragging their too, too solid flesh across the stage too much of a strain, one cannot tell.'[16] Delightfully put, and we can take our choice—a bit of both, perhaps. Incidentally Clara Novello revealed that it was many years before she could bring herself to sing Gilda on account of 'the man's attire' and 'exposure of person'. But Gildas have been known to take exception to other matters besides sacks and transvestism. Once Melba was billed to appear at Covent Garden with Scotti, but the latter being indisposed, Ruffo took his place at the dress rehearsal. It was early in his career, and anxious to succeed he sang his part too well. Melba promptly demanded and got his withdrawal, on the grounds that he was too young to play her father. But many years later, when he was internationally famous, Melba felt no antipathy to appearing with him. Ruffo refused. She was too old to play his daughter. (Or so the pleasant story goes!)[17]

To revert to Bernard Shaw and the Melba–Ancona performance at which the final duet was reintroduced; it is well worth while quoting his comment, for it is a rare testimonial to Verdi's ability to surprise us with his less familiar music:[18]

Its orchestration is celestially pretty, so much so, that as I have not a full score within my reach, I will not undertake to swear that it has not been touched up by Mancinelli, or someone with all the latest discoveries at his fingers' ends.

Mancinelli was Covent Garden's leading conductor, and was in charge of the orchestra at the first performances there of *Falstaff* and *Tosca*, besides the débuts of both Melba and Caruso. He also tried his hand at composing operas, one of them to a libretto by Boito. Rather than believe he tried to re-score the final duet of *Rigoletto* I personally take pleasure in visualizing the rapt concentration of Bernard Shaw on hearing for the first time the dramatic contrast between the dying Gilda with her weak, pizzicato pulse and delirious arpeggios, and the distraught buffoon with his heavily-orchestrated outpourings of despair. It is more a duologue than a duet. They are not united by their music, but kept ruthlessly apart. For Verdi saw that they were not to be reconciled. The daughter has disobeyed her father to die for loyalties quite beyond his comprehension. The father is overwhelmed by stark facts quite inexplicable to him. So they go their separate ways: she to her mother in heaven—a mother she does not know; he—whither? Back to the Court to hear 'Questa o quella' and 'La donna è mobile' all over again? To make horn-gestures at fat Ceprano and endure Marullo's epigrams? Or will he change the direction of his *tremenda vendetta* and go in search of Sparafucile?

We began with Hugo's own version of his plot. Let us end with the brilliant commentary of our own Ralph Vaughan Williams. On the occasion of the fiftieth anniversary of Verdi's death, the Editor of *Opera* invited some eminent English composers to contribute their own observations. One might have supposed, superficially, that the nearest Vaughan Williams ever got to Verdi was being his immediate neighbour in alphabetically-compiled reference books. But not at all. At the same age at which Verdi wrote *Falstaff*, this doyen of English symphonists wrote:[19]

Verdi wrote operas. He did not add music to plays full of superficial philosophy or bogus psychology. He carried on his drama by means of lyric song. His orchestra, it is true, has a wonderful sonority, but it is the voice on which he counts to elucidate the situation. He realised that song can carry on a plot in a way which words alone can never do.

A good example of this comes from the last Act of my favourite Verdi opera, *Rigoletto*. In case readers are not familiar with the opera I will briefly rehearse the story of the last Act (from memory, I fear, for I have lost my copy of the score).

A wicked Duke has seduced (or is about to seduce, I forget which) the daughter of his Jester, who planning revenge with several 'R's', persuades his friend, the keeper of a disreputable inn, to invite the Duke to his house, offering as a bait his, the innkeeper's, own daughter, who is quite ready to become seducee No. 2. The Duke is to be murdered and his body in a sack is to be thrown out of the window for the Jester to play with.

On the night appointed the Duke arrives and sits at a table in the inn garden, drinking wine and making love to the innkeeper's daughter, and singing to her the famous *La Donn' é* mobile, an obvious and banal tune, which it is impossible to forget. Having sung his prologue the Duke leads the girl into the house.

At this moment the Jester's daughter, Gilda, arrives and rushes into the inn after them, and it is she who gets murdered and not the Duke. Finally the Jester appears waiting outside the window. The sack is thrown down, but as he is gloating over it the Duke's voice is heard in the distance singing *La Donn' é mobile*. He has escaped! The Jester tears open the sack and finds in it the body of his own daughter!

Here is a situation which with the aid of a striking tune can be made clear in a very short time and with very few words. Without music this would have entailed a lot of boring explanation and perhaps an extra scene. This is real music drama.

Reading this superb acknowledgment of one genius by another, we cannot help feeling that, by having 'lost his copy of the score', Dr Vaughan Williams had the advantage of us all. Who would presume to tidy up his narrative? The immortality of *Rigoletto* is enshrined in his five-word verdict: 'This is real music drama.'

NOTES

1 Hackett, *Francis the First*, p. 118.
2 *Heptameron*, Day the Third, Novel XXV.
3 Lady Jackson, *The Court of France in the Sixteenth Century*, vol. II, ch. 6.
4 Ibid., ch. 4.
5 Ibid. ch. 6.
6 Morley, H. *Clément Marot*, ch. 2.
7 Coignet, C., *Francis the First and his Times* (tr. Twemlow), ch. 10.
8 Brinton, S., *The Gonzaga Lords of Mantua*, chs. 8, 9 and 10, *passim*.
9 Francis Hackett (*Francis the First*, p. 179) tells us that Francis I did in fact once meet Federigo Gonzaga in Milan. Hearing from him that his mother Isabella d'Este had a maid of honour so attractive that she had been locked up for safety in a convent, he sent the Bishop of Nice with a forged papal brief, for the purpose of abducting the girl. But a band of Spaniards fell upon the Bishop and rescued her. A splendid 'operatic' story, and an intriguing link between the real King Francis and the real Duke of Mantua—with a dash of *Trovatore* spice thrown in!
10 Brantôme, *Les Dames Galantes* (*vide* Henderson, *Dianne de Poytiers*, ch. 9, p. 67).
11 Gatti, *Verdi*, vol. I, p. 31. Others were Giuseppe Demaldé, Verdi's first biographer, and Canon Demaldé, the School Inspector at Busseto.
12 Walker, *The Man Verdi*, p. 216.
13 *The Record Collector*, vol. XII, nos. 10 & 11. 'The Rigoletto Quartet on Records' by Carl L. Bruun.
14 *Copialettere*, Appendix CVII, p. 497. Verdi to Borsi.
15 Shaw, *Music in London*, vol. III, p. 244.
16 Hussey, *Verdi*, p. 77.
17 Rosenthal, H. *Two Centuries of Opera at Covent Garden*, p. 299; and *vide The Record Collector*, vol. VI, no. 6, where Aida Favia-Artsay tells the story in greater detail but slightly differently.
18 Shaw, op. cit., p. 244.
19 *Opera*, vol II, no. 3. Ralph Vaughan Williams in *A Verdi Symposium*.

9

AZUCENA

He went off without saying anything to me, without even looking this way. How selfish! And yet he does not know the truth. . . . May he never discover it. . . . If I were to say to him, 'You are not my son. You belong to an illustrious family; you have no ties with me. . . ,' he would turn against me and abandon me to my lonely old age. He came very near to finding out . . . but he must never, never know. What does his existence matter, if he can't go on being my son?

IN THE MIDDLE of the *El Trovador* of Gutiérrez Azucena speaks this touching soliloquy. It is the cruelly insoluble nature of her problem that makes her so pathetic a figure. Verdi found her dilemma dramatically compelling. There were many plots with tenor hero, soprano heroine and baritone villain; but only one had an Azucena. She could bring a new and fascinating dimension to an old tale. Assembling his cast for the Rome première, he was easily able to find singers for Manrico, Leonora and Di Luna; but, as he admitted in a letter to the librettist, 'I still haven't anyone to do Azucena—that Azucena I'm so keen on!'[1] He had previously written to Cammarano expressing his particular interest in her as a character 'with her two overwhelming passions—*filial and maternal love*'.[2] Yet he never conceived the idea of writing for her a special 'grand aria' at the footlights. Her part developed in his mind as an essay in declamatory brooding, a smouldering fire that could spurt and splutter and smoke; but not a conventional heroic role with cavatina and cabaletta and claque.

Many commentators have read into Azucena a moving tribute from the composer to his mother's memory; for she had recently died. Certainly Manrico's 'Riposa o madre' is as beautiful a tribute as any mother could wish from her son; but are we to suppose that Verdi, had he not just been bereaved, would have written something with less feeling? Azucena the desperate gipsy, haunted by her mother's pyre and her own infanticide (her remorse stemming, not from having flung a baby into the flames, but having flung her own baby instead of her enemy's) is surely no model, however devoted, for Luigia Verdi! This

Trovador Azucena is an operatic 'natural', translated from the Spanish Theatre to the Italian Opera House without model, offspring of her own self.

Il Trovatore is traditionally supposed to have a very complicated plot. This is because it is based on events that took place before the curtain rises. (So are *Agamemnon*, *Hamlet*, and *The Importance of Being Earnest*.) But a sort of obscurity does pervade this opera, partly because it seems to be historical yet it is not the history we were taught at school; and partly because in its clash between a just establishment and a selfish rebellion law and order are represented by the baritone villain, while the heroic tenor is on the side of the trouble-makers. So we get a topsy-turvy picture of events; our loyalties are misdirected; our comprehension misled.

We have on the one hand a royal palace full of faithful retainers and ladies-in-waiting, with mention of a queen in residence. But their authority is challenged by an ill-defined force, eager to spring to arms at the bidding of their troubadour hero, yet expressing military and political allegiance to someone named Urgel. Neither the king nor this Urgel comes forward in person. The spotlight is on the romantic wrangle between the king's commander and the rebel's hero; but for all their ranting they seem to be pawns in a bitter civil struggle which must really be far more important than their personal animosity.

It is, in fact, a fairly straightforward situation. The king is Ferdinand I of Aragon. Before being invited to ascend the vacant throne he was a Castilian prince, but his grandfather had been king of Aragon, so he had a good claim. Opposed to him was Jaime, Count of Urgel, whose great-grandfather had been king. So Ferdinand's claim was lineally one stage superior to Urgel's. The dead king, however, had left a grandson, excluded from succession by the pope on account of illegitimacy. We could forget him, except that his title was Count de Luna. Civil war between the supporters of Ferdinand and the followers of Urgel seemed certain. Ferdinand had the backing of the pope. Urgel attracted the Catalans of his own domains, plus the disaffected and the adventurous; and perhaps he would have gained an overwhelming advantage had he not, as a demonstration of defiance towards his rival's pontifical backer, involved himself in the cold-blooded murder of the bishop of Saragossa. At once a prudent and scrupulous commission formed itself for the purpose of electing a new king without bloodshed. The result was a majority vote for Ferdinand. He therefore became king of Aragon, and immediately made friendly overtures to Urgel. The latter, however, did not accept the verdict of the panel, and resorted to arms. He did not manage to raise the support he expected, failed in his attempt to overthrow the regime, and ended up in prison. So Ferdinand the Just became undisputed ruler of Aragon, to be succeeded by his better known son Alfonso the Magnanimous. Of the Urgels no more was heard.[3]

This then is *Il Trovatore*'s background. The Count Di Luna leads the army of Ferdinand the Just. Manrico is a guerrilla commando on the side of Jaime, Count of Urgel. So when his supporters, at the end of Act II, burst into the convent shouting 'Urgel viva!' it may puzzle us, but it need not, for their cause is hopelessly doomed. Unfortunately Ferdinand the Just has placed his affairs in the hands of a very unjust steward. (Or is he all that bad?) He is, of course, nothing to do with the young Count de Luna who might, but for the pope, have put forward a strong claim to the throne. The pope, Benedict XIII, an Avignon pope (one of three popes at that moment) was himself an Aragonese, and what was his real name but Pedro de Luna! Furthermore, the powerful supporter of Urgel who assassinated the bishop of Saragossa was . . . Antonio de Luna. Students of fifteenth-century Aragonese history can emerge somewhat dizzy—which is so frequently claimed for those who get to grips with the plot of *Il Trovatore*.

We are asked to believe in a hero who displays all the qualities of an old Spanish *hidalgo*; chivalry, courtesy, breeding, culture (only the bluest of blood bred troubadours—they were not street-singers); and yet who could rally his armed rabble to charge through the cloisters of a convent shouting 'Urgel viva!' and consort with gipsies to the odd extent of accepting one of them as his mother. Verdi saw at once what a good tenor role was waiting for him here; but all his outpouring of romantic melody does not make Manrico any more credible. We are asked to believe in a queen's lady-in-waiting who, though in love with a tenor serenader, confuses him in the dark with a recitative-declaiming baritone; who, assuming her lover to be dead simply because he has not serenaded her lately although she must know he has other commitments, gives up her secure and privileged appointment in the royal household to blight her romantic youth by taking the veil in a nunnery; who, having been rescued from that fate, arranges for an even more catastrophic one by poisoning herself when she is in fact on the winning side, rather than become the bride of a man who does not appeal to her, and from whom she could surely have escaped by going to see her mistress the queen and putting the facts before her. Really, the behaviour of these two makes the

Count Di Luna rather a sad, maligned figure. It is no crime to love a lady who prefers someone else. And if it is sacrilegious to enter a convent for the purpose of preventing a novice from committing herself, it must be conceded that he only failed because he behaved more discreetly than his rival and was overwhelmed by sheer numbers. As for the Scarpia-like theme of 'if you become mine I will spare your captured lover'—well, Manrico was not only a prisoner-of-war, but a prescribed rebel of the sort who got little shrift in the Middle Ages anyway; and a marriage between a royal lady-in-waiting and a handsome captain of the guard has romantic possibilities if the lady will only rid herself of a disloyal obsession and see reason and duty. The tragedy of Di Luna is his inability to time things accurately. His warm-hearted aria 'Il balen' is a glaring example of the right song in the wrong place. He embarks on it after a brief recitative that opens with the words 'Tutto è deserto'. If this is so, why waste such a passionate aria? Surely the time for it was in the Aliaferia garden, when he spent precious minutes recitativing, only to let the troubadour slip in a serenade just as his own aria should have been starting. Had there then been a song contest, with 'Il balen' balanced against 'Deserto sulla terra', at least he would have obtained a fair hearing and, who knows?, perhaps Leonora's serious consideration. As it is, his tender outpouring is heard only by Ferrando, Verdi's nearest approach to Gurnemanz, and his wholly obedient followers.

It is a relief to turn to Azucena, that crazed creature who seems to live perpetually in the past, and a lurid past at that. She belongs to another world, a sort of Brechtian fantasy. In *El Trovador* she speaks prose, as though she belongs to a low-life sub-plot. But she is in fact right in the centre, a timeless projection of the bizarre and the profound, a phoenix beating the air with portentous wings, a disturbance teasing the imaginations of those who have little to tease. So amid their comparative puppetry she waxes the more realistic, and her eccentricities concern us far more than the moral scruples or lack of them which guide those characters whom the play is chiefly about.

Azucena, alike in play and opera, brings disquiet to disrupt the romantic flow. Verdi spotted at once that she was vital to his plan, a ready-made chance for a mezzo-soprano to be matched against the big rôles; not an in-and-out bird of passage like Federica, Duchess of Ostheim, or a last-act cabaret-turn in the manner of Maddalena; but a creature of equal status with tenor, baritone and soprano, with her own arias and a major share in the duets and the top line in an ensemble. He saw at once her dilemma, her inner conflict, her vital thirst for vengeance wrapped in inescapable doom. And Verdi saw, and warned Cammarano, that she must not be mad; worn out and wandering perhaps, but not mad. Not for her a grand *scena* with coloratura fireworks, but a dreamy drift of exhaustion.

Verdi's opening follows Gutiérrez closely. The play opens in prose, with the night sentries discussing the old tale of the witch and the baby, the evil spell, the burning of one witch and the vengeful kidnapping and destroying by another, her daughter. All this has to be told to the audience, though one is always tempted to comment that the retainers all know it so well that there is no need for them to recount it to each other. Verdi had seized his chance to let the story be told and at the same time give us a musical introduction to his opera; for this first scene may well be called a *prelude with voices*. Although absorbed into Act I, it could have been a prologue, for it neither concerns nor contains any of the principal singers. Ferrando's long bass aria with choral comments by the guards is indeed a dramatic prologue to the story, for it tells of events which took place many years before. And its theme is Azucena and her remote mother.

Once we are past that superb operatic launching, the triple drum-roll, the flamboyantly descending fanfare, the muffled horn-call, less than thirty bars of Tennysonian narrative magic, we are listening to sombre matters solemnly discussed. Clarinet and bassoon predominate in the recitative, and successions of semitones give eerie shivers. The aria which somewhat buoyantly started with the words 'Abbietta zingara' is soon slipping into emotive language—'ammaliato' . . . 'fattucchiera' . . . 'strega' (bewitched . . . witchcraft . . . witch). And its postlude is a chromatic slither. Soon Ferrando is telling in depressing monotone how witches can take on various shapes in the darkness, accompanied by the strings mournfully undulating in semitones, the same device being used by the chorus *come un lamento* as the narrator lets his nocturnal imagination run away with him. Suddenly a bell strikes midnight with an alarm-like urgency that so startles the semi-hysterical retainers that one fears for the safety of the king and queen, were Urgel's rebels to choose this moment for an attack on the palace. The whole scene is deliberately planned towards this Gothic climax. We are no better for not believing in witches. These people certainly did. Less than thirty years earlier a queen of Aragon had been put on trial for witchcraft, and not many years later in Castile the Constable, Alvaro de Luna (wonderful Verdian name!), was accused of bewitching the king and executed. Azucena, in her bloodthirsty quest for vengeance, had certainly laid herself wide open to the suspicion and the charge. But apart from the ghoulish suggestiveness in the music, the most memorable thing about this opening scene is the collection of unison choral snatches that comment on Ferrando's narrative. They have a brevity, an informal spontaneity, that quite suddenly brings into the *Trovatore* score something not usually connected with it—the fragmentary *Falstaff* manner. If their effect errs on the side of jauntiness it would seem that Verdi, faced with a long bass solo and all-male chorus, was at least making a conscious effort not to be dull.

Azucena does not appear in the play until the beginning of the third act, which opens with the song recalling the burning of her mother. This song, compelling enough in the Spanish play, is a 'natural' for the librettist, and has easily become Cammarano's 'Stride la vampa'. But although transferred from a spoken drama to an operatic text, the stage directions still preserve the instruction *canta*, as though she is to be thought of as not merely telling her own lurid story, but giving voice to some ancient and fatalistic rite. The camp full of gipsies is an irresistibly operatic ingredient, an invention of Cammarano's, and skilfully brought forward for colourful contrast at a point where it is needed. These gipsies in the Biscayan mountains live unfettered by the cloistered and balustraded protocol of their civilized betters. The music tells us this at once, sprightly and with plenty of trills, scored without brass but made piquant by the addition of a triangle. It has an immediate, forward drive, a sort of lively expectancy, as it builds up to the big tune, so famous the world over, in which Verdi uses eighteen different instruments, straightforward in harmony and percussion but rich in range if not in symphonic texture. The anvils, metallically clanging an octave apart in turn, artlessly rivet the rhythm. They are some years in advance of Nibelheim, and very innocent by comparison with Alberich's forced labour camp. These happy gipsies swing democratic hammers, and when their works foreman bids them pack up, they obey cheerfully and depart, singing into the distance like Disney's dwarfs.

We should notice, however, the ingenuity with which Azucena herself has been isolated from the chorus. She could so easily have been given two operatic stanzas with choral refrain, as Lady Macbeth's brindisi or Eboli's *canzone del velo*. Doubtless Verdi would have supplied an applause-catching number; but he saw the necessity for contrasting

her morose morbidity with the carefree levity of the gipsies. So she takes
no part, but as soon as their song is over she begins hers, and a fine piece
of melodic character painting it is. But the most interesting feature of her
song is the way in which it balances Ferrando's 'Abbietta zingara'. The
key is the same. It has a similar semiquaver figure running through. It has
a parallel downward structure. It describes the same event. How then do
we feel compelled to listen attentively to her, whereas Ferrando may not
have succeeded in capturing our attention? The secret lies in the scoring.
While Ferrando's narrative is assiduously backed up throughout by the
whole orchestra (less brass), Azucena has an accompaniment more
carefully and economically worked out. The strings thrum the 3/8 time,
but violins alone take her melodic line, trills and all, to be replaced in the
middle by clarinet and bassoon chords; and when at the end of the stanza
she trills on one note held over four bars, the bassoons are with her while
the clarinets undulate in thirds, pencilling in the *strega*-complex that so
terrified Ferrando's listeners.

It is characteristic of Azucena's obsessed mind that she repeats herself as
ideas revolve through her troubled head. Now, when the gipsies
comment on the sadness of her song, she echoes in gloomy triplicate the
notes addressed by them:

Then at once she turns towards the hitherto silent Manrico and calls out
to him:

This echo of her burning mother's desperate cry rears at intervals in
her suffering memories, a haunting motif that will never leave her.

When the gipsies have departed, Azucena has Manrico to herself at last. She still has plenty to tell him. Cammarano follows Gutiérrez closely, turning his ample prose speeches into a striking passage of dramatic verse, twenty-four consecutive lines each of fourteen syllables. On this formidable foundation Verdi has built his famous *andante mosso* in 6/8 time, 'Condotta ell'era in ceppi'. The rhythm is deliberate, reinforced with a pitiless repetition of suppressed horror from oboe and violins with here and there an underlying touch of drums. This type of rhythmic insistence sticks to Azucena and singles her out as though Verdi was well aware that a Spanish gipsy must be portrayed in such a manner, though well past the age for castanets.

As she recalls past horrors and *mi vendica* comes back to her, Verdi fans the fires of her mental anguish by using his orchestra to depict her ghastly memories. There are *staccato* strings and woodwind flickers impelling her on, until the violins divide and splutter out the 'Stride la vampa' theme while she dwells on the grisly picture of her mother's burning; then the writhing *strega* thirds are added, working up to a *tutti* climax as *mi vendica* is hurled out, A in alt, with an octave drop and a wailing orchestral descent. With a pitiless, throbbing accompaniment she tells Manrico how she threw the wrong child into the pyre, each phrase punctuated by an uprush. The whole orchestra *fff* blazes as she cries *straziante*:

Again the repetition so characteristic, as the crisis of her terror subsides with the woodwind thirds and string tremolo descending, murmuring, dying to *pppp*. Azucena drifts on, exhausted, mechanical:

It is a point beyond which things emotionally cannot go; and at once a change creeps in. Assuring Manrico that he is indeed her son, she skates to safety on a rapid recitative almost *secco*, telling how she nursed him after he had been wounded in battle, lavishing true maternal care on him. Manrico, with a show of conscious heroics, affirms how he stood his ground alone against Di Luna's assault, his own men having been routed, and how he received his wounds in front. Azucena wonders why, thus set upon in battle and left for dead, he failed later to kill Di Luna when he had him at his mercy. If we are attentive to this important passage, set modestly between two musical climacterics, we will learn something to our advantage. Firstly, there had already been a battle at Pelilla between the king's army and the Urgel rebels, in which, despite Manrico's personal bravery, the rebels had been driven from the field. Pellila is on the Ebro, some forty miles downstream from Saragossa. Yet thanks to Azucena Manrico had sufficiently recovered from his wounds to have been fit enough to break through the royal lines, serenade Leonora, and engage in a duel with Di Luna. We hear now for the first time the result of that duel (which followed off-stage at the end of Act I). Azucena tells us that he won the fight but spared the Count, and she cannot understand why he did. Again the repetition:

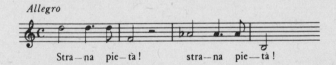

Allegro

Stra—na   pie—tà!   stra—na   pie—tà!

Then begins the duet 'Mal reggendo all' aspro assalto', which shows as fine a contrast as a duet possibly can between two people ideologically out of touch. Manrico's stanza, pulsing and epic, tells how his sense of chivalry prevented him from slaying his beaten foe. Something inside him forbade the *coup de grâce*. His voice drops as he relates this strange warning. But it is quite lost on Azucena, who counters his *cantabile* with a new, deliberate tune of her own, not exactly taunting him, but reading him a firm lecture on the proper way to deal with one's defeated enemies. Even in the middle of this stern homily she can revert to her repetitive mannerism, this time as though driving home her point (see page 238). This fine passage is enshrined for us in Louise Homer's two records, one with Caruso, the other with Martinelli—what a lucky Azucena to have had such 'sons'! Listening to it we can study what is a

Allegro meno mosso

com—pi, o fi—glio, qual d'un Di—o, com—pi, al—

—— lo—ra il cenno mi—o...

high-water mark of Italian operatic construction—emotional conflict
stated in music by two quite different tunes, the voices blending only at
the end when Manrico agrees to act next time as she now bids him; yet
like Hamlet over Claudius, he never pulls it off.

Hard on the close of this section a horn is heard off-stage. It sounds a
third drop, from G to E. It is the signal of Ruiz the messenger; and
Manrico at once sounds his own horn in reply, E to C. Some exchange a
little more exuberant and exciting would not have come amiss at this
point; not necessarily Siegfriedian, but less lugubrious. But if Verdi has
missed an opportunity, Azucena does not. She slips in another *mi vendica*.

The messenger enters and hands Manrico a letter. He intones its
contents, which makes it sound more urgent than the conventional
operatic letter-reading (as with Lady Macbeth). The news, that Leonora
thinks him dead and is about to enter a convent, may well cause him to
cry 'Oh giusto cielo!' as the music becomes *agitato mosso* and the strings
rip along in urgent summons. His impetuous resolve sweeps Azucena's
lame protests aside until, with the time switching to her 3/8 and the
marking *velocissimo* she forces him to listen to her. Using her favourite lilt
she tries craftily to disarm him and call a halt to his tempestuous mood.
Her subtle plea:

Velocissimo
con passione

No, sof—frir-lo non pos—s'i—o il tuo

sangue è sangue mi—o!

is a forerunner of Iago's (È un'idra fosca, livida, cieca'! Azucena is using simple gipsy cunning as against Iago's distillation of malignity; but the original guile is there. However, it is lost on Manrico, who allows her to end with a frantic and wholly justifiable cadenza and then plunges ahead with his terrific 'Un momento puo involarmi' prompted by Verdi's written instruction that the two notes on which its opening is based must be well accented. This must sound, Verdi saw, like the rhythmic gallop of a ride to the rescue. So he has written tearaway stuff full of true operatic excitement. Operatic, since only a tenor would open out his lungs for 95 bars when he should be in the saddle and down the mountain-side. But what bars! All Azucena's build-up, her gory narration, her maternal cosseting, her anxious plea and subtle cajoling—all have been of no avail. Filial love gives way to sexual. What a pity there is no record of Caruso singing this. He did make one with Homer but it was never published. As a substitute one can take pleasure in the version by Zenatello and his wife Maria Gay.

So ends this powerful scene, a galaxy of emotional crises and contrasts, seemingly set to just the right music from start to finish. It provides a fine long session for the mezzo-soprano, with a chance to sing passionately and act fiercely. She can easily stop the show, but it must be by her singing, not her histrionics. The latter have only too often been used to bolster up the former!

Manrico dashes off from the remote Biscayan mountains to the Convent of Jerusalem on the other side of Saragossa. But if we have been listening attentively to Azucena we may have heard her warn him that he is running the risk of re-opening recent wounds which have not properly healed. What wounds? Not, of course, those sustained on the field of Pelilla. These must be from his duel with Di Luna, whom in fact he overcame and refrained from killing. We are left to assume that this duel was of such intensity that even the victor sustained serious injuries. But we must accept that there is a touch of Superman about Manrico, with his melodramatic ability to arrive in the nick of time; and sure enough he arrives at the convent just as Di Luna is poised for the kidnapping of Leonora on the threshold of her last vows. Yet we should note that, although neither the Count nor the troubadour has any regard for the fact that the place whereon they are standing is holy ground, yet Manrico, Ruiz and the rebels far outnumber Di Luna, Ferrando and the palace retainers. So much so that the latter unanimously concede the contest. Here, surely, is Manrico's chance to keep that promise he made to Azucena, 'Yes, I swear I'll plunge this sword into the villain's heart.' Now, in the suburbs of Saragossa at night, might he do it pat. . . .

The message that told Manrico of Leonora's intention to become a nun also informed him that the rebels had captured the fortress of Castellor and its defence had been committed to his charge. We must assume that he considered the abduction to have priority over his military appointment; but that, once Leonora was safely in his clutches, he once again assumed his responsibilities, reporting to Castellor and taking her with him. The heights of Castellar (the Italian libretto indulges in a minor spelling variant) lie roughly twenty miles north-west of Saragossa. Manrico would have crossed them on his dash to the convent; and now he has had to retrace his steps. The rise of the curtain at the start of Act III shows us the royalist camp of Di Luna pitched before the rebel stronghold, 'with the fortifications of Castellor in the distance'. The occupation of this high ground dominating the upper Ebro would be a considerable threat to the king's headquarters and seat of government at Saragossa. It is imperative that Urgel's army be dislodged and Castellor regained for the Crown. The banner of Count Di Luna hangs above his tent, and Ferrando, now apparently sergeant-major, passes on the Count's orders for a dawn attack, adding as his own personal incentive that there will be 'fat booty'. The assembled soldiers greet this with the fine chorus full of threat and swagger, the ripe fruits of a self-assured Verdi in the late thirties. Less well-known around the world than the Anvil Chorus, and certainly less so than the Soldiers' Chorus in *Faust*, it occupies its conventional operatic position at the beginning of an act, but does more than this. For its full-throated vigour warns us that the rebels, in spite of their strategic superiority, are about to face a determined onslaught that may well wrench their position from them.

The warriors retire (as operatic choruses often do when their number is over—without any clear reason) and the Count Di Luna strides out of his tent into the *praetorium*. He glares at the towers of Castellor, but his recitative informs us immediately that he is not engaged in a tactical survey. Leonora is up there and he is consumed by passion. But the poor Count, just as in the gardens of Aliaferia, is robbed of a certain aria by a sudden turn of events. 'Oh! Leonora!' he has exclaimed, but before the phrase can be resolved, *Odesi tumulto*, and Ferrando rushes in over a torrent of dotted quavers. A gipsy spy has been caught in the precincts of the camp. It is of course Azucena. She has wandered down from her hide-out in the mountains in the wake of Manrico, hoping to catch up

with him and prevent him from doing anything rash. She knows he has
been ordered to defend Castellor, but somehow she has lost the way and
has been picked up by the royalist patrols, the very worst thing that
could have happened to her.

The entry of Azucena restores to the extrovert music that subtlety
characteristic of her part. It is all histrionics now. Her hands are tied and
she is struggling and protesting, as well she might, for they are already
calling her *strega*. Before the interrogating Count she is both alert and
uncommunicative, as befits a prisoner-of-war. When Di Luna enquires
about her movements, she is vague, and claims a gipsy's right to exist on
free range. But she is craftily playing for time. To the Count's question
'Ove vai?' she replies 'Nol so.' She then continues in phrases broken by
little comments on the strings, as though in her perplexity she is pausing
to think what to say next. If we turn to the score of *Otello*, where the
Cassio-Montano brawl has brought in the Moor, and he turns to ask Iago
what is going on, we will find Iago replying 'Non so.' Then, just like
Azucena in Di Luna's camp, he goes on explaining very carefully, with
almost the same string comments sounding the ticking-over of his wary
mind. So thirty-five years later Verdi was still ready to utilize an old
Trovatore trick. Possibly not many *Otello*-lovers notice this; but it is
there.

The short passage is marked *adagio*. Yet as soon as Ferrando begins to
suspect, four bars of *allegro* take its place, denoting a sudden upsurge
of interest. Then, with Azucena returning to her self-defence, there
is a switch to *andante mosso*. These tempi are deliberate and expressive.
We may smile at the old operatic device of a casual place-name setting
the dramatic ball rolling. Here it is Biscaglia; in *Boccanegra* it is Pisa; in
Forza del Destino Calatrava. But clearly Azucena has made a serious
mistake mentioning her geographical origins, and she senses it; for at
once she tries to cover up by spinning them a touching tale, but she is
back to her favourite 3/8 and the same key as her narrations in the
previous act. However, deliberate guile it is, and its opening four bars
may be compared with the opening of another and more celebrated
gipsy also putting on an act:

Andante mosso
con espress.

Giorni   po-ve——ri vi——ve-a

and

Allegretto

Près des rem— parts de Sé—vil——————— le

The slow waltz-like tune developing, first on the violins and then with the aid of flute and piccolo, brings an air of unreality into her apologia. Such sugary proceedings surely cannot last. Nor do they. For suddenly there is a dramatic break-off as Ferrando recognizes her. The tempo switches to *allegro* as they all taunt and challenge her. Defenceless now she casts aside all the ingenuity of pretence in an outburst that is moving in its long-drawn simplicity:

Allegro

E   tu non vie-ni, o   Man-ri—co,o fi—glio mi—o?

Non soc—cor—ri al—l'in-fe—li—ce   ma—dre tu–a ?

Immediately the full orchestra crashes in with a punch of uninhibited vulgarity, and the distraught victim turns at bay amid her heartless captors and lashes at them in a sort of mini-cabaletta of superb venom. Soon the Count and Ferrando, backed by the chorus, are striking back vigorously, with a trumpet ripping along to rivet their abuse and their fiery threats of destruction. It is a little *tour de force* for the mezzo-soprano who, ringed round by male warriors can fling up her manacled arms and behave like a newly-caged tigress, throwing about in their midst her lone woman's body and female voice, with two As to back up her hysterics. The ensemble is short, turgid, and wholly convincing, and it brings down the curtain with a fine, whirring orchestral postlude as the pinioned Azucena is dragged off and the Count returns to his HQ tent with a Number One hostage to his credit.

The straying of Azucena into the royalist perimeter provides the turning point of the story. The rebel espionage is at once fed with this vital information, and Ruiz conveys it to Manrico, who in spite of the certainty of an impending attack is losing no time in arranging his marriage to Leonora up in the chapel of the fortress he is commanding. The intelligence thus disseminated by the Count pays instant dividends. Manrico Superman deserts his bride, summons his commandos, and charges down to the rescue. His ill-considered sortie from his fortified eyrie into the royalist-held plain is just what Di Luna hopes for. The action is not described. When the fourth act starts we hear at once of his capture, for he is in the dungeon at Saragossa. The Count, as we learn later on, has followed up his destruction of Manrico's attack by a counter-strike at Castellor and has taken the fortress. He has failed to find Leonora; but he has wiped out the rebel foothold up-river from the capital, and among his prisoners are the very ones he most wished for.

When we next meet with Azucena she is in prison, a broken old woman, all her spirit exhausted; her reputed son Manrico, himself under sentence of death, doing his best to comfort her. We have meanwhile come to know and appreciate Manrico much more. We have heard him as the lover ('Ah si ben mio'); the hero ('Di quella pira'); and the troubadour ('Ah che la morte'). In the first of these, an aria drawn from a very passionate and poetical speech in Gutiérrez, he has strayed into the cavalier realms of Suckling or Lovelace, distilling loyalty and gallantry to his lady in a passage so richly phrased that it seems as it unfolds to touch on the intensity of Siegmund's 'Spring Song'. Yet within a few bars he has plunged into 'Di quella pira', electrifying us with the single-minded devotion of a commander about to lead a forlorn hope, a sort of Sebastopol charge with only disaster ahead. No wonder Camillo Cavour, hearing that the Austrians were about to embark on a similar military mistake, feeling the urge to burst out singing automatically tackled 'Di quella pira' in his excitement. He was celebrating, whether he was aware of it or not, the impending doom of the Austrian armed forces rather than the diplomatic triumph of his own engineering.

The voice of Manrico floating out through the little barred window of his dungeon reduces us at once to compassion. This is an inverted serenade, for the minstrel should always be on the outside. But the theatrical *coup* belongs to Gutiérrez. What Verdi has added is the monastic *Miserere*. Gutiérrez was content with a single voice reciting a two-line prayer, a very modest effect compared with the musical version, which sets the anguish of Leonora and the sorrow of Manrico in an almost apocalyptic framework, a horrifying ante-mortal requiem. It is noteworthy that the Church is portrayed throughout as firmly on the side of the Establishment. This serves to emphasize the esoteric and irresponsible nature of Manrico's entanglement with the vagrant world of the gipsies. But there is one facet of this *Miserere* not generally noticed. When after the first chorus the throbbing accompaniment for Leonora begins (where Verdi has written in 'Although this passage is scored for the full orchestra it must be played very quietly'), we have already been prepared for this in the previous act. When Manrico and Leonora are together in Castellor, and he warns her that the fortress is to be attacked at dawn, she fears a threat to their marriage but he replies 'Il presagio funesto, deh! sperdi, o cara!' Beneath her nervous words the 'cellos and basses play, *pp*, the same theme that now, in the *Miserere*, accompanies Leonora's 'Quel suon, quelle preci, solenni funeste', as though the terror she momentarily felt before has now fatefully returned. It was, on the threshold of her wedding, a passing premonition. Now it is reality, the entire orchestra ramming home what before was thinly suggested by the deep strings alone. These are almost Wagnerian musical tactics, but in a score noted for its plethora of splendid tunes, such little subtleties tend to pass unnoticed.

Now in the final scene we have once again the full orchestra playing soft, lugubrious chords, darkly depicting what the stage directions call an 'orrido carcere'. The wandering of Azucena's mind is ghoulishly portrayed by *tremolo* and *staccato* strings, and over them the flickering woodwind recalls 'Stride la vampa'—one flute, one clarinet, one bassoon in a kind of nightmare obsequy. Again we hear that desperate uprush that played such an emphatic part in the monologue 'Condott'ell'era in ceppi', and there is the same exhausted dying away after the hysterics. Then, calm of mind, all passion spent, Azucena glides back into her indigenous 3/8 for 'Si, la stanchezza'. Verdi is here at his lyrical best. Here he struck a universal chord. Our own Victorians loved 'Home to our mountains' as they loved 'Home sweet home'. Professor Dent's translation retained the words; as does the recent one by Messrs Tucker and Hammond. We cannot conceive Azucena without 'Home to our mountains'. More effective, really, is Manrico's refrain 'Riposa, o madre'. He is a troubadour, and this is in effect his last and most moving serenade. Very sensitively does Verdi put across the drowsing and dropping off to sleep of the old gipsy, while he caresses her with his

lullaby, the violins divided and muted. At this point of rest, we may
think

> Fear no more the heat o' the sun,
>   Nor the furious winter's rages;
> Thou thy worldly task hast done,
>   Home art gone, and ta'en thy wages. . . .

Gutiérrez, after the usual scene in prose, his regular medium for
Azucena-Manrico duologues, breaks beautifully into verse as she sleeps
and he watches:

> Duerme, duerme, madre mía,
> Mientras yo te guardo el sueño,
> y un porvenir más risueño
> durmiendo allá te sonría.

Coming after the prose it must have a stirring effect. It easily becomes an
Italian libretto; but it needed a Verdi to match it in song. The tragedy is
that this well-earned repose is so soon to suffer a catastrophic awakening,
yet too late for her to save her Manrico's life by telling Di Luna who he
really is. So by lulling the old woman to sleep Manrico has signed his
own death warrant. This is real pathos, real irony.

The end of *Il Trovatore* is somewhat brittle. The arrival in the cell of
Leonora, the inevitable misunderstanding, the subconscious crooning of
Azucena (this last a touching musical interpolation into the
story)—these combine to roll the opera along to its conclusion. But with
the entry of Di Luna we have another trio. In the play Leonor dies before
the Count's arrival. Verdi has to keep his soprano going right to the end,
so she dies in his presence. The last pages, accurately copied from the
play, are abrupt and tuneless. It amounts to a sort of disintegration of
musical formality. Yet it is true to the text. A series of ejaculations
punctuated by a series of downward orchestral plunges, and it is all over.
Azucenza, suddenly very much awake, tells the Count he has executed
his own brother; then remembers her own filial pact and cries:

With her exultant B flat ringing across the dungeon she falls beneath the window through which she has been compelled to watch Manrico beheaded. In the play, she dies. Verdi does not commit himself. His Azucena collapses, leaving the Count to remark somewhat tamely 'And I survive!' It is no doubt meant to be remorseful; but it is usually drowned by the last orchestral chords; nor do we, in the opera house, care very much what the Count is thinking. Events have moved too fast, both for us and for him. But we ought to emerge from the theatre disturbed by that last cry

Sei vendicata, o madre!

For she, who has lived for vengeance, by achieving her goal has lost her all. And that is the story of *Il Trovatore*.

NOTES

1 *Copialettere*, CXXII. Verdi to Cammarano, 9 September 1851.
2 Ibid., CXVII. Verdi to Cammarano, 9 April 1851.
3 Chapman, *A History of Spain*, chs. XI and XIV.

10

THE GERMONTS

Once more La Traviata sighs
Another sadder song.
Once more Il Trovatore cries
A tale of deeper wrong.

ALFRED NOYES[1] HAD not been reading the Covent Garden prospectus, but had been within earshot of a London barrel-organ. 'The music's only Verdi', he commented; but at least he recognized it, and not only recognized it but was able to differentiate between *Il Trovatore* and *La Traviata*. When I once asked an Italian restaurant band to play some *Trovatore* they beamed delightedly and embarked on *Traviata*, and I had not the heart to confide in them that I knew they had got it wrong. But one of the mysteries of operatic music is surely the way in which Verdi made two entirely contrasted masterpieces using almost exactly the same methods. The deeper wrong and the sadder song have similar ingredients, like techniques, indistinguishable formats; yet the one pulses through and through as an heroic horror story, while the other breathes the follies and intimacies of the salon and the boudoir, and the results seem to be quite distinct.

It is almost impossible to put one's finger on precisely what creates this distinction. Verdi appears to share with Shakespeare that uncanny flair for suffusing his art from within by means of natural tinctures absolutely suited to the theme on hand. *Trovatore* glows with Tennysonian heroics. *Traviata* scintillates and dims with the chandeliers and shadows of promiscuity and disillusion. Yet both are fashioned in the same idiom. There are passages in *Traviata* in which Verdi displays a new care over instrumental details, and pulls off tricks of musicianship more adroit than anything in *Trovatore*; but it is in the main a thing of conventional cavatinas, cabalettas, choruses and ensembles, stylistically backward compared to the new writers of contemporary French literature. In spite of this Verdi's music has taken Dumas' story round the world, to regions where his novel and his play perhaps have never penetrated.

Although in this story nobody draws a sword, shoots a pistol, lives in a castle, or puts on armour, and no one is stabbed or poisoned, it instantly appealed to Verdi. It came within his own personal experience, which cannot be said of the many historical melodramas he had so successfully adapted. Many conjectures have been made about how much Verdi translated his own emotions into the music of *Traviata*, how many of his own first-hand memories are enshrined in the score. He never met or even saw Marie Duplessis, for she died five months before his first visit to Paris. But it is by no means impossible that Peppina may have remembered her. There may have been many live links between Verdi and Peppina on the one hand, and Marie and her clientèle on the other. We know that Ranelagh, a Parisian playground by Passy, attracted such as escorted Marie on expeditions of pleasure. Roqueplan met her there in the company of a Count,[2] and Roqueplan was the director of the Opéra who, as soon as he heard Verdi was in Paris, invited him to write something for his theatre. There must have been many in the artistic world of Paris who could have gossiped with Verdi about Marie Duplessis. When he began to live at Passy, he was doing what the artists did—sharing bed and board with a woman not his wife, and a woman, let us face it, well versed in this kind of living. Their mutual arrangement rubbed shoulders, however respectably, with that Parisian permissiveness in which Marie Duplessis and her kind flourished. We know, from a letter of Peppina's, that important hostesses giving parties in the winter season would hire her to sing. Although she admitted that she did not care to become involved, and used to hurry home quickly afterwards, she at least met Society— and who knows whom she met?

So when the novel *La Dame aux Camélias* came into the bookshops, Verdi and Peppina must have read it with interest; and when Dumas turned it into a play they must have been haunted by its undertones that struck chords of conscious understanding. No wonder, really, that Verdi felt the stirrings of composition. He was familiar with the environment, the sort of people, and something of their problems. Such faith had he in his ability to make an opera of it that he automatically engaged Piave to construct a libretto based on the play, evidently accepting Piave's competence to do the transcript. His verses are quite conventional, typical of the style Verdi had been so at home with since *Ernani*, but totally alien to the modern prose conversation-drama of Dumas. Over this structure of stanza, rhyme and metre, so familiar to Verdi, *Traviata* grew into a high-romantic melodrama, soaring buoyantly above the hammer-and-chisel workmanship of *La Dame aux Camélias*. For although Dumas' novel has a fragrant charm as it unfolds its tainted adventures, his subsequent play creaks with laboured construction, for all its brittle story and sad end. The novel has inspiration: the play has technique. Had Dumas been a poet, what a distillation of tragic beauty his play might have been! Verdi, in a way, has supplied what was wanting. He has liberated the caged soul of Dumas' drama, lifting it into realms beyond its deserts.

I once had the good fortune to attend on one and the same day a matinée of *La Dame aux Camélias* and an evening performance of *La Traviata*. They seemed to me two totally different works. The play was a slice of real life, so shot through with familiarity as to be disturbing, but not in the least uplifting. The opera was more than the same story through rose-coloured glasses; it was grand, bright, lofty, epic—a pinnacle of experience. The play, which had scandalized the French Theatre on account of its photographic realism, was still pitiful and tragic. But it showed mundane, earthy, doomed people. The opera, familiar to the point of staleness, sang of souls rather than bodies, immortality rather than death, hope rather than despair. That, it then seemed to me, is what Verdi has done for the Lady of the Camellias. Dumas has left her marbled in Montmartre. Verdi has raised her in stained glass against the light.

But this accolade of respectability was far from apparent at the time, at least in England where the norm had become puritanical. When in 1857 Lord Campbell introduced to the House of Lords his Bill which was to become the Obscene Publications Act, the pornographic example he displayed in his hand to his fellow peers was not *Fanny Hill* but *La Dame aux Camélias*. According to Norman St John-Stevas,[3] when *La Traviata* was given at Covent Garden 'a note on the programme informed patrons that no English translation of the libretto was available' (a more inoffensive libretto than Piave's could scarcely be imagined!). But it was the essence of Victorian prudery that any reference to the existence of prostitution was certain to corrupt. Cyril Pearl[4] quotes the *Lancet*:

> The daughters of Dives, knowing all about the plot of the *Traviata*, visit the Opera to witness the apotheosis of a consumptive prostitute, and drive home through the Gehenna fair nightly held in the Haymarket—yet we are expected to credit that they lay their heads upon their pillows without considering what it all means.

As for *La Dame aux Camélias*, just as the novel was displayed in the House of Lords as a warning, so the play was banned by the Lord Chamberlain through what the French called *le cant anglais*. The critic Francisque Sarcey observed that when at last it was permitted, the raising

of the ban had been instigated by the Prince of Wales. This critic said
jokingly to an English official, 'Now you've put on our *Dame aux
Camélias*, you'll agree that the morals of old England have not
deteriorated.' The reply he got was, 'Ah, but it has only had two
performances so far. You wait!'[5]

We are all familiar with how *The Times* objected to *Traviata*'s 'foul
and hideous horrors' and dismissed its music as 'of no value whatever'.[6]
We recall that the *Illustrated London News* found nothing better to say
than 'It has pretty tunes, for every Italian has more or less the gift of
melody; but even the tunes are trite and common. . . .'[7] We smile at the
Athenaeum's 'The music of *La Traviata* is trashy . . . the poorest music,
poorly sung. . . .'[8] Henry Chorley had nothing but contempt for both
Piccolomini and for *Traviata*. He wrote of the prima donna, 'Her
performances at times approached offence against maidenly reticence
and delicacy—They were the *slang* of the musical theatre;—no other
word will characterize them:—and *slang* has no place in opera. . . .'[9] He
wrote of *Traviata*, '"La Dame de Camelias" [*sic*] was a story untenable
for music. Consumption for one who is to sing! A ballet with a lame
Sylphide would be as rational.'[10] So *Traviata* was damned for its obscene
plot, its vulgar music, and (because nothing must be right) its poor
performance. Yet the 'daughters of Dives' and a good many other
daughters too, flocked to Her Majesty's, to the Lyceum, and to Covent
Garden, intent not only on being depraved and corrupted, but also on
hearing lovely music brilliantly sung.

But it took an Englishman, Benjamin Lumley, to come out in print, in
The Times' correspondence columns, with a pious and moral defence of
Dumas' story as represented in his own theatre. He claimed that such a
portrayal of the punishment of vice could but have a salutary effect on
those who witnessed it. Of course he had one eye on his own box-office,
but by offering it to his public as a reforming tract he perhaps made many
new converts. For although it is a story of a woman, immortalized on the
one hand by such as Doche and Duse, Bernhardt and Garbo and
Feuillère, and on the other hand by Piccolomini and Patti, Melba and
Tetrazzini, Farrar and Ponselle and Galli-Curci, it is, as perhaps Lumley
perceived, a story for *men*. A galaxy of female stars of the first magnitude
have given it a glittering progress in theatre and opera house; but it is at
bottom a man's tale—a reminiscence of youthful follies and a warning
that the facts of life weigh heavily and disastrously against the dreams of
temptation.

That is why it is as well to look at the story as the Duvals or the Germonts make and break it. *La Dame aux Camélias* or *La Traviata* is the title. Our own Elizabethan theatre could have provided an alternative more picturesque and accurate: *'Tis Pity She's a Whore*. How Verdi came to select the name *Traviata* we do not know. He wrote in one of his letters, 'I am setting *La Dame aux Camélias* for Venice. Its title will be, perhaps, *Traviata*.'[11] In her dying prayer at the beginning of the last act Violetta refers to herself as 'traviata'. In her Act I hey-day (her virginity of vice, as Dumas provocatively put it) she called herself 'franca, ingenua'. But before the last curtain rises she has obtained absolution from a priest, and now at last she acknowledges that she has 'erred and strayed'—which is precisely what *traviata* means. Devotees with a classical education could, with a slight grammatical liberty, construe it with a Rabelaisian directness not inapposite to the lady's profession. However, in London the Italian word began to be borrowed as a euphemism for courtesan, harlot, or worse; for we read, 'It is nicer phraseology than that of coarser days.'[12] One certainly cannot dispute that Giuseppina Strepponi was every inch a *traviata* at that time. With two bastard children by a *primo tenore* to her discredit, she had now graduated to a liaison with a composer. It is curiously satisfying to realize that, if there *was* a subconscious identification of her with Madamigella Valery, in her case Violetta's prayer was favourably answered:

> Della traviata sorrido al desio,
> A lei, deh perdona, tu accoglila, o Dio.

For if ever a *traviata* was granted pardon and benediction, it was surely Giuseppina Strepponi! But if it were not for *men*, women would neither err nor stray. Had not Verdi, since setting up house with Peppina, written the opera *Stiffelio*, whose finale turned on the biblical quotation 'He that is without sin among you, let him first cast a stone at her'?

It must be admitted that *Traviatas* are always remembered for the coloratura star of the evening, Bosio or Bellincioni, Carosio or Caniglia or Callas, Sembrich or Sutherland; and rightly so. But those two Germonts—obdurate, obstinate, old-fashioned father and smug, selfish, short-sighted son—represent the immoral and moral forces that wrongly and rightly interfere with the chosen status of the heroine, divert her from self-sufficiency to insecurity, and hasten her physical destruction. Each, in his own separate way, might be called *Il Traviatore*.

One of the most striking features of *La Traviata* is the rise of the curtain after the first Prelude. The orchestra has played what is, in poetical effect, a sonnet in music, delicately shaped and chiselled, but having about it a sort of noble sadness—nothing cloying or pathetic—a tale of tragic resignation. Then suddenly the whole orchestra rears up as though roused from a reverie, *allegro brillantissimo e molto vivace*, and we are looking at the sumptuous interior of a demi-mondaine's *palais*, glittering with crystal and mirrors, candelabra and silverware, and thronged with elegant gentlemen escorting partners quite indistinguishable from ladies. The switch from subdued tranquillity to convivial brillance makes one sit up, which is a very good way for an opera to start. Verdi had already played this trick with *Rigoletto*; but in *La Traviata* the impact is magnified by subtler scoring and greater contrast. It is not Dumas, who opens his play quietly enough in Marguerita's boudoir though the cast gradually assembles and a party develops. The mould is the traditional operatic one. Dumas' scenario has been poured into it, stirred round, and concocted with all the trimmings of an opera night. Verdi has made no concessions. The ingredients are new but the treatment is as before.

Yet Verdi's complete confidence in his own formula, his certainty that his style could absorb a revolutionary story, achieves one early and emphatic stroke of encouragement. These contemporary Parisians can enjoy themselves to contemporary music. When they dance there can be an up-to-date waltz—no searching about among minuets or perigordini or knocking up a *festa di ballo* quite out of touch with the period costumes. Violetta Valery's hired band would give the composer no problems at all. The waltz was the order of the day, and Verdi contributed his own, quite lively and tuneful enough to join the standard repertory (though it never has). One of Marie Duplessis' favourites was Weber's *Invitation to the Waltz*. In the novel Marguerite has a go at it on her piano, if somewhat unsuccessfully, for she comes to grief in the middle and hurls the music across the room as a gesture of despair at her inadequacy, for Gaston R. and the Comte de N. both play it well. 'How on earth can I manage eight sharps in a row?' she exclaims. She would have found less difficulty with Verdi's, for it holds no such terrors.

Having puffed up Marguerite's informal little supper party into a crowded ball, Piave has found himself in difficulties over his text. There has to be movement and animation. The old, static introductory chorus will not do. So to give the impression of a swinging evening he divides the chorus between those who arrived on time and the late-comers. Thus the opera starts with the tenors reproving the basses for being late, and the basses explaining that they became involved in another party—at Flora's. How Mlle Valery has lured all the tenors, while Mlle Bervoix has attracted the basses, we can only conjecture. Dramatically it is a silly enough start; but its intention is to convey that the night-life of Paris is fluid and irresponsible and without ceremony. At any rate, the absentees have timed themselves not to be too late for supper; for Violetta soon has them at their ease and their delinquent hostess Flora, who has come with them, is welcomed without a word of reproach.

Meanwhile Verdi has himself been making sure that the opening gambits are not drowned by his orchestra; for he has laid down in the score that during the personal and mutual introductions the accompaniment is to be limited to two 1st and 2nd violins, two violas, one violoncello, and one double bass. By the deft use of this string octet he ensures that we know who Flora is, and that we do not miss the important introduction of Alfredo by Gastone, with the latter's information about his friend's interest in Violetta and his attentions during her recent illness. Such key exchanges must not be swallowed up in the general gaiety and Verdi does his best to prevent this, while continuing the flow of music uninterrupted. When Baron Douphol is brought into the conversation (to be deliberately embarrassed by Violetta) an oboe is added as though mockingly. As Douphol shows his touchiness we hear the horns; and then gradually the scoring thickens and builds to the unanimous 'beviamo'. Violetta reveals an unexpected wisp of classical culture by likening herself to Hebe as she pours wine for Alfredo, who neatly caps her allusion. Gastone, perhaps impishly, asks Douphol to give the company a brindisi, but '*Il Barone accenna che no*'. So he coaxes Alfredo. It may be the primo tenore's due, but this sudden limelight is inappropriate for a young guest not yet received as a privileged member of Violetta's clientèle. However, he readily accepts the invitation to sing in front of them all, and one can say that at this point the preludial matter is completed and the drama has begun. As the orchestra crashes out a few chords before the switch to the brindisi, the champagne corks pop and all is set for a convivial evening.

In these few introductory minutes we have learnt, amid a spate of gay and delightful music, most of what need be known for the launching of the story. The heroine, 'calme et retranchée dans son dedain', as Jules Janin wrote of Marie Duplessis,[13] has been ill but is resuming her thirst for social entertainment. Her admirers include a Doctor (perhaps unofficially on duty), a Marquis, a Viscount, and a Baron. But plain M. Germont is likely to supersede them and is already distrusted by the Baron—himself by no means the lady's favourite, nor Flora's either. We may wonder in pasing how diplomatically this Italian version of a French story has adopted a group of picturesquely hybrid names—Violetta Valery, Flora Bervoix, Gastone de Letorières, Alfredo Germont—but we know all we need for a start, with the exception of one crucial point. Neither Piave in his libretto nor Verdi by musical implication has given the uninstructed student the slightest clue that the magnificent salon revealed before him is not the interior of a stately château, nor that the sumptuous beauties raising their champagne glasses are neither the sisters nor the fiancées of the debonair gentlemen with whose arms they have linked their own. The soprano's interesting occupation is so far suppressed. The general agreement that a party should be enjoyable and alcoholic by no means presupposes sexual liberality. A producer can allow the infiltration of erotic by-play, elderly roués with monocles pawing their chosen tarts, the furtive fumble and the saucily-invited licence. But Verdi has made strictly sure that his music is absolutely innocent of any such innuendo, while Piave's words conjure up visions no more dangerous than those of Milton's

> Meanwhile, welcome joy, and feast,
> Midnight shout, and revelry,
> Tipsy dance, and jollity,
> Braid your looks with rosy twine,
> Dropping odours, dropping wine.

However this did not prevent Camille Bellaigue from identifying in the music something 'a bit topless' (un peu débraillé).[14] And Bruno Barilli, dreaming of *Traviata*, could muse,[15]

> You can sense amid the sleepy echoes wafting in the air the soft rustle of clothes being taken off, of combs and pins and wispy bits of whalebone springing from corsets. And then you seem to hear the sigh of a husky and tear-laden voice, and the quiver of a ripe bosom leaping free of its clasps—and with a rich, downward swish of gauze, the slither of a warm petticoat as it drops to the floor.

But undertones of D. H. Lawrence aside, it is quite certain that Verdi

was not seeking to shock or titillate, being quite happy enough with a
musicabile plot, *avant-garde* though it may have been in the 1850s. If we
turn to the novel of Dumas, we read this of Marguerite's supper party (as
recalled by Armand):

> At this supper we ate, drank and were merry. It wasn't long before the
> blue jokes and four-letter words began . . . much relished by Nanine,
> Prudence and Marguerite. Gaston too was thoroughly amused. I tried
> to turn a deaf ear and a blind eye to what was going on, and to join in
> the fun that seemed part and parcel of the meal; but I gradually
> detached myself and left my glass untouched. I was quite upset
> watching this pretty young thing of only twenty drinking away,
> using the language of a bargee, and laughing more and more loudly as
> the stories got dirtier.

At the play one will listen in vain for any smut. The gaiety is
inconsequential and forced—mere padding (to tell the truth) and dull
enough to be tiresome. Operatic convention has certainly given the
scene a face-lift, taking it altogether out of the uncertain hands of Dumas
and planting it firmly in the world of musical entertainment. When
Alfredo Germont, abandoning his initial shyness, takes the central
position on the stage and limbers up for the brindisi, we are teetering on
the edge of the realm of Offenbach. But when the tune starts—that tune
with the uplift that launched young Victor Gollancz on a lifetime of
Verdi-worship (and goodness knows how many thousand others)—
then we are really at the heart of Italian Opera. Its sturdy 3/8 pulses
unerringly beneath Alfredo's stanzas. This he sings *con grazia, leggerissimo*
and with repeated *pp* reminders that it is not so much a boisterous
drinking song as an invitation to love. For Alfredo has one eye on the
general company and the other on Violetta, whom he toasts openly.

It was at this point that Geraldine Farrar once, in a provincial German
opera house, casting aside her champagne glass in order to take Alfredo's
hand, inadvertently threw it down into the prompter's box, and next
morning was presented with a bill for breakages—25 pfennig.[16]

For all the élan of this brindisi, with its enthusiastic choral refrain, the
real moment of impact is Violetta's taking up of the second verse. This is
as piquant as it is unexpected. Operatic drinking songs are usually for
solo voice. Violetta's intervention saves it from being a static number
and swings it right into the unfolding drama, particularly when, after the
guests have transposed the tune down a fifth, she lifts it again in a short,

intimate dialogue exchange with her impetuous wooer, her vivacity being neatly answered by his persistence. This rescues the brindisi from flourishing as a musical item detached from the score. It is welded in securely. It has not often been singled out for a separate gramophone record, though Caruso, who recorded no other excerpt from the opera, did the brindisi with Alma Gluck. The late Sir Victor Gollancz, who clearly held it in high esteem (once mentioning the music in the same breath as a Bach violin concerto), recalled this record as being by Caruso and Farrar.[17] But it was Gluck; and his memory continued to wobble when he added to his list of favourites one of the Nile Duet by Zenatello and Destinn. How collectors would have loved this! They never made it. . . .

With the brindisi joyously concluded, Violetta's hired band starts up in her adjacent ballroom. Curiously, its sounds seem to mystify her guests, who unanimously enquire 'What is that?' When Violetta invites them to come dancing they all comment 'What a good idea! We'd love it!' Not often can an operatic chorus have to utter anything more inept. Piave seems to be nodding, for hardly have they reached the communicating doors when they are arrested by a cry from their hostess who is 'smitten by sudden paleness'. How he expected a prima donna to carry out this stage instruction one can only wonder. No doubt the florid Fanny Salvini-Donatelli on that unhappy night in Venice made very little of it. But as Violetta is obliged to sit down we can all assume that something has come over her without bothering to check up on whether she has succeeded in turning pale as Piave would have her do. At any rate the guests are persuaded to carry on dancing. Their distressed hostess is left to cope with her personal problems alone (but of course not quite alone, for Alfredo, most concerned, has remained behind).

The waltz then comes into its own, swinging along for over 30 bars without any singing. We can catch glimpses of the swirling couples in the ballroom; while Violetta, in pathetic contrast, stares at her reflection in a mirror and remarks how pale she looks. Her conversation with the deeply concerned Alfredo is neatly superimposed on the waltz, which has several themes and excellently conveys the spirit of enjoyment denied to the unhappy hostess and ignored by her loyal admirer. This is certainly more dramatic than in the play, where Gaston sits at the piano, starts playing a polka for the party to dance to, until Marguerite after a few steps is unable to continue. She asks for water and suggests the others go into the next room, leaving her to get over it. Indeed the selfish

Prudence expresses her irritation as she goes. So Armand and Marguerite have their first intimate conversation. It is not highlighted, as in Verdi, by the sounds of revelry. We soon forget Gaston, Saint-Gaudens, Olympe and Prudence as the long dialogue unfolds. But the skill of Dumas prompts one slight break and reminder. He brings Prudence back after a while to ask what on earth the two are up to. Marguerite says they are just coming, and Prudence withdraws. This little intrusion is lifted into the opera by Piave, but it is Gastone who appears at the door, enquires, laughs, and retires. Spike Hughes thinks this is pointless;[18] but it could be a necessary link, however tenuous, between the merry guests and their missing hostess. Hofmannsthal later employed a similar piece of stagecraft when he brought in Faninal and the Marschallin to interrupt briefly the final duet of the young lovers. Pure stagecraft it is; elaborately rococo in the Strauss opera, swift and straightforward in the Verdi. In each, a point is made.

Before the interruption by Gastone we have been listening to the duet 'Un di felice, eterea'. This is Verdi at the top of his form, showing us two people with entirely opposite approaches to the same problem, and therefore having totally different music. The earnest Alfredo sings of his love *con espansione*. All the interest is in his vocal line, which is almost a serenade with the barest orchestral foundation. The wayward Violetta replies *brillante*, with near-coloratura embroidered into her tune, patterned with flute and clarinet. His passionate approach and her elusive denial are deftly interwoven as he persists with his emotional phrase while her triplets ripple away like shallow surface reflections of his ardour, a metallic glitter rejecting his romantic glow. His almost Swinburnian obsession with 'croce e delizia' is firmly rebuffed by her mercurial repudiation of all things deep and permanent. We are captivated, and it really does require the jovial intrusion of Gastone to remind us that there are many others under the same roof, romping away full of *delizia* and quite free of *croce*. Indeed we probably did not notice that the waltz stopped as soon as Alfredo began his declaration of love. Now, on Gastone's appearance at the door, the band starts up again, though its repertoire must be somewhat limited, for it plays the same old number for the next dance.

However, it breaks up the lyricism of the tenor and the soprano, who now revert to snatches of conversation. Alfredo is about to leave. Violetta plucks a flower from her corsage and hands it to him. In the play it is specifically a camellia: in the opera, just a flower. No camellias for

Miss Valery. . . . Even the play side-stepped the clinical innuendo of the novel, in which the reader has already learnt that Marguerite always wore a bunch of white camellias, except at certain recurrent periods when she exchanged them for red ones. At this crucial point in the story they are red. Armand asks, 'When shall I see you again?' 'When this camellia changes colour,' she replies cryptically. 'And when will it change colour?' 'Between eleven and twelve tomorrow night.' Such *badinage dérobé*, though indigenous to French literature, even Dumas could not repeat on the stage. Had Piave tried, ever so slyly, to work it into his libretto, Verdi would certainly have had none of it. But *La Dame aux Camélias* loses something of its demi-mondaine decadence with the excision of this insinuating motif. Violetta's dizzy pallor was perhaps not entirely due to her chronic malady. But that was quite rightly to be no business of operatic audiences.

So she tells Alfredo that he may visit her again when the flower has faded. With the ecstatic realization that this will be on the morrow, he grasps the flower and cries

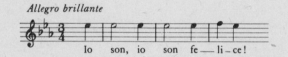

and we in the audience, at least if we are men, can suddenly share his sense of elation at the overwhelming good fortune that has come his way. Giddily he repeats the phrase, just as we would have him do and Verdi knew he would do, while the waltz swirls on to its close. In a moment Alfredo is gone and all the guests are pouring in to thank their hostess for her lovely party. Piave insists that they enter uproariously, flushed from drinking and dancing. He is hopefully opting for some realistic measure of dissipation. But Verdi merely repeats the opening music, giving them all a well-ordered crescendo (which they really ought to bungle after Violetta's champagne) and sends them packing without the slightest hint of disorder. Had Piave been reading Thackeray?[19]

The four thousand guests whirled screaming, reeling, roaring out of the ballroom in the rue St Honoré, and tore down to the column in the Place Vendôme, round which they went shrieking their own music. . . .

It was nothing in those days for parties to last all night and end with a mad, drunken *galope* in the streets. Dumas knew all about this at first hand. Verdi may have done. But in his safe hands Violetta's *fête de nuit* ends with decorum conducted in strict common time. Producers may add their dissolute snatches of horse-play; but the score trundles on regardless. In the play the tawdry little get-together ends with nothing more daring than Saint-Gaudens exclaiming that he is having a fine time, as *Prudence puts on a man's hat, Gaston a woman's, etc.* (!)

The great closing scena for Violetta is a Piave-Verdi invention, and brings a bravura climax to the act quite beyond the scope of Dumas, whose curtain-fall, as related above, is absurdly tame. When it rises again on the same interior we hear Marguerite calmly planning her romantic liaison with Armand and arranging how her rich and elderly 'protector' will finance the escapade. But in the opera Violetta Valery shows far more independence of spirit than Marguerite Gautier. Her long, brilliant set-piece is memorable for its superb portrayal of a vacillating mind. She weighs up the advantages and drawbacks of such a liaison. In her cavatina she carefully explores the possibility of a romantic entanglement. In her cabaletta she blows the idea sky-high in a burst of deliberately forced gaiety, against which Verdi has cunningly laid the *strophe* of Alfredo, singing his love-theme somewhere outside as he wanders homewards at daybreak, his head full of exciting promises, his heart bursting with impatience. The intrusion of Alfredo's voice is a musical bonus. The libretto makes no mention of it. Piave seems not to have planned it. Verdi is repeating his recent *tour de force* outside the Aliaferia dungeon, where he had achieved such a hit with Leonora on-stage and Manrico's voice floating in from the wings. Yet Violetta, although she hears Alfredo twice, does not succumb. Her irresponsible roulades bring down the curtain with the clearest possible understanding that whatever may be the young man's emotions, it will be nothing more than a brief and giddy holiday for her.

Underpinning the whole scena is Alfredo's love-theme:

He has already sung it to her; and now, left alone, she repeats it to herself. But it is an echo, an intriguing memory. She is exploring the possibility

of something she does not herself feel. This theme is a man's declaration.
Hers, the woman's 'whole existence', is expressed only in the Prelude
and once after that in the course of the opera—when she is faced with
losing him for ever:

A— ma-mi Al– fre – — do,   a — ma-mi quan-t'io t'a —— mo

a —— ma–mi Al–fre—do   quan-t'io   t'a— mo, quan-t'io   t'a———

mo   Ad — di ———— o ! . . .

These themes are inter-related. They share the same key. They start
and finish on the same notes. But whereas the course of Alfredo's is
elegant, studied and gracious, her theme by contrast soars and plunges
in that total surrender which is the crux of womanhood. Within and
around that F major octave lie both the measured gallantry of his
petitioning and the whole-hearted flood of her acceptance. As Alfredo
repeats his love-theme outside her window just as she is abandoning
herself to the easy way out—the restless search for brittle pleasures—he
would seem to be taking a calculated risk. And indeed she does not
appear to have accepted the bait, as her coloratura whirls on its axis. But
Alfredo is leaving no stone unturned. He has even procured a harp to
thrum beneath his serenade. Now where on earth did he get that? . . .

Among the several 'new' elements introduced by Verdi into Italian
Opera during the course of La Traviata is this long, full-blown aria
bringing down the curtain at the end of an act without any choral
support. To spotlight a soloist for a finale was almost an
innovation—not quite, for Rossini had done it in Cenerentola, and
perhaps other instances could be found; but here in Traviata it is
deliberately contrived for dramatic effect, and what an effect it has! Later
it would become a commonplace, particularly with the German
composers and those influenced by them. The repertoire is heaped with
great solo finales, mostly for sopranos, but not always. Against

Brünnhilde, Isolde, Aida and several Strauss heroines one can set Wotan, Falstaff, Otello, Canio, and Boris. The danger for the composer, if his solo-finale is not at the very end of the opera, is how to maintain the level when the curtain rises on the next act. In *Traviata* Verdi did not solve this problem very successfully. For at the rise of the curtain on Act II we have immediately another full-blown solo, this time for the tenor. Alfredo's aria is so inferior to Violetta's that the second act can never start without a sense of anti-climax. Furthermore, Alfredo is now happily installed in the love-nest that readers of Dumas know all about, while listeners to Verdi who do not know the story will be most surprised, for they have left Violetta carolling away about her preference for absolute freedom, 'Sempre libera . . .'

A later composer would have felt the necessity for linking the scenes with an orchestral intermezzo, something on the lines of the *Thaïs* Meditation. In the novel Armand says:

I could easily have glossed over the start of our liaison, but I wanted you to know what steps led up to it, how I agreed to all her suggestions, and she became unable to carry on without me.

The steps that led up to the liaison are fully presented to the audience in the play's second scene. But Verdi and Piave, unlike Armand in the novel, have indeed glossed it over. For here, suddenly in sporting get-up and carrying a shot-gun, he is in the country cottage Violetta has rented. His opening recitative does indeed give us a précis of how this change in his fortunes has come about. It contains one or two tender phrases, but in the main it is desiccated stuff, as is the aria which follows. That Verdi is not writing at his inspired level is only too apparent. This young man in love and living *à deux* should surely have music more rapturous than this. It is possible to argue that when he was the eager pursuer there was more passion in him than there is now, with the consummation behind. This may be accurate psychology, but it is not good romantic opera. Either Rodolfo or Manrico could have taught him what to sing under these happy circumstances. But it may also be argued that Armand is, by any social standards, something of a 'wet'; so why should Verdi's Alfredo blossom out into a Great Lover? As for the gun and the shooting-kit, this must have been borrowed by Piave from an episode towards the end of the novel when Armand, temporarily back home with his father, goes

out on a shooting party, but cannot get Marguerite out of his head. 'I was
shown where to stand,' he recalls, 'but I put down my unloaded gun and
began to day-dream.' Piave's borrowing, though it may strike us as
superfluous, may in fact add to our realization that all his leisure and
pleasure is disastrously mortgaged; for the day of reckoning is at hand.
This we soon learn, for immediately after his aria Violetta's maid Annina
comes in. Her dress betrays she has been travelling. Alfredo is curious,
and to his enquiries she replies that her mistress has sent her to Paris to sell
horses, coaches, everything. The upkeep of the household has drained
her resources. Piave and Verdi are silent about the elderly nobleman
who was coaxed into financing the project and has since withdrawn his
support. Such demi-mondaine ethics are not for their honest approach.
But Alfredo is naturally shattered, and when he learns how much
Violetta is in debt he tells Annina he is off to Paris at once to put things
right. He does not tell us how, and we may wonder, in the opera house,
how he is going to balance the budget if he has not so far made any
tangible contribution. Dumas of course explains these mundane details.
The libretto jettisons them. Alfredo pours out his remorse in a cabaletta
at the climaxes of which all the orchestra pounds vigorously as though
something really drastic is afoot. But all Alfredo is doing is telling us
(twice through) that he is thoroughly ashamed, and his sense of honour is
urging him to make immediate amends. At the conclusion of this
prolonged outburst he dashes off to Paris. One may wonder how.
Dumas, in the play, realizing that he must be marooned since the horses
and carriages have been sold, arranges for him to say he will take a cab.
Later Annina, followed by Violetta, will be leaving for Paris as well. So
however deep in the country they are, there must be a rank not far
beyond the gate.

Unfortunately for us, it is customary to omit from performances not
only Alfredo's cabaletta but the whole dialogue with Annina that leads
up to it. This senseless cut is the rule rather than the exception, and stems
from the widely held suspicion that Verdi's cabalettas (except a few
lucky ones) let the score down. It does not seem to occur to producers or
conductors that operas have words, and that when they prune the notes
they are also snipping away the sense. Even Toscanini aligned himself
with this disastrous tradition.

Straight upon Alfredo's precipitate exit Violetta comes in with
Annina, who had left the stage empty for the tenor to enjoy his cabaletta
(if permitted). She tells her mistress that he has gone to Paris but will be

back before the evening. A servant, Giuseppe, enters with a letter which
he hands to Violetta, then goes out with Annina (why did she come in at
all?). Giuseppe, incidentally, has by-passed the play, coming direct from
the novel. He was Armand's servant. ('My servant was called Joseph,' he
tells us, adding somewhat patronizingly, 'all servants seem to be called
Joseph.') But the arrival and departure both of people and of messages in
this scene are very arbitrarily handled by Piave. It is one of the most
loosely constructed scenes in any Verdi opera. In the course of a few dull
bars we must appreciate that Violetta is expecting a man 'on business';
that the letter delivered by Guiseppe is from Flora inviting her to a party
that very evening, having at last tracked her down to her secret cottage;
that she has no intention of accepting. Whereupon Giuseppe is back,
announcing the arrival of 'un signore'. Had he carried out his duties
correctly, he would have enquired the gentleman's name and business
and conveyed them to Violetta. In the play Nanine makes the same
error. So Violetta, assuming it is her lawyer arriving for his
appointment, is taken back when a complete stranger walks in. It is
Alfredo's father, and now Verdi really has to pull himself together, for
on his stage are two proud protagonists who must battle it out mightily.

We are on the threshold of one of the longest duets that Verdi ever
wrote, and it must be agreed that Piave, with a straightforward scene of
Dumas to adapt, has produced an excellent slice of libretto for Verdi to
work on. This is one of the great duologues of the operatic world. Lifted
from the prose of the play to the lyrico-heroic plane of the opera it
becomes like one of those marvellous scenes of Elizabethan dramatic
poetry that so ennoble the pages of Shakespeare and his best
contemporaries. How coldly, disdainfully calculating are its opening
gambits, studiously exchanged without any accompaniment save an
occasional punctuating chord! This tense orchestral silence lies between
two phrases played with deliberation by all the strings. The first,

Allegro

ushers Germont in, bourgeois, condescending and pompous. One cannot
but recall a like entry—that of Ochs into the Marschallin's boudoir. In

three bars we have a fine miniature of calculated self-assurance. The second,

depicts that studied control suddenly rocked off balance as Germont reads the receipts that show who has been keeping whom. We catch a glimpse of his mind, fortified by pride, yet insecure in the presence of a female he thought would be transparent but whom he already finds himself unable to see through. In between these two string phrases lie the tentatively sparring exchanges as they face each other, unaccompanied—a passage less for the conductor than the producer. For this is dramatic dialogue alive with nuances. The very opening words of Germont,

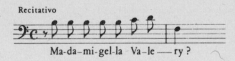

carry a sort of inconclusive hesitancy. As though it is distasteful for him to pronounce the name Valery, he drops from D right down to F. In ordinary dry recitative he might have simply reverted to B, or gone up a semitone. But this drop of a sixth is a cunning piece of craftsmanship by Verdi, and gives father Germont a subtle start to his rôle. He is solid and ultra-respectable. He has never so much as spoken to a courtesan before,

and for all his outward show of composure he is ill at ease. The phrase
lets us into this secret. But we soon learn more; for when he has perused
Violetta's papers he lets slip the truth he must have intended to
conceal—that he is at heart a sentimental old thing:

Ah il pas—sa—to   perchè,perchè v'ac—cu—sa!

The lyrical style and aroma of this phrase will recur as the duet unfolds.
Having thus revealed himself, he has no great difficulty in slipping into
his first stanza, 'Pura siccome un angelo'.

It was traditional in the French theatre for M. Duval to show his moral
superiority and contempt for his son's ill-chosen mistress. Entering the
house, he would take off his hat, but on finding that it is Marguerite to
whom he was speaking, he would ostentatiously put it back on his head.
This so incensed the critic Sarcey that he claimed to have cried out,
'Remove your hat! Don't you see who it is you are talking to? It's Mlle.
Sarah Bernhardt!'[20] The opera house took up this tradition, as amusingly
reported by Bernard Shaw:[21]

> He (Maurel) came in rudely with his hat on; and when he found that
> Violetta had a noble soul, he took the hat off, like a gentleman, and
> put it on a chair. I instantly foresaw that Albani, when next overcome
> by emotion, would sit on it. So breathless became my anticipation
> that I could hardly attend the intervening duet. At last she did sit on it;
> and never would that hat have graced Maurel's temples again if it had
> been historically accurate. This, then, I presume, is the explanation of
> the anachronism on Maurel's part. Albani must have refused to give
> up the business of sitting on Germont's hat, thereby forcing him to
> adopt one that would bend but not break under an exceptional
> pressure of circumstances. . . .

The opening gambits over, Germont proceeds to enlarge on his
daughter's coming marriage and tells how her fiancé will break off their
engagement rather than acquire a brother-in-law who brings shame on
the family by so scandalous an absence from its bosom. With admirable
composure he refrains from expressing the charge that his son is not only

living *with* a prostitute but actually *on* her earnings. In a stanza that is openly sentimental he dwells on his daughter's future rather than his son's present. The tune derives expansively from the phrase quoted on page 267 as Germont brings simplicity to bear on what is a complex problem. In the play M. Duval puts forward his argument with reasoned logic. Piave cuts across all this with the charming, if unlikely, phrase

> Deh non mutate in triboli
> Le rose dell'amor.

But it carries a fine irony perhaps lost on Piave. For what Germont asks Violetta not to do to his daughter is precisely what he himself is proposing to do to his son.

The dramatic result of this straightforward plea is marvellously handled by Verdi. A comfortable tune played by the violins in the manner of Donizetti tells us that Violetta is generously disposed to listen to him, and to leave Alfredo alone for a while. But as soon as Germont hints that he has further demands, the music accelerates until everything is thrown into a deperate *tutta forza* of resistance. A significant *pausa lunga* enables the distraught Violetta to recover and begin her 'Non sapete' section which, with its broken phrases and orchestral punctuation during the rests, admirably conveys her mounting agitation. Then as realization grows she becomes overwhelmed by the unpalatable truth and bursts out in the passage marked *ancora più vivo*. Here, letting her emotions rip over an orchestral surge that includes all three trombones, cimbasso, and timpani a-roll, she suddenly fills the theatre with a streaming nobility of sound far beyond the confines of any previous Verdi heroine.

Germont, bowled over by what he has triggered off, answers with a repeated phrase that sounds heavy after her glorious outburst:

But he too is given a *pausa lunga* in which to collect his wits, and he is soon continuing his persistent arguments. His new mode of attack is to probe into the future. What hope will she have, when time has sapped her sexual ripeness, of retaining the love of a man not united to her in the eyes of heaven? It is an argument that would carry no weight today; but put in the mouth of an upright, unimaginative provincial, a god-fearing, frock-coated, respectable bourgeois gentilhomme, it comes both naturally and inevitably. The tune Verdi gives Germont here carries the marking *con semplicità*. But though simple, it is by no means naïve. These are deliberate tactics. Through the stanza runs, with variations, a figure:

The prominence of this may almost irritate us, but it is clearly meant to work on Violetta in the manner of a Chinese water-torture—wearing down her resistance. This it does; and her sad 'Così alla misera' with its oboe and deep pizzicato is one of the most moving moments in the score. Here, really, is her surrender, her tragic climax. The serenity of 'Dite alla giovane' communicates the peace of mind she has found on making her decision; but it is this flood of womanly resignation after Germont's insinuating jabs that clutches our emotions in the theatre. Germont has thrown her, wrestling within the rules, yet by a moral foul.

Has she thrown in the towel too soon? That same Francisque Sarcey who objected so vehemently to M. Duval's hat wrote that if he had been Dumas *fils* he would have made her reply,[22]

Come now, you silly old man, you won't get me to believe that a girl isn't able to be married because her brother has a mistress and is having fun with a pick-up! You must take me for an absolute goose!

O that Marguerite had answered thus, and Violetta too!

In her touching *andantino* she sings her lovely rising and falling tune against the barest rhythmic accompaniment; but when Germont comes in with his *piangi, piangi* the woodwind section supports him. The scoring is carefully detailed as though Verdi is trying to ensure that Germont is fairly treated in a scene throughout which the audience is certain to be rooting for Violetta. But against her *fil di voce* his insistent baritone cannot but carry with it the overtones of a bully who has put his weapon down only because he has already won his fight.

From here to the end of the duet we marvel at the dignity, restraint, and refinement of this *donna traviata*; and really all Germont can do is mouth platitudes of grateful sympathy. Expansively, with full orchestral backing, he acknowledges her generosity and asks what he can do in return. Over a thrummed pizzicato she talks of death. We are suddenly aware of the tragedy his interference has set in motion. Whatever fine sentiments he expresses now will be all in vain. He has killed not only his son's liaison but his mistress too. Her pathetic phrase 'Conosca il sacrifizio che consumai d'amore' borrows a pale, sad reflection of his own first expression of humanity (page 267). Once again there is a *pausa lunga*, which has almost achieved the status of a non-motif. This splendid final *allegro* concludes, as it started, with a measured exchange of short, telling phrases—single words, some of them—punctuated rather than accompanied, galvanizing the audience into attentive silence. So the broken Violetta and the embarrassed Germont part; her romance shattered, his Pyrrhic victory won.

Many have been intrigued by the fascinating possibility that when Verdi composed this duet he was only too conscious of his affair with Giuseppina Strepponi and his father-in-law Barezzi's disapproval of it. We may think it inconceivable that he and Peppina could have attended Dumas' play in Paris without savouring its romantic affinity with their own position. They had taken a small country house at Passy. Armand and Marguerite did likewise at Auteuil, the next place down the Seine beyond Passy. This scene in the play must have reminded them of their own riverside hideaway. *La Dame aux Camélias* was much relished by unmarried lovers, among whom we can with certainty include Verdi and his ex-singer. With what irreverent amusement they may have looked upon the unsympathetic Duval, disapproving exactly as Barezzi seems to have done of a liaison which violated his provincial code of morality. Verdi wrote, in the course of his famous letter to Barezzi (dated 21 January 1852),[23]

> In my house lives a lady. . . . Neither I nor she owes an account of our actions to anyone.

In the novel of Dumas Marguerite writes (of Duval's visit),

I had to remind him that I was in my own house, and I did not owe
an account of my life to him. . . .

This youthful attitude of revolt against parental 'narrow-mindedness'
Peppina and her lover may have deliciously shared with Marguerite and
Armand. The late Frank Walker went so far as to detect in Peppina's
letters 'a melancholy, sick-room atmosphere not unlike that of the last
act of *La Traviata*'.[24] This is perhaps excessive seeking for parallels. But
we cannot help recalling that Verdi's first wife once pawned her jewels
when the rent could not be met, just as Marguerite Gautier found herself
compelled to do. The composer must surely have remembered this, and
perhaps it is one of the reasons why La Traviata's name did not become
Margherita. . . .

Verdi possessed nothing of the complex that could produce *Intermezzo*
and the *Sinfonia Domestica*. A passing awareness there must have been,
when he and Peppina read Dumas' novel and saw his play, that they
themselves had had first-hand experience of some of the situations
described therein. Of course all creative artists draw on their own
memories of life, on their acquaintances and environment, their
pleasures and pains. But Verdi's *Traviata* was never conceived as a
manifesto or proclamation on behalf of extra-marital passion, or against
the stodgy interference of 'square' parents. Verdi's music, quite devoid
of sexual dalliance or rebellious spite, simply deals with a dramatic
conflict, as it did in every one of his operas. That is why the music of
Giorgio Germont is so steady and restrained that Varesi, the creator of
the rôle, found it too boring. His dislike was its testimonial; for its
transparent, bourgeois tunes aptly hit off the old-fashioned provincial
citizen to whom Paris spells Babylon. One is tempted to recall how
Strauss was ill at ease with his Jochanaan and openly confessed his muse
to be out of touch with 'holy Joseph'. One may suspect that Verdi, only
recently demobilized from being the 'helmeted musician', had to
struggle to provide tunes for Germont Senior that would be palatable to
his public, which expected his baritone at least to carry a sword, if not to
draw it. But the homely airs of Germont are the musical equivalent of
'plain speaking', and their persuasiveness carries the day with Violetta.
The key-note of their long duet is restraint. When Violetta's emotions
burst out of this restraint we are not only all the more moved by her
predicament, but we also appreciate the more the unflappable self-
control of Alfredo's father. Verdi's music ensures this. He has not only

directed his baritone to sing *con semplicità*, he has composed his part *con semplicità* as well.

With the departure of the elder Germont Piave and Verdi begin again to get into difficulties with their stage business. Violetta scribbles a letter during four orchestral bars, rings for her maid Annina and tells her to deliver it herself. Annina expresses surprise ('oh!') on reading the address. We in the audience are more surprised that Violetta has had time even to write the address, let alone the note it accompanies. We of course are supposed to know what it is all about, though Verdi and his librettist have not given us the slightest clue. So poor Annina, who has already been sent to Paris once in this scene by Alfredo, is now summarily despatched thither again by Violetta, who then proceeds to write another letter. This one, obviously, will be for Alfredo, though she does not openly tell us so. A solo clarinet plays while she writes; and what it plays could be a dirge-like variation on part of the brindisi. 'Nessun maggior dolore. . .'

But Alfredo comes in, having returned from Paris. The agitated strings quiver with Violetta's confusion, as she hides her letter from him. But he has had another letter—from his father, whose arrival he now expects. This somewhat unsatisfactory spate of letters is to be found in Dumas' play. But the spoken word can gloss around the awkwardness with comments and explanations unattractive to a précis-minded librettist, who treats it all tersely. At this point Verdi fully makes up in that superb passage of love and farewell for his heroine which is one of the most glorious meteors in the operatic firmament (page 262).

It may be thought strange and a little disappointing that the first months of Verdi's open union with Giuseppina should have produced nothing more inspired than *I Lombardi* re-hashed into *Jérusalem* and the generally abused *Il Corsaro*. Yet it is precisely here that we can find the swelling bud of Violetta's inflorescence, in the orchestral prelude to Medora's aria in *Il Corsaro*. Soffredini noticed this, but proceeded to compare it unfavourably with the mature outpouring of Violetta.[25] Nevertheless, the phrase is an expression of loyalty and devotion. Medora's, played by strings, is shown opposite. It introduces her harp-accompanied song (overheard by Corrado) which is closely adapted from Byron. In fact Byron's third verse,

Remember me—Oh! pass not thou my grave
Without one thought whose relics there recline;

The only pang my bosom dare not brave
Must be to find forgetfulness in thine

strangely pre-echoes the pathos of abandoned Marguerite-Violetta. Her
full-throated love-cry is the passionate blossoming of that melancholy
phrase floating from where poor Medora 'loved and sung'.

When Violetta has left the stage after this emotional climax, we in the
theatre are so overwhelmed that our hearts go out with her, and we
cannot help it that our eyes are idly bent on the wretched Alfredo,
thinking his prattle to be tedious.

And what, indeed, does Alfredo do at this climacteric in his personal
drama? *He sits and opens a book!* This may astonish us, but it is borrowed
from Dumas. However Dumas, with a Parisian audience to understand
his story, explains that Armand is thumbing through *Manon Lescaut*.
When he finds the passage he wants he reads it aloud, and it contains a
pointed parallel with his own affairs. In the novel it was the dead
Marguerite's copy of *Manon Lescaut* coming under the hammer at the
auction that triggered off the entire tale. Dumas could not resist bringing
this book, whose story was related to his own, into his play. Piave either
missed the point or decided that Italian audiences would not appreciate
it. Puccini was not even born!

So Alfredo spends four bars silently contemplating a book—*any* book, then fidgets and looks at the clock, wondering whether his father will come after all. To him enters Giuseppe *frettoloso*. The strings agitate as he tells Alfredo that Violetta has left for Paris in a carriage that was waiting for her, Annina having already gone ahead. (How did Violetta suddenly get hold of this carriage, having sold her own?) Piave is rapidly losing his grip on details, for he now has to bring in a special messenger with a note just given him by a lady in a carriage. Alfredo tears it open nervously, almost deserted by Verdi who throws in a scatter of perfunctory string chords and tremolos. Then, as the truth dawns, the whole orchestra floods for seven bars as the father returns and embraces his son. Here Dumas brings down the curtain, having managed the business of Violetta's departure and note very much better; for he has retained Prudence as well as Nanine, thus having an extra character to play with. Verdi and Piave, however, skating over the thin ice of their wobbly scenario, settle down to a final scene of their own contriving.

Alfredo sits down with his elbows on the table and his head in his hands while his father coaxes him by calling up memories of his abandoned home in Provence, the bright sun and the Mediterranean which he has given up in exchange for dishonour. He has brought sorrow to his father and has cast a shadow over the household. Such is the gist of his appeal, set to a sentimental, disarming tune which is sung twice through, embellished with *acciaccature* which are also echoed in the woodwind accompaniment, as though insinuating his appeal to his son. But Alfredo remains immobile throughout. Here is no splendid tenor-baritone duet; instead, a tableau of doubtful plausibility. Alfredo is behaving like a spoilt child; his father is coming very close to making a fool of himself. For 'Di Provenza' surely wanders uncomfortably near to the borderline beyond which live those songs whose sentimentality is an embarrassment to listen to. Small wonder that, when his two verses are done, he has to add as an anti-climax not without its funny side: 'Have you no answer to your father's love?' This suddenly stings Alfredo to cry out: 'A thousand serpents are eating my breast! Go away!' and then, as his father protests, he adds the important aside 'Ah it was Douphol!'

This is one of those curiosities typical of Piave and accepted by Verdi in which a crucial link or allusion is thrown away in an odd bar or two. We are to understand that Alfredo suddenly suspects that Violetta has left him for Douphol. But the name Douphol has not previously been uttered in the course of the opera; so unless we have studied the *personaggi* we will not know what he means by 'Ah it was Douphol!' He is in fact the Baron who, at Violetta's party, expressed his distaste for Alfredo and then refused to sing the brindisi when invited. But then he was always referred to as *barone*.

It is now time for Giorgio Germont's cabaletta, for musically it is his due. This cabaletta is almost always omitted from performance. The producer either considers that by now everyone has had enough of these Germonts, or has decided that the music is inferior and the scene ends better without it. On the former count he is possibly right; on the latter definitely not. The sudden cessation of argument after 'Di Provenza' never sounds natural; for the very shape of things cries out for such a climax as only a cabaletta can give. There is no chorus to round off the scene, and no tenor-baritone duet to bring down the curtain; for Verdi has decided that the father shall be persistent and garrulous, and the son by contrast inarticulate. Furthermore, its excision robs us of a telling bridge passage of four bars in which the first and second violins play in thirds a sudden theme so at variance with what is going on that we may wonder how Verdi came to insert it. But surely it is Violetta-music. While the Germont men stand on the stage at odds and out of sympathy with each other, this serene phrase steals like a bitter-sweet smile, a fleeting wisp of Grasse perfume elusively wafted above their heads and beyond their reach. . . .

It is fragmentary, momentary, for at once Giorgio Germont is at it again, coaxing his son in a two-verse cabaletta to come home again to domestic happiness. But he is still up to his persuasive tricks; for throughout his music he continues using (almost abusing) a variant of that phrase (page 269) with which he so persistently worked on Violetta in his duet with her. But on Alfredo it has no effect. For no sooner is his second verse finished than his totally inattentive son spots the letter which Violetta received early in the scene and cries out 'She is at the party! I'm off to get even with her!' And he is gone. Once again Piave has asked us to surmise the contents of some undivulged correspondence. As for Alfredo's father, he goes in pursuit. But if Verdi had been faithful to Dumas, we should never have seen him again. He went back to his country home. But an operatic baritone cannot disappear thus when there are still two important scenes ahead. So we follow both the Germonts *alla festa*.

The *festa* both gains and loses by being blown up to operatic proportions. In the play Olympe is having a party in her 'elegant salon', where her guests cannot be expected to vie in glitter and performance with an operatic chorus. Verdi and his music can magnify the occasion. In the novel Olympe's ball plays a rather different part. Armand goes to it with the deliberate intention of letting Marguerite observe him negotiating openly with his hostess whom he describes as 'plus belle que Marguerite'. Indeed, her 'gorge éblouissante' gives promise of pneumatic bliss; and he takes a cruel pleasure in wounding Marguerite (who is with Varville) by his blatant pursuit of Olympe. Marguerite, very pale, goes home. There is no baccarat, no confrontation with Varville, no flinging of winnings at her feet. All this Dumas invented for his play, and Verdi follows it closely, once the musical padding is over. What he and Piave have invented for themselves is a new dramatic continuity to the story. There is a time-lag in both novel and play; but Flora's party is that very evening and Alfredo goes straight to it from the country retreat. This is why the next scene properly belongs to the same act, and it is wrong to call it Act III as is so often done. The libretto makes better theatre, and obviously helps us to accept Giorgio Germont's intrusion into Flora's salon. He is still hot on the scent. What we do lose is the necessary insinuation that Violetta is now established as Douphol's mistress, and has consequently earned by her professional services the redemption of horses, carriages, jewels, etc., recently pawned for Alfredo's maintenance. She has now pawned her heart for the luxury of Douphol's purse, and this is an important facet to the cruel dilemma in which she has been placed by old Germont's interference.

The operatic version plunges us straight into the garish demi-monde complete with private cabaret and casino. We are spared the artificially constructed conversation that Dumas had to invent for Saint-Gaudens, Anais, Prudence and the like. Verdi's pleasantly innocuous choruses take its place; and if they are not quite what one would have looked for chez Marie Duplessis, Thérèse de Paiva, Alice Ozy, or Cora Pearl, there is really not much else that Verdi could have done to entertain us pending the arrival of Alfredo alone followed closely by Violetta on the arm of Baron Douphol.

At this point a new tension is injected into the score. Hitherto the opera has been either jolly or sentimental, with one or two brief emotional outbursts. Now there are strained relations, brittle conflicts, snapping tempers. Alfredo and his old cronies sit down at the card table and begin to gamble intently, while Flora greets the newly-arrived Violetta and Baron Douphol, the latter noticing Alfredo and urging Violetta not on any account to speak to him. Our attention is momentarily drawn from the card game by their conversation with Flora and each other. Then, as though a studio camera has been swung from one group to another, we find ourselves concentrating on Alfredo and his mounting luck, for he is winning and boasting of his prowess and good fortune. Then the baron, hearing a reference to his new and jealously guarded mistress, joins Alfredo and challenges him to a game. The baron and Alfredo now assume the central position of our interest. Alfredo continues to win, first 100 louis, then 200. Fortunately for the baron, a servant announces supper, and all go to the next room, Alfredo and the baron still exchanging correct but sub-acid courtesies. The whole of this scene is carried on over a restless foundation of orchestral bristling, a persistent nagging of strings in 6/8 like an *idée fixe*. It is a masterly inspiration, seeming to catch all the characters in a vice and hold them firmly, writhe and gesticulate how they will. Only Violetta remains partially outside this captured group. Three times she sings a long phrase of her own, expressing her anguished misgivings; but this is not the prima donna's moment, and the conductor should restrain her from dragging out Verdi-heroine climaxes for herself. Alfredo is of course behaving very badly, but one notices with passing sympathy how, when he brags that he will use his winnings to return to the country (taking Violetta away with him) he sings a phrase that recalls his moment of excitement when she first gave him the flower from her bosom:

When all have gone in to supper except Alfredo and the baron, while the nagging theme in the orchestra still persists, Douphol's suppressed anger is remarkably suggested by his singing only the note C, as though holding himself back from exploding. Then they join the others, and the gambling theme dies away, *ppp*, to be replaced by an uprush of strings and a great *tutti* crash as Violetta comes back into the salon, followed by Alfredo, whom she has called to join her alone.

Verdi immediately pulls off another *coup*. Hot on the rhythmic structure of the gambling scene he now gives the strings another insistent, pulsing foundation for the hectic conversation between Alfredo and Violetta. Not long after composing *Traviata* Verdi wrote to Somma about *Re Lear*, 'It is extremely difficult, when writing nothing but dialogue, to put across its effect in music.'[26] Difficult he may have found it, but no one can say he did not here find a workable formula. In the first act Alfredo and Violetta could converse over the strains of a waltz being played by a band in the next room. But here there can be no such device. Their dialogue, just as the previous dialogue among the card players and those watching them, has to be thrashed out musically in a structure that is superior in fluidity to mere recitative. The problem is brilliantly solved. The orchestra throbs on as they exchange phrase after phrase in growing desperation. Everything is taut and tense. Again we have the impression of characters caught in shifting quicksands that will not let them go; when all of a sudden Alfredo extricates himself by shouting to the other guests to come and join him. An orchestral *tutti* brings them in. He has his desired limelight now:

Then he launches into the angry tune that, though delayed, has been inevitable.

His leap up of a sixth and back again on 'tal femmina' conveys desperation. Amneris will make the same leap up when confronting the priests after the trial of Radames. The ensuing stanza, though directed in cowardly fashion at a defenceless woman, brings out some show of spirit. Alfredo's anger is certainly more notable than his romantic dalliance. Hardly portrayed as one of opera's more attractive lovers, he surely wins a prize for impetuous tantrums. His mounting scorn is admirably put over within the framework of this short *arioso*, short because, like a bad lover, he cannot control himself, and just as his music is getting exciting he hurls his winnings at the feet of the fainting Violetta and his spent rage is drowned in the swift and sonorous comments of the ensemble. At which point his father comes in.

The appearance of Giorgio Germont amid these Parisian frolics has often been stigmatized as ridiculous. His presence, without invitation, in a private house full of upper-crust prostitutes and their titled clients is always a butt for the shafts of those who look for the ridiculous in opera. But although Dumas sent him home for ever after the country-house scene, Piave and Verdi had over-riding reasons for bringing him on. He is no Athanael bent on the conversion of a fallen woman; he is out to recapture the affections of his own wayward son, hot on whose heels he has dashed to Paris. Obviously he has seen Alfredo enter Flora's house, and he sees no reason in the world why he should not fetch him out. Musically, of course, there must still be a primo baritono for the big finale. The confrontation between outraged father and outrageous son is a dramatic moment of considerable interest. And how well Verdi has dealt with it!

Hard on the exasperation of the ensemble comes Germont's lone voice, *con dignitoso fuoco*. At first his phrases, broken by his own emotion, are punctuated by string *pizzicato*. Then as he collects his self-control, the strings are bowed to give him surer support, a device as simple as it is deft. But Verdi has not turned him into a ranting baritone; he is still the sentimental, open-hearted provincial. In his phrase, marked *grandioso*:

we can detect the substance, if not quite the melody, of 'Di Provenza il mar, il suol'. Alfredo's remorse is expressed in striking contrast, with a series of shamefaced ejaculations, each unaccompanied save for the last two notes under which the strings jab tersely as though depicting his father's frowns:

Ah si! che fe - ci!   ne sento orrore!   Gelosa smania, de-lu-so amore

The rebuke and the self-pity are two short but powerful solos, spotlighted on the threshold of the great finale, which starts with a general comment out of which breaks Violetta's poignant plea. But in the bars before her 'Alfredo, Alfredo' we should notice how Verdi has striven to preserve the *hauteur* of the insulted Baron Douphol with a vocal line all his own. The finale is beyond praise, a moving element which only opera can give to such a story. Though superficially similar to the big ensemble in *Macbeth*, its details are richer. The chorus does not swallow up all the minor characters. The sadness of Flora and Gastone can be separately traced. The baron, the marquis and the doctor get together while the chorus makes its own staccato comments without, until the very end, soaking up anyone else's part. Under Violetta's exquisite top line Alfredo repeats his dejected monotone. Then, by a subtle arrangement he sings a rising phrase in unison with his father, only to continue it in unison with Violetta, as if torn between his loyalties (see opposite). Somewhere along the line, not specified in the libretto, Baron Douphol strikes Alfredo with his glove or makes some such gesture to indicate that a duel will follow. We know from the story that Alfredo won this duel and wounded the baron. We may guess, from our operatic acquaintance with the two gentlemen, that it carried with it no great feat of arms.

The contrast between the final curtain of the second act and the opening of the last is one of the operatic theatre's most moving experiences. Verdi would repeat in *Don Carlo*, and more strikingly in *Otello*, this device of following a full ensemble-finale with an emotional prelude leading to a tragic solo. But here in *Traviata* he seems to excel over the others by harking back to the first notes of the opera and bringing us once again that passage scored for sixteen violins divided into four parts which so achingly expresses the pity and the terror of the heroine's inner decay. 'Poor and pale, consumptive music,' wrote Chorley with brittle contempt.[27] What a splendid epitaph for Violetta and diploma for Verdi!

From the rise of the curtain to the end of 'Addio del passato' a sustained elegiac sadness persists. The score abounds in careful instructions for the deployment, not only of the solo violins, but the violas and violoncellos, while the wind instruments, particularly during the aria, are deftly and delicately chosen. Here Verdi comes nearest to the intimacy of *La Dame aux Camélias* which is the novel's special quality. Here, by his flow of melody and refined scoring he paints the fear of death and the horror of loneliness which made up this girl's tragedy. The true pathos of Marguerite Gautier's story lies in the macabre auction sale of her worldly treasures, which surrounded her useless while she wasted away on her death-bed, while her relentless creditors waited without. Jules Janin tells us of an antique clock 'which had struck the hour for Mme Pompadour and yet again for Mme du Barry'; of Buhl cabinets, Sèvres china, and a host of ornaments and figurines in bronze, enamel and terra-cotta, not to mention paintings and furniture.[28] All the more was she to be pitied, dying there amid the silent mockery of all the choice luxuries no longer of avail to her, all acquired by the salacious mortgaging of that body which death was now moving to foreclose.

Although in his play Dumas depicts Marguerite reduced to loneliness and poverty at the end, and Verdi does not contradict this, the opera usually fails, by reason of its large stage, to convey anything like death in a garret for Violetta. She is no drab little Mimi. The pathos and wastage of her decline are physical rather than financial, and how mournfully this is conveyed by the music, particularly if she is allowed both verses of 'Addio del passato'! Its truncation is inexcusable. All through these pages there lurks an uneasy sense of doom. Though the dying Violetta laments that

> There'll be no tears when I am in my grave;
> No flowers, nor cross, nor epitaph I'll have,

we cannot but think of Montmartre cemetery, of Dumas' ghoulish exhumation, of the marble tomb of the real Alphonsine Duplessis and the flowers that people still put there because of her sad story imperishably enshrined by Dumas and by Verdi. In these pages of the opera we suddenly become aware, as we never did in the previous acts however sumptuously staged, of all *la fille entretenue*'s glamorous equipage and the physical intimacies that procured it.

> Addio, del passato bei sogni ridenti . . .

The haunting oboe tells us wearily that the unsubstantial pageant is
faded, and her little life is rounded with a sleep. The scene in fact is
rounded with a chorus in the street down below. This chorus is an
operatic device, piquant in that it serves to contrast the careless carnival
revels with the grim interior of impending death. Music can readily be
adapted to this. It must be admitted, though, that Verdi does not seem to
have applied himself very studiously to its actual composition. However,
the chorus shambles past with all the evanescent foolery of a Mardi Gras
parade, with the prize ox led in fancy-dressed procession. But a sinister
thought arises. For as we detect the effervescent rattle of tabours and
tambourines, we recall how they were used in the cabaret at Flora's
party. Does this rabble of revellers include those prostitutes and wastrels
who have already demonstrated their pleasure at dressing up and
performing antics and singing about the fat ox of Paris? Is Gastone down
there in the street? And Flora? And D'Obigny and Douphol? Are they
all passing by on the other side, while Violetta dies?

After this the orchestral excitement which heralds the arrival of
Alfredo acts as a tonic, if a bitter-sweet one. We are conscious of echoes
of the first Prelude, and of the work-up to the 'Amami Alfredo' of the
second act; and with a characteristic *tutti* burst the lovers are in each
other's arms. As the orchestra races along, the ecstasy of their short
exchanges makes up for the brittle slanging match of their previous
dialogue. They reach a noisy climax; there is a pause; quiet chords by
bassoons, clarinets and oboes; and a modulation into 'Parigi o cara'. This
duet is another instance of Verdi at his operatic best. The music is simple,
the emotion inescapably accurate. How long ago since they last sang a
duet! Then Violetta was coquettish and wavering; Alfredo began with
one tune and she followed with another in carefree contrast. Now they
are re-united, tragically too late, they share his tune, their divergent
ways in harmony at last. It is old, romantic Alfredo who tells her

The old, eager, impetuous youth who cries excitedly

Pa-ri-gi,o ca——ra   noi   la-sce-re——mo. . .

Throughout this duet Verdi is still dividing and re-uniting his violins with care and precision; and when the *andante* movement is over and the *allegro* suggests a growing cheerfulness in Violetta a sudden figure *ff* for first violins and double basses,

cuts like a spasm warning her that all is not well, and she has to sit down. Then she pulls herself together, trying to rally her spirits, the woodwind and first violins trilling in support; but a new agitation creeps into the accompaniment as she makes an heroic attempt to dress for Alfredo, but finds the effort beyond her. Here the full strings repeat four times a phrase that depicts her resolute persistence:

Alfredo meanwhile can only utter short, bewildered exclamations, and tells Annina to get the doctor. As the orchestra seems to be preluding another climax for the struggling Violetta, she bids Annina let the doctor know Alfredo is back and she desperately wants to recover; but instead of a vocal climax Verdi suddenly shakes the whole theatre with a full brass chord *tutta forza*—four horns, two trumpets, three trombones, and a cimbasso—the only moment in the whole score given over to the brass alone; and what a shattering effect it has! It is in fact nothing more than the dominant C major chord, but unleashed thus without warning it is like a grave yawning at Violetta's feet. The cabaletta of the duet, 'Gran Dio! morir sì giovane', is led by her, desperately resigned now to the approach of death. Alfredo takes up her tune. He can find nothing new for himself. Through their exchanges and the reprise she continues to lead; for this is no rapturous love duet, but a doomed woman's frantic hold on life and her man's helpless support.

At the end the doctor comes, and with him Alfredo's father. Once again librettist and composer have yielded to the musical convention of having a baritone to balance the finale. Nor can we argue that Giorgio Germont's presence is unlikely. After all, he wrote her a kind, understanding letter (and maybe now Alfredo is back in Paris he feels the necessity of keeping a paternal eye on his movements). But how different is his opening 'Ah Violetta' from that first, cold 'Madamigella Valery'! Finding the bitter truth, he is overwhelmed with remorse, and after a forceful outburst he observes quietly, and solely on the note B, 'Oh malcauto vegliardo! il mal ch'io feci ora sol vedo!' It is high time he knew it, we may think.

So the finale begins, with the whole orchestra doing *ppp* very much the same as it did in the *Trovatore* 'Miserere'. In fact Verdi gives identical instructions: 'This passage must be played very quietly by the whole orchestra.' Like the tread of pall-bearers it crunches under the vocal lines. Though Annina and the doctor are at her bedside with Alfredo and his father, it is really only Violetta we are concerned with. When the short ensemble breaks off for her last spasms, it is Alfredo's love-declaration that we hear played by two solo first violins, just as it was earlier when she read his father's letter to herself. *Alfredo*'s love—not her own deeper-felt theme. For this unselfish girl goes to her Madelaine and her God with only her inadequate lover in her mind. It is all over swiftly, the brass-laden orchestra dragging down the curtain with pugnacious chords. Many have wished that Verdi had closed this tragic scene quietly. A few years later he might have done. The very end of *Traviata* looks crude on paper; but in the theatre, when we have succumbed to the cathartic powers of the last half-hour, those hefty chords do much to drive away our tears and put a brave face on us before the lights go up.

La Traviata is the only one of all Verdi's operas which takes place wholly indoors. Producers, finding this a restriction, have moved the country house scene from the drawing-room to the garden; and some have held Violetta's opening party on a patio or terrace. These are mistaken attempts to liberate the drama from its domestic setting and lend it an *al fresco* freedom it is not meant to have. This is an opera, not of claustrophobia, but of carpet and cushion and chandelier, of marble and mirror, of escritoire and chaise-longue. It is an interior, a domestic problem, a ménage. The outside rarely obtrudes. The rapture of Alfredo floats into Violetta's deliberations at the end of the first act. It lures and tempts her and opens up for her a new horizon. Through the long windows of the next scene we glimpse the garden, the gate and the hedge beyond which runs the road to Paris, to the real world beyond present dreams, to disaster. In the last scene of all, when Annina pulls back the curtains to let in the daylight, Paris *en fête* clatters riotously by with mocking indifference. All else is *chez* Violetta, or *chez* Flora Bervoix—the boudoirs, salons, and *chambres à coucher* of the demi-monde from splendour to eclipse.

In Verdi's life it seems to close an epoch. It is as though his genius had struggled through the confines of his historical melodramas, straining to meet the contemporary challenge, nearly surfacing once or twice, and now at last fully emerging in this Parisian tale acted out behind the doors and shutters of the very boulevards he had sauntered along with Peppina on his arm. It was proof he did not have to write about conquering kings and castle walls. And having proved it, with growing leisure, never again working on two new operas at once, he reverted to medieval stories, to the conspirators and crusaders, the daggers and the poisoned cups. But from now on there was a ripening maturity, a deeper emotion, a surer technical grasp. The people in Verdi's later operas are more richly fashioned in their developing three-dimensional range; and it is because his inspiration had been tempered by the living magnetism, the attraction and repulsion, the frailties and the fortitudes, of Madamigella Valery of Paris and the Germonts of Provence.

NOTES

1 Noyes, *The Barrel-Organ*.
2 Prasteau, Jean, *C'Etait la Dame Aux Camélias*, ch. 5.
3 St John-Stevas, *Obscenity and the Law*, ch. IV, p. 68.
4 Pearl, *The Girl with the Swansdown Seat* (Signet edn), p. 43.

5 Sarcey, F. *Quarante Ans de Théâtre*, vol 5; *Les modernes*, p. 189.
6 *The Times*, 26 May 1856.
7 *Illustrated London News*, 31 May 1856.
8 *Athenaeum*, 16 August 1856.
9 Chorley, *Thirty Years' Musical Recollections*, vol II, p. 236.
10 Ibid., p. 240.
11 *Copialettere*, CXXXIX, Appendix. Verdi to De Sanctis, 1 January 1853.
12 Pearl, op. cit., p. 80. In Webster's Bible (1833) the expression *to go a-whoring* was replaced by *to go astray*. *Vide* Fryer, P., *Mrs. Grundy, Studies in English Prudery*, p. 28.
13 Janin, Preface to *La Dame aux Camélias*.
14 Bellaigue, *Verdi*, p. 54.
15 Istituto di Studi Verdiani, *Verdi*, no. 2. Gian Paolo Minadri, *Frammenti Verdiani di Bruno Barilli*, p. 794.
16 Told by her during a broadcast commentary on *Traviata* at the Metropolitan Opera, New York, 5 January 1935.
17 Gollancz, op. cit., p. 27.
18 Hughes, op. cit., p. 176.
19 Thackeray, *The Paris Sketch Book*.
20 Sarcey, op. cit., p. 197.
21 Shaw, op. cit., vol. I, p. 179.
22 Sarcey, op. cit., p. 202.
23 *Copialettere*, CXXV, p. 130. Verdi to Barezzi, 21 January 1852.
24 Walker, op. cit., p. 207.
25 Soffredini, op. cit., p. 110.
26 Verdi to Somma, 12 July 1853, quoted by Mario Medici, *Lettere sul Re Lear*, in *Verdi*, No. 2 (Istituto di Studi Verdiani), p. 773.
27 Chorley, *Athenaeum*, 3 May 1856.
28 Janin, op. cit.